REVOLUSI
INDONESIA INDEPENDENT

REVOLUSI!
INDONESIA INDEPENDENT

HARM STEVENS, AMIR SIDHARTA,
BONNIE TRIYANA, MARION ANKER

IN COLLABORATION WITH
ANNE-LOT HOEK, REMCO RABEN,
YUDHI SOERJOATMODJO,
AMINUDIN T.H. SIREGAR

RIJKS MUSEUM | ATLAS CONTACT

CONTENTS

7   FOREWORD
      TACO DIBBITS

8   FACES OF THE REVOLUTION
    PERSONAL TESTIMONIES AND COLLECTIVE EXPERIENCES
      HARM STEVENS

18   THE SPIRIT OF THE REVOLUSI
    PERSPECTIVES ON INDONESIAN INDEPENDENCE
      REMCO RABEN

50   PROKLAMASI
    INDEPENDENCE CAPTURED
      YUDHI SOERJOATMODJO

76   FREEDOM THE GLORY OF ANY NATION
    REVOLUTION IN THE STREETS AND ON PAPER
      HARM STEVENS, BONNIE TRIYANA

98   THE SIGNAL TO RISE UP
    MENACE AND VIOLENCE AT THE START OF THE REVOLUTION
      HARM STEVENS, MARION ANKER

120   PROPAGANDA FOR THE REPUBLIC
    AT THE FOREFRONT OF THE INFORMATION WAR
      AMIR SIDHARTA, HARM STEVENS

140   CAUGHT IN THE NET
    THE DUTCH HUNT FOR INFORMATION
      HARM STEVENS, BONNIE TRIYANA

166   DIPLOMASI AND AGRESI
    THE UNCERTAIN PATH OF NEGOTIATION AND CONFLICT
      MARION ANKER, ANNE-LOT HOEK, AMIR SIDHARTA,
      HARM STEVENS, BONNIE TRIYANA

200   COMRADES OF THE REVOLUTION
    ARTISTS AND THE INDONESIAN REVOLUTION
      AMINUDIN T.H. SIREGAR, AMIR SIDHARTA, HARM STEVENS

230   FOUR TIMES 365 DAYS
    SUKARNO'S RETURN TO JAKARTA CAPTURED
      YUDHI SOERJOATMODJO

250   NOTES
259   LIST OF ILLUSTRATIONS
266   MAP
268   INDEX

FOREWORD

On 17 August 1945, after more than three centuries of colonial domination, Indonesia declared itself a free nation. It was the start of a revolution, a struggle for independence that would last four and a half years and determine the fate of the country and its inhabitants. The exhibition in the Rijksmuseum and this book centre on people in the *revolusi*: fighters, artists, diplomats, children, politicians, journalists and others. Their lives tell the history of the independence struggle, through their experiences, via objects and eyewitness reports. Indonesia was one of the trailblazers on the road to independence after the Second World War. Many countries would follow in the next two decades. With this, Indonesia takes on a crucial role in the history of the twentieth century.

A team of Indonesian and Dutch researchers has been working intensively on this project in Indonesia and the Netherlands since 2019. Research and exhibitions in the Netherlands often focus on the Netherlands' role in this period and its consequences here, but with this exhibition we aim instead to provide an international perspective. Historical research, the search for stories never told before, and sources never shown before, form the basis for this. This work included discussions and intellectual exchanges with people within the museum, but above all outside it. The process of listening *beyond* the walls of the Rijksmuseum – the conversations with descendants of the people who went through the Indonesian revolution, and with historians and researchers in the Netherlands and Indonesia – brings the various points of view together. We are conscious that the eyewitnesses in the exhibition and this book cannot represent all the lives of the time, but we hope that *Revolusi!* will provide an impetus to enrich the nation's gaze on the past with more personal experiences. These also include the stories of people in the national histories of the Netherlands and Indonesia that were previously denied proper attention, a silence that is painful for many to this day.

We are grateful to all the institutions and individuals, in Indonesia and in the Netherlands, who by lending their objects, telling their stories and making pictorial material available contributed to the exhibition and this book. The Rijksmuseum also thanks all benefactors for their contribution. The appointment of the Indonesian curators Amir Sidharta and Bonnie Triyana has been made possible by the Johan Huizinga Fund/ Rijksmuseum Fund. The additional programme accompanying the exhibition with room for dialogue has been made possible in part by vfonds and DutchCulture.

Revolusi! is not the end of the line. In the future we would like to build on the good (inter)national working relationships that developed over the course of this project. The Rijksmuseum aims to contribute to a broader history of the Netherlands, to mutual understanding and connection among the numerous groups in Dutch society upon whom the Indonesian revolution has had a significant and lasting influence, such as the Indo-Dutch, the Chinese community with roots in Indonesia, the Moluccan and the Papuan communities.

Taco Dibbits
General Director, Rijksmuseum

FACES OF THE REVOLUTION

PERSONAL TESTIMONIES AND COLLECTIVE EXPERIENCES

HARM STEVENS

REVOLUSI!

Our brain as camera. There's always something left out of the picture.
—Merapi Obermayer

A good way to get to know the faces of the Indonesian revolution (1945–1949) is to open this pocket-sized photo book, seized during the revolution, and leaf through it carefully [1]. On the third page, the original owner of this book of friends gazes at you out of the corner of his eyes. 'S. Nasrudin (Sutarso)' is written in pencil under the small snapshot [2]. Nasrudin was part of the Siliwangi Division of the Tentara Nasional Indonesia (TNI, Indonesian National Armed Forces), which fought for an independent Indonesia from 1945 to 1949. This much can be learned from the text written on the first few pages. Later on in the little book, Nasrudin's comrades pass before your eyes: young men proudly posing in a photo studio somewhere in Java, alone or in a group [3]. In another photo, three women stand behind two small boys sitting in a chair, two of them wearing a *selandang* (head covering) [4]. Might they be relatives of Nasrudin? Two pages later, a placard at the feet of soldiers in a group portrait bears the words (in Indonesian): 'In honour of the hari raya holiday [the Islamic breaking of the Ramadan fast] we are united on 26-8-48 in our struggle for the fatherland' [5].[1]

Less than two months after this holiday, Nasrudin made a note elsewhere in the book. It would be the last. The note concerned the suppression of a communist uprising in the city of Madiun in East Java by troops loyal to Sukarno in September 1948. Nasrudin, presumably in agreement, quoted a newspaper in which the communists in Madiun were labelled collaborators: '*Sadar* newspaper of 9 October 1948: Indonesians who worked with the Dutch: 1: Muso. 2: Amir and co., working with van Muk [Mook]. 3: Djokosajano. 4: Setyadjit Sugondo. 5: Wikana.'[2] The note is dated 20 October 1948. Not long afterwards, Sutarso Nasrudin was probably taken prisoner by the Dutch military, somewhere in Central Java.

At that moment this highly personal pocket-sized book became a source of information. The confiscated album, upon Nasrudin's arrest, most likely came into the possession of an intelligence unit attached to the Dutch military. Nasrudin seems to have been conscious of the risk that the book and the identity of his friends might fall into the hands of the enemy, for the word *Pembakaran* (burn) is written on one of the last pages. This was most likely an instruction to family and friends to destroy the book if it was in danger of falling into enemy hands.[3] The agents of the intelligence service left their mark on various pages in the book: here and there a few words in Dutch or the addition of a name and sometimes an ominous question mark by a portrait of one of Nasrudin's friends [6]. Whether this meticulous intelligence work led to the arrest of the comrades of Nasrudin gathered in the book is unknown, but the possibility cannot be excluded.

There is no uncertainty about the fate of the book's owner: Sutarso Nasrudin was executed by Dutch troops. The book's cover bears a sticker, probably added years later, with the words 'owner executed'. Some words in pencil are still just visible under the sticker: 'S Nasrudin, executed by Capt. Janssen v E[…]'. The name is barely legible after the 'E'.[4]

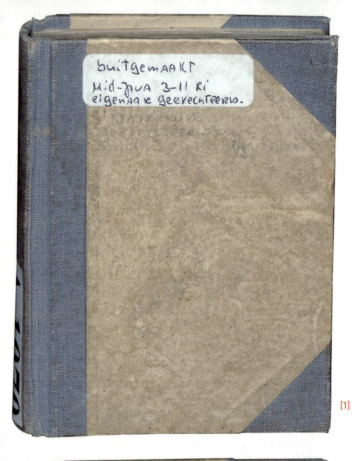

[1] Cover of Sutarso Nasrudin's book of friends, c. 1948. Sticker added later with the words 'owner executed'

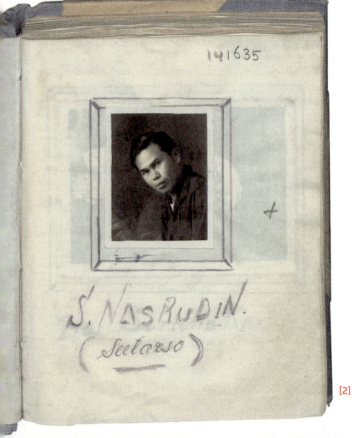

[2] Sutarso Nasrudin, portrait from his book of friends, c. 1948

[3]　S. Munif, portrait from Sutarso Nasrudin's book of friends, c. 1948

[4]　Three women and two boys, portrait from Sutarso Nasrudin's book of friends, c. 1948

[5] Group of soldiers, portrait from Sutarso Nasrudin's book of friends, 26 August 1948. Left to right, standing: Nasrudin, Soedjijo, Boedikadjo, Oemar; seated: Sugianto and Ichsani

[6] Three men, portrait from Sutarso Nasrudin's book of friends, c. 1948. Annotated by the Dutch intelligence service with names and a question mark

The album must have been brought to the Netherlands in 1949 or shortly after the end of the war in Indonesia, probably by a Dutch soldier. After various peregrinations, Nasrudin's book of friends was acquired in 2004 for the photo collection of the Royal Netherlands Institute of Southeast Asian and Caribbean Studies (KITLV). Since 2014 it has been held in the Special Collections of the Leiden University Libraries (UBL), as part of an extensive loan from the KITLV.[5]

The book of friends shows that the patrimony of the Indonesian revolution in Dutch public collections (archives, libraries and museums) can come from a murky source and as a result elicit great unease. An unease that has more recently been fed by public discussions about looted art and the restitution of colonial collections, and the attention devoted to this in the media.[6] From private album to instrument of intelligence work to public asset: these are steps that are far too jarring. Is such a personal object, once secured in an acid-proof box in the Special Collections and labelled with a sticker bearing the library's logo, neutralized into patrimony? The answer to this question is of course no. The conscientious way in which Anouk Mansfeld, curator of photography, has written about this sensitive document shows that both the UBL and the KITLV recognize the problem of this possession. 'From a desire to redress past injustice', Mansfeld writes, 'the present owner of the friends book, the KITLV Association, is conscious of the need for expert and independent provenance research, so that it can be determined in what way Nasrudin's photo album might be eligible for restitution'.[7]

To return to this chapter's opening sentence: to get to know the faces of the revolution, one must, in spite of all the issues involved, leaf through this album. In order to see the men, women, boys and girls who fought for the independence of their nation. In order to glimpse something of the spirit of the revolution and of the pride and conviction that Nasrudin and his friends exude in the snapshots in the album. However, it is also imperative not to become entirely enthralled by 'the blinding light' of the revolution and exclusively consider Indonesian experiences and faces.[8] Alongside the Indonesian story (which consists of a myriad of individual stories), those who put together this book and the exhibition at the Rijksmuseum at the same time bring Dutch faces and points of view closer, and therefore also show the perspective of the Indo-Dutch, the diffuse group of Dutch citizens (often with Indonesian ancestors) who were born in the pre-war Dutch East Indies or in any case were closely tied to it, and who ended up between two fatherlands, as it were, after the Second World War. Other groups also come up. We focus our lens, for instance, on an Indonesian-Chinese family and show a fragment of their life in the extremely uncertain initial phase of the revolution in Jakarta.

A RANGE OF EXPERIENCES

Revolusi! presents a range of experiences, which are illustrated and told from multiple vantage points: from Indonesian and Dutch perspectives and those of the groups and individuals who fall between the two, with an eye towards the international power arena and foreign observers, and attention to personal testimonies and collective experiences. These perspectives, testimonies and experiences diverge, contrast with and overlap one another. Together, all these stories form a fragmented and incomplete history of revolution and decolonization. The reader and visitor look through the eyes of the people who went through the revolution and are therefore invited to constantly move the markers.

Violence and the threat of violence are highly present in the personal histories recorded here, and become visible in a variety of ways, black on white in a typed list of the dead, or in the frayed shreds of a shirt shot to pieces. Amid this violence, a modern visual culture developed in the ranks of the young Republic of Indonesia, which encompassed propaganda posters, photography, film and painting. Until now these creations, aside from a few exceptions,[9] have remained virtually entirely ignored in the Netherlands. The representation of the revolution by painters and other artists, as well as the course of their careers in the turbulent period between 1945 and 1949, are extensively examined in this book and the exhibition it accompanies. *Revolusi!* allows contemporary works of art, posters, objects, documents, photos and films to speak (and at times contradict one another).

The story of the revolution is also told by famous and less well known photographers who, camera at the ready, spread the news from Indonesia around the world. Often they were thoroughly infatuated with the looks and swagger of the young Indonesian revolutionaries in the streets, who exuded youthful idealism. In their photos we see how an (extremely photogenic) Indonesian revolutionary self-image developed [7].[10]

OUTSIDE THE PARAMETERS

Based on the idea that this revolution is world history, we have endeavoured to broaden the traditional gaze the Netherlands has cast on the colonial past until now, in which it is seldom Indonesia that is discussed, and mainly Dutch actions in Indonesia instead.[11] With allusions to the Dutch 'presence' in Asia, 'the Netherlands overseas' or the 'Dutch encounter with Asia', these actions have been rather eu-phemistically highlighted. The Rijksmuseum has traditionally also made use of this limited, unilateral approach.[12] Because this book and the exhibition concern revolution and decolonization, it is important to open our eyes to the Indonesian aspects of this history.[13]

The research for the exhibition and the book, which began in the spring of 2019, has been conducted from the outset by Indonesian and Dutch researchers. Art historian Amir Sidharta and historian Bonnie Triyana worked on the project in Indonesia, as well as during two working visits to the Netherlands. Marion Anker and Harm Stevens, both curators of history at the Rijksmuseum, did the same in the Netherlands. The curators were assisted by two consultants: historian Remco Raben and art historian Aminudin T.H. Siregar, each of whom made significant contributions to the exhibition and the book based on their own expertise. Yudhi Soerjoatmodjo wrote two chapters in this book, forming the opening and closing chords in our narrative of the Indonesian revolution. Anne-Lot Hoek contributed to the chapter 'Diplomasi and Agresi'. Extensive use was also made of expertise on specific sub-topics from

[7] Three young Indonesians on the street in Yogyakarta, photo by Hugo Wilmar, December 1947. The armed young men belong to the militia group Kebaktian Rakjat Indonesia Sulawesi (KRIS, Service of Indonesian People from Sulawesi)

researchers and heritage and museum professionals in the Netherlands and abroad, bringing Indonesian stories, documents and objects into sharper focus. This book has no single author; it was written by a collective and came into being thanks to a joining of forces and the generous exchange of information.

Yogyakarta-based artist Timoteus Anggawan Kusno made a gallery-sized installation for the exhibition entitled *Luka dan Bisa Kubawa Berlari* (Wounds and Venom I Carry as I am Running).[14] He seeks, finds and presents the unheard and unseen in objects in the Rijksmuseum to which the museum hitherto always applied, in registration, descriptions and ways of display, a dominant colonial stamp: flags captured by the colonial army and navy in various regions in the Indonesian archipelago and the portraits of the colonial governors-general, which were brought to the Rijksmuseum from Indonesia at the end of 1949 and as such literally and figuratively became history, museum pieces instead of justifications for colonial power. Among the relics of the colonial period, the artist lets anti-colonial voices and images, connected to the spirit of revolution, resonate.

In the process, this research project – Timoteus Anggawan Kusno's work too is based on provenance research, documentation and registration – has been an exercise in thinking outside the parameters of the museum and the walls of established institutions. The tangible history of the Indonesian revolution and the stories about it are not contained exclusively in the acid-proof boxes of library archives or in museum depots. The research for *Revolusi!* has taught us that it is precisely by looking beyond these institutional storage places that stories can be found, from then and now, that enrich the perspective on the revolution. (Family) stories are being told at Dutch kitchen tables and in Indonesian homes, where black-and-white snapshots and historical documents are spread out. It is then evident that this history is still very much alive, seventy years later.

WORK, WORK AND WORK

The title of this book and this exhibition is *Revolusi!*, the Indonesian word for revolution, which for many (but not all) Indonesians is an apt reference to the years 1945–1949, the period of the Indonesian struggle for independence on which we focus in the exhibition and book. The story begins with the big bang of Indonesian independence: the *Proklamasi* (independence proclamation) issued by Sukarno just after 10 a.m. on 17 August 1945. As a coda, we have chosen a historical reportage closely recording Sukarno's entry into Jakarta on 28 December 1949. An important aspect of this is the representation and staging of both historic days, which seem to mirror each other. While the triumphal march of 28 December 1949 can be seen as a thrilling apotheosis of a popular revolution, we are conscious that aftershocks of the political and societal turbulence continued for a significant time. It soon became clear that the circle had not yet been completed on 28 December 1949, either in Indonesia or in the Netherlands. There were still all kinds of unresolved problems and conflicts created in the revolution, often rooted in the period of colonial occupation. These continued to affect relations between the two countries, as well as the position of specific groups in the Netherlands and Indonesia, for instance people in the Moluccan, Eurasian and Papua communities.

Sukarno knew only too well that there was still a lot of work for the young nation of Indonesia to do when he ascended the steps of the terrace of the Istana Merdeka (freedom palace) in Java for his address to a crowd of 250.000 people. Before the first president of the Republik Indonesia Serikat (RIS, Republic of the United States of Indonesia) concluded his speech with the words 'sekali merdeka, tetap merdeka' (once free, always free), he reminded the Indonesian people: 'Now we have to work, work and work, for the reconstruction of our nation'.

This exhortation to 'work, work and work' can also serve as inspiration for the Rijksmuseum today, for there is still a great deal of work to be done in order to arrive at a decolonized narrative about Indonesia and the Netherlands, a history in which an Indonesian voice resonates but also the voices of the Javanese, Moluccans, Dutch, Balinese, Eurasians, Sumatrans, Peranakan Chinese and Papuans. This work must be done by joining forces, bringing together researchers from the Netherlands, Indonesia and other countries, as well as Dutch and Indonesian museums. In this light, the exhibition and the book *Revolusi!* provide a blueprint for what still has to be done. The work is never finished.

THE SPIRIT OF THE REVOLUSI

PERSPECTIVES ON INDONESIAN INDEPENDENCE

REMCO RABEN

REVOLUSI!

What was the Indonesian revolution? The question has no straightforward answer. In a superficial sense, it was a struggle for Indonesian independence, a conflict between the Republic of Indonesia and the Netherlands. But what was Indonesia? The country existed on paper, as well as in the minds of Indonesian nationalists. The war against the Dutch was merely part of a much larger process, namely the invention of Indonesia. This process was more chaotic and complex than is suggested by the prevailing image in Indonesia, that of a united struggle against the former colonial power. The revolution was much more than a war between Dutch colonizers and Indonesian freedom fighters. This introduction examines the *revolusi* in search of its spirit. It does not offer a streamlined historical narrative but reveals – from different perspectives – the excitement, confusion and misery experienced by the people involved.

ARENA OF HOPE

The revolution was no ordinary war. The parties to the conflict were not two sovereign nations. Indonesia, in the years 1945–1949, was an arena in which the struggle for Indonesia's future was fought out, a struggle between different conceptions of Indonesia. What was at stake in the conflict was not simply whether independence (or greater autonomy) would be achieved, but who would decide the country's future and what that future would look like. This is the briefest possible summary of the 'revolution'.

The idea that Indonesia had to be built from the ground up was tremendously powerful. A wave of creativity, experimentation and hope washed over society. The best illustration may be a photo of the artists' group Gelanggang Seniman Merdeka (Arena of Independent Artists) from 1948 [1]. The Dutch cameraman Charles Breijer had travelled to Indonesia in 1947, made contact with the artists and photographed them. This photo shows a group of poets, writers and visual artists, all very young, relaxed and self-confident. Their boldness seems to leap out from what is doubtless a posed picture. These children of the shock waves that were rolling across Indonesia had grown up in the period of Dutch and Japanese occupation and had witnessed the birth of Indonesian independence. In their art, they were trying to give shape to the need for renewal. Every one of these men – and the few women among them – would set the tone for a distinctly Indonesian art scene. Perhaps not all their work was equally original, but that is not relevant here. Gelanggang was striving towards a new language for the new Indonesia.

Gelanggang propagated the spirit of the revolution from its base in Jakarta. Many other artists followed President Sukarno to Yogyakarta when he went there in January 1946 to form his nation, beyond the reach of the British and the Dutch. At the president's request, artists in and around Yogyakarta used their talents to depict the spirit of the revolution. Gelanggang's members seemed more emphatically open to influences from the Western world: in their 1950 manifesto they called themselves 'the rightful heirs to world culture'.[1] At the same time,

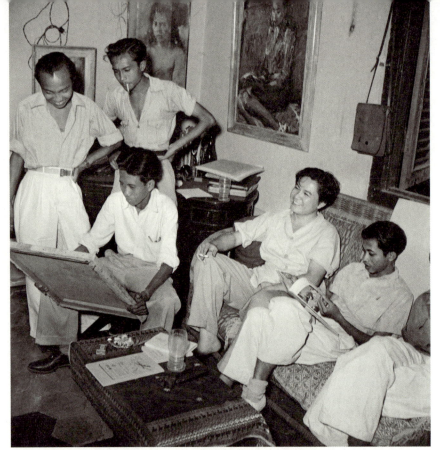

[1] Gelanggang Seniman Merdeka (Arena of Independent Artists), Jakarta 1948.
Left to right, standing: Mochtar Apin, Asrul Sani, Baharudin;
seated: Henk Ngantung, Chairil Anwar

they were every bit as nationalistic as the painters in Yogyakarta. The young poet Asrul Sani, one of the central figures in the Jakarta group, for instance, fought in the Tentara Pelajar (TP, Student Army) in Bogor (then Buitenzorg) before moving to Jakarta and joining Gelanggang.

The youthful artists of Gelanggang and elsewhere were already referred to as the Angkatan 45 (Generation of 1945), even during the revolution.[2] Perhaps the best-known voice of this generation was the poet Chairil Anwar. In 1944, before the end of the Japanese occupation, he wrote in his poem 'Siap-Sedia' ('We're Ready'):

> Our blood is forever warm,
> Our bodies are forged of steel,
> Our spirit is strong, is brave,
> We'll repaint the skies,
> We're the bearers of real happiness.
> ...
> Friends, friends,
> Let's swing our swords toward the Bright World![3]

No talk of an independent Indonesia here – the Japanese occupying regime would not permit that – but there is a spirit of hope. Chairil Anwar was the great voice of renewal and of experimentation. In late 1945, when the revolution was already under way, he wrote in his famous essay 'Hoppla!!': 'Hoppla! A jump great enough to fulfil the promise of this young nation of ours. ... The Word is Truth!!! ... And anyone who won't contribute we're prepared to shove along ... Let us be brothers, carving an alabaster monument in honour of a perfect Indonesia. A perfect world...'[4] If anything expressed the spirit of the revolution, the need for truth, the necessity of renewal and self-development, it was the words of this leading member of Gelanggang.

PROCLAMATION

The greatest seismic shift in Indonesian history was, without a doubt, the declaration of independence by Sukarno and Mohammad Hatta on 17 August 1945, two days after the Japanese capitulation. The proclamation itself was an event thrown together in haste, with an audience of a few hundred.[5] There were prayers – it was a Friday morning in the month of Ramadan – solemn speeches and cheering in Japanese fashion, with both arms raised in the air, as we can see in Frans Mendur's photographs of the gathering [SEE P. 72 [18]]. Etty Abdul Rachman, a young woman who worked in an office in Jakarta and maintained close links with the nationalists, attended the proclamation and later described her feelings: 'I was moved. I wanted to cry, but no tears would come. Only my throat hurt, as if it had a big lump in it that I couldn't swallow.'[6]

This was a glorious moment: the birth of Indonesia. The event did not come out of nowhere; it had been the subject of reflection and discussion for more than three decades, and in the final months of the Japanese occupation independence had actually been planned by the

Panitia Persiapan Kemerdekaan Indonesia (PPKI, Preparatory Committee for Indonesian Independence), a panel of prominent Indonesian nationalists, under Japanese supervision. But on that day, 17 August, an independent Indonesia existed only on paper. Beyond the typed sheet with the words of the proclamation, it had yet to become a reality.

Despite opposition by the Japanese, who were assigned responsibility by the Allies for maintaining order in Indonesia, the news of the proclamation spread quickly. That same day, the text of the independence proclamation was disseminated among the people of Jakarta in hurriedly printed pamphlets. An Indonesian employee of the Japanese radio broadcaster, Mohamad Jusuf Ronodipuro, managed surreptitiously to broadcast the news that same evening, spreading it to other parts of Java.[7]

Not everyone could believe it, or dared to. Minarsih Wiranatakusuma, the daughter of a regent with nationalist sympathies and a leading activist in the women's movement, wrote in her diary on Friday 17 August: 'Today the independence of Indonesia was announced. Not everyone knows yet. People are confused and do not yet understand. Indonesia is free – on paper. ... We cannot yet be certain what is really going on. People talk a great deal, but they do not know what to believe.'[8] From other parts of Java, people were sent to Jakarta to verify the news.[9] And even when the reports turned out to be true, it was not clear to everyone what independence meant. Above all, it was unclear how much power the Japanese still had.

Gradually, red-and-white flags, the symbol of a free Indonesia, began turning up everywhere [2]. Groups took up arms, and not always with the noblest of intentions. To many people, the cry for freedom was irresistible, even though it was not obvious what it entailed. Yet over time the situation did become clearer. The recently formed Indonesian government, under President Sukarno, moved quickly to build a state system. The government in Jakarta called for the establishment of local 'national' committees (Komitee Nasional Indonesia), and local leaders responded at once. In many places, there were elections to the local administration and the local national committees. A distinct spirit of democracy was often present.[10] In some areas, however, the transition of power involved the use of brute force against the old aristocracy, which had been responsible for local administration under Dutch and Japanese occupation. This was especially true on the north coast of Java (Pekalongan), in West Java (Banten) and in North Sumatra, where the call for independence led to a social revolution in which many members of the old elite fell victim to violence.

It took the Dutch many weeks to realize that the Indonesian playing field had changed radically, and even longer before they understood that something irreversible had happened. Only gradually did the news trickle into Dutch administrative circles in Australia – where the colonial administration of the Dutch East Indies had been based during the war against Japan – and in The Hague. The Dutch hardly had any idea what had gone on in Indonesia under the Japanese

[2]　On 19 September 1945, barely more than four weeks after the proclamation of independence, a first mass gathering was held on Ikada Square in Jakarta. The banner reads: 'One nation, one will, always freedom'

occupation, or what a sense of liberation had resulted from the Japanese capitulation and the proclamation of independence. Even Europeans who had struggled to survive for several years in the Japanese internment camps turned out to be unaware of what was brewing in Indonesian society. The Eurasian Elien Visscher, the daughter of an employee in the sugar industry in East Java, was interned in a Japanese camp for two years before finding herself in the streets of Semarang again for the first time in August 1945. 'Outside we ran into Indonesians, who offered friendly greetings. But a few times we saw trucks pass by, carrying men who shouted something in an unfriendly way. They were shouting "merdeka". I didn't know the word, and at first I couldn't even make out what they were saying. It turns out to mean "freedom".'[11]

By August 1945, the Dutch East Indies no longer existed – except perhaps under international law as interpreted by the Dutch. But in Indonesia, colonialism had run its course. Indonesians were looking towards a wide-open future, whereas the Dutch saw their options dwindling. In its weakened state, the Netherlands mainly searched in the Indonesian war of independence for a strategy to retain some influence; to the Indonesians, the war was an explosion of expectations.

OPPRESSION AND RESISTANCE

The proclamation of independence was such a profound event that it overshadowed all that had preceded it. It was the big bang of the Indonesian state, the wellspring of Indonesian history. To nationalists, it was the moment of truth, which, as Chairil Anwar wrote, would wipe away the deceitful words of the past. This was a new beginning [3]. Yet as sudden and radical as the revolution seemed, it cannot be explained without some knowledge of the historical history of repression and resistance under the Dutch and Japanese regimes.

The Dutch often wondered where the revolution and the violence of 1945 had come from so suddenly. Most Dutch people believed that the Indonesian struggle for freedom, and the spirit of violence and revolution among its youth, was rooted in Japanese anti-Western propaganda. It is true that the revolution would have been unthinkable without the Japanese occupation. The Japanese had mobilized and trained the young in paramilitary organizations and quickly readied an army of volunteers to defend the country. The Japanese had also set up the Preparatory Committee for Indonesian Independence in the final months of their occupation, which naturally heightened the expectations of politically engaged Indonesians. What may have been most important was the simple fact that the Japanese occupation made freedom imaginable for large groups of Indonesians. The Japanese had defeated the Dutch regime in early 1942 without much effort, many Dutch had been imprisoned, and Indonesians had been given positions that had been unattainable in the Dutch period. The Japanese policies had plunged the country into unprecedented economic hardship. There was famine on a massive scale, and a

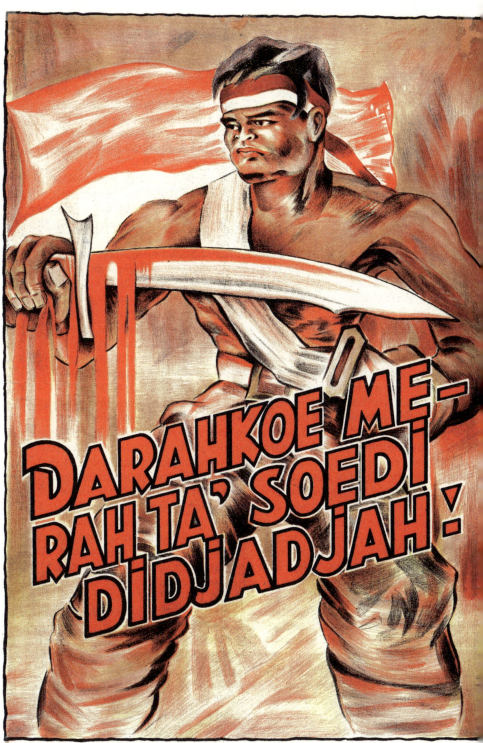

[3] Indonesian propaganda poster: 'My blood is red, unwilling to be conquered!', by Kompoel Sujatno, c. 1945–1949

generation grew up in an atmosphere of state violence, with no prospects for the future. This reinforced their realization that foreign domination only brought misery.[12]

The Dutch belief that pernicious Japanese influence was the cause of the revolution is understandable, but it also reveals the inability of the Dutch to question the effects and legitimacy of their own colonial occupation. Most Dutch officials felt that Dutch colonialism had been sanctioned by law and had harboured only the best intentions for the Indonesian people. They denied or ignored the undercurrent of discontent and resistance created by the colonial administration.

There had been resistance ever since the Dutch conquest of much of the archipelago in the late nineteenth and early twentieth centuries. In Dutch circles, the idea of a Pax Neerlandica – a peaceful society under the Dutch flag – predominated, but this disregarded the existence of all kinds of dissatisfaction, protest and actual resistance. Large-scale uprisings were rare. There had, however, been parties and organizations in the Dutch East Indies speaking out in support of independence since 1912. There were also many acts of vandalism targeting the colonial authorities or the business sector. For years, sugar growers grappled with cane fires, unions organized strikes and people rose up in protest against the tax burden. New religious movements, sometimes messianic, emerged here and there under the authority of local leaders. Such manifestations of discontent were rarely described as anticolonial, but they all carried the seeds of resistance against the established colonial order.

The image of the peaceful colony also disregards the systematic violent oppression of people who turned against Dutch rule. Banishment without trial and internment, but also censorship, espionage and intimidation, were among the weapons in the arsenal of the colonial state to suppress political aspirations that could weaken colonial authority. Much of this activity was cloaked in the mantle of justice, as defined by the colonial government. In her novel *Buiten het gareel* (Out of Line), the writer Soewarsih Djojopuspito provides a detailed account of the intimidating police surveillance imposed on nationalists.[13] The book tells the story of Soewarsih's work at a 'wild' school, which was not supported by the colonial authorities, who were in fact constantly keeping watch over it and interfering with its operation. Police spies, raids, teaching bans and confiscation of printed materials made this type of education practically impossible.

There were, of course, 'progressive' Dutch people who realized that Indonesian demands for autonomy were justified. Often these were officials filled with a sense of responsibility for the development of the Dutch East Indies. In the 1930s, a small group of progressive colonial officials of this variety came together in the association De Stuw (The Dam) and its magazine of the same name. A strikingly large number of them would later become leading Dutch figures in the era of revolution; examples include Huib van Mook, the lieutenant governor-general, and Johann Logemann, the minister of overseas territories. But even these progressives were wary of the spirit of revolution. Without exception, they thought in terms of gradualism and paternalism, and saw the Netherlands as taking a leading role in the development of Indonesia into a modern society.[14] The idea that Indonesians had the right to decide their own fate was alien to them.

Most Indonesian nationalists realized sooner or later that the Dutch would never take the step of offering unconditional independence. That became clearer than ever during the Japanese occupation. In a speech on Radio Oranje, the radio broadcast by the Dutch government in exile, on 6 December 1942, Queen Wilhelmina hinted at greater autonomy for Indonesia, but within the Dutch empire. She also said: 'I know ... that the partnership that has developed over many years offers the Indonesians the best guarantee of a return to peace and happiness.' What the queen evidently did not realize, or was ignoring, was that the Indonesians had never seen this partnership as equitable. When Dutch officials returned to their positions in the autumn of 1945, they had this speech in the back of their minds. But the train of Indonesian nationalism was already well past that station.

Ironically, many nationalists were in various ways children of the colonial state. Almost without exception, they came from the rising lower middle class; their parents worked in government and education. Sukarno was the son of a schoolteacher and an upper-caste Balinese woman; Chairil Anwar's father was an official in North Sumatra. Most leading nationalists had completed some form of secondary education, become competent speakers of foreign languages and developed a very cosmopolitan outlook. They had insight into global affairs. The nationalists were keenly aware that the Second World War had been fought in the name of freedom and self-determination.

Even Dutch politicians had heard and understood that message, but their deeply entrenched colonial mindset made it impossible for them to share their authority. The conflict between the Republic and the Netherlands that broke out in the late months of 1945 was not primarily about whether Indonesia deserved greater autonomy – although there were Dutch people who contested even that. More than that, the conflict was about the degree of autonomy, and above all about the degree of paternalistic guidance in attaining it.

THE SPIRIT OF SELF-DEVELOPMENT

Not only the spirit of resistance but also the spirit of renewal had been present in Indonesian society for some time. After 1900, Indonesian society had changed at a dizzying pace. Colonial conquests, the rise of capitalism, technological innovations, education and the growing intervention of the colonial state in everyday life opened up new horizons for many Indonesians. This was not by any means solely the consequence of Western or colonial influence; it emerged from a globalizing world in which Muslim and intra-Asian networks played just as important a role. The process of reflection on the future shape of Indonesia had already begun amid the cacophony of these years before the Second World War. No topic was excluded: religion, the position of women, national identity, language, concepts of race and culture, Indonesian art, the ideal form of government and, inevitably, the relationship between East and West.

This intellectual foment gave rise to the concepts of the new Indonesia to be constructed in the revolution. The history of the revolution is often viewed as a struggle between Indonesia and the Netherlands, but many Indonesians saw it much more as a time of self-discovery and collective self-development. In large parts of Indonesia, the Dutch seemed very far away. In 1945, what mattered most to Indonesians was to construct a state and rebuild the economy, but radical changes also took place in many other domains – for example, in the social role of women. It was not that all women suddenly had a different position in society or harboured new expectations, but they were starting to demand a more prominent place. As part of the struggle for freedom, women were expected to expand their role as carers to encompass the greater cause.[15] Many supported the struggle, for example through their work in the communal kitchens set up to nourish the guerrilla fighters, or else provided nursing. Some joined the student army Tentara Pelajar although few actually participated in combat.[16] Others became politically active. Women received the right to vote in 1946. Soon afterwards, there were women in parliament and even women ministers – Maria Ullfah led the way in 1946, ten years before the Netherlands reached that milestone.

In the arts as well, it was a period of frenetic activity. The few composers in Indonesia wrote revolutionary songs. Daljono and Kamsidi, for example, wrote a song in praise of the notorious *bambu runcing*, the bamboo spears used as weapons by many fighters, and the famed musician Ismail Marzuki devoted numerous songs to the struggle. In some of them, he mentioned the women fighters; a case in point is 'Melati di Tapal Batas' (Jasmine on the Border) from 1946:

> You are called Srikandi,
> a real woman warrior.
> You follow the trail of the *pemuda*,
> follow to protect the nation.[17]

This atmosphere of furious creativity was especially striking in and around Yogyakarta, where the presence of numerous artists led to a flourishing, effervescent period in the arts. Painters had workshops there, and the theatre blossomed.[18] The artists who had followed Sukarno to Yogyakarta played a central part in shaping the image of the revolution. Sukarno invited them to contribute to the struggle by expressing the revolutionary spirit. One of the many artists who responded to this appeal was Affandi. In 1946 he painted five *laskar rakyat* (people's militia fighters) huddled over a map, discussing their strategy [4]. This is not a documentary painting but a symbolic representation of a struggle actually taking place at a great remove from the community of painters. The fighters are examining a complete map of Indonesia; we can clearly see the outlines of Sulawesi and Borneo. Affandi thus showed that the conflict in progress in Central Java was a struggle for the entire archipelago.

[4] *Laskar Rakyat Mengatur Siasat I* (The People's Militia Decides Tactics I), by Affandi, 1946

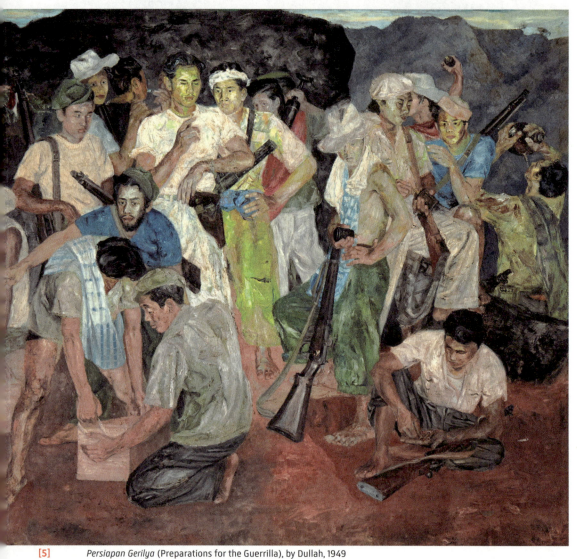

[5] *Persiapan Gerilya* (Preparations for the Guerrilla), by Dullah, 1949

Seko Perintis Gerilya (Prambanan) (Guerrilla Vanguard, Prambanan), by Sudjojono, 1949

Other artists, such as Dullah, Hendra Gunawan, Sudjojono, Soedibio and many more, likewise idealized the *pemuda* (young freedom fighters) in their paintings [5, 6]. But they also made themselves useful in other ways. A large number of artists designed posters and made banners to spread the message of freedom, mobilize the population and let the outside world know that the Indonesians had a right to liberty. Many had gained relevant experience during the Japanese occupation, when they had supported the propaganda and public information activities of the Japanese military regime, and that experience came in very handy. After the proclamation of independence, for instance, the painter Hendra Gunawan from Bandung joined the circle of radical students surrounding the journalist and prominent nationalist Adam Malik in Jakarta and made posters there. He also fought at the front in Bekasi and other parts of West Java before leaving in early 1946 for Yogyakarta, where he joined the painters' colony.[19] The poster production methods of the painters' studios there can be seen in a series of photographs of the Pusat Tenaga Pelukis Indonesia (PTPI, Powerhouse for Indonesian Painters) taken in Yogyakarta in 1947 by Cas Oorthuys. This was the headquarters of a group of artists who had a close working relationship with the ministry of information.[20]

It is not surprising that Yogyakarta was entirely caught up in the spirit of the revolution. Not only had the Republican government taken up residence there, but refugees were constantly arriving, more than doubling the city's population [7]. It was teeming with soldiers, intellectuals and artists. Yogyakarta may have been the place where the new society was being constructed in the most deliberate manner. This was in stark contrast with the image that Dutch administrators tried to paint of the Republic as a chaotic region with an incompetent administration. In Dutch circles, Yogyakarta was called the pesthole.[21] In 1947, Lieutenant Governor-General Van Mook described Yogyakarta as a 'hotbed of disorder and insecurity'.[22] When the social democratic journalist and member of parliament Frans Goedhart in August 1946 became the first Dutch reporter to travel to Yogyakarta to investigate the situation there, people in Jakarta told him he was out of his mind.[23] 'Their so-called Republic is one great chaos, rife with murder, looting and pillaging', one major is said to have shouted when Goedhart revealed his plan. What Goedhart witnessed, however, was an orderly society with a stable government system and a productive agricultural sector. All the people he interviewed professed great loyalty to the Republic.

Republican authorities were undertaking serious attempts to make the government system more democratic. For instance, the sultan of Yogyakarta, Hamengkubuwono IX, introduced a new administrative structure for his province in February 1946, the Daerah Istimewa Yogyakarta, in which local and regional officials reported to *majelis desa* (local village councils) or *dewan perwakilan* (regency councils).[24] Yogyakarta was now the centre of the new Indonesia, where the influence of the Republican government was greatest. In other places, the Republic's authority was weaker. In South Sulawesi and parts of Sumatra, for example, the revolution sparked attempts by rival rulers and communities to resolve local conflicts by force. Similarly, the situation in West Java became turbulent, with not only the returning Dutch authorities vying with the Republican authorities, but also the Darul Islam movement, which fought for an independent Islamic state.

Circumstances in the Republic were difficult and sometimes disorderly – of that there can be no doubt. The Dutch put Republican territory under great military pressure, many men took up arms, autonomous groups of fighters were active in numerous areas, and the trade boycott by the Netherlands hit the economy hard. Dutch military activity, especially the large-scale occupations after the offensives of July 1947 and December 1948, destabilized the country. Even so, over the years the Republic had managed to set up a well-organized administration. In the final year of the revolution, when all of Java was formally under Dutch rule, it became clear that the Republic and its guerrilla warfare could count on overwhelming support. Ultimately, the Dutch had to acknowledge that Republican authorities in many places had their house in order, and furthermore that the authority of the Republic had been embraced by a large majority of the population.

BETWEEN DIALOGUE AND VIOLENCE

For four years, the Republic of Indonesia was in armed conflict with the Netherlands. The Republic desired immediate and complete independence, as proclaimed on 17 August 1945, while the Dutch hoped to go on pulling the strings, and some even wished to retain control of the entire colony. One of the many perspectives on the revolution was that both parties could resolve their differences through dialogue. And plenty of dialogue took place, almost constantly [8]. Delegates and politicians travelled back and forth by air and by rail between Jakarta and Yogyakarta. The daily train from Jakarta to Yogyakarta and back had a *kereta luar biasa* (special wagon), which transported the negotiators between the two cities. The correspondence between the two parties was never-ending, often going by way of negotiating committees and intermediaries, and also in many cases through the foreign observers sent to Indonesia by the United Nations after August 1947. At the same time, armies on both sides were perpetually pursuing military advantage in a kind of parallel world, the Republicans by means of infiltration and underground resistance and the Dutch through gradual annexation, purges and aggressive patrols. Combat and dialogue were two sides of the same tussle.

The Indonesian Republic and the Dutch spoke different languages, however. The Dutch denied the Indonesian claims, along with the Indonesians' capacity to wield power. The Republicans refused to grant the Dutch any military authority over Republican territory. Yet negotiators on both sides were consistently doing their best to resolve the conflict by diplomatic means. A few times they even came close.

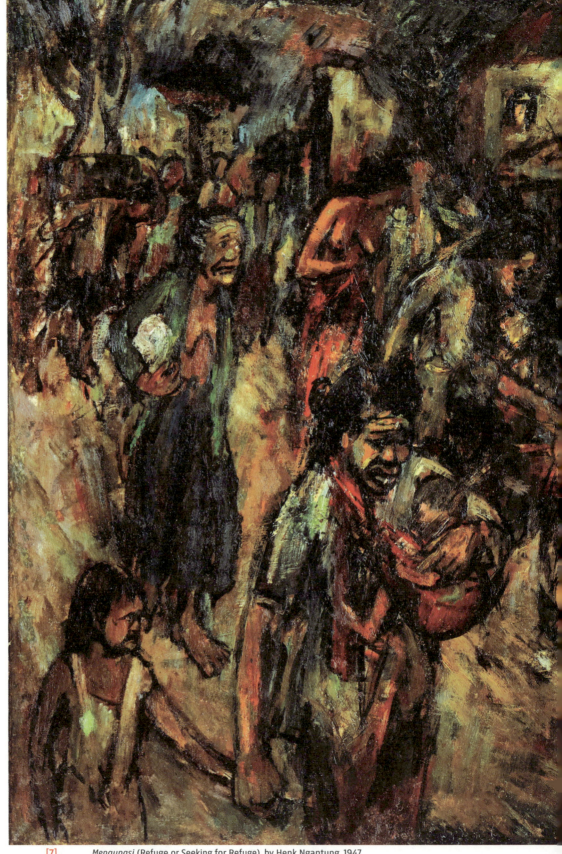

Mengungsi (Refuge or Seeking for Refuge), by Henk Ngantung, 1947

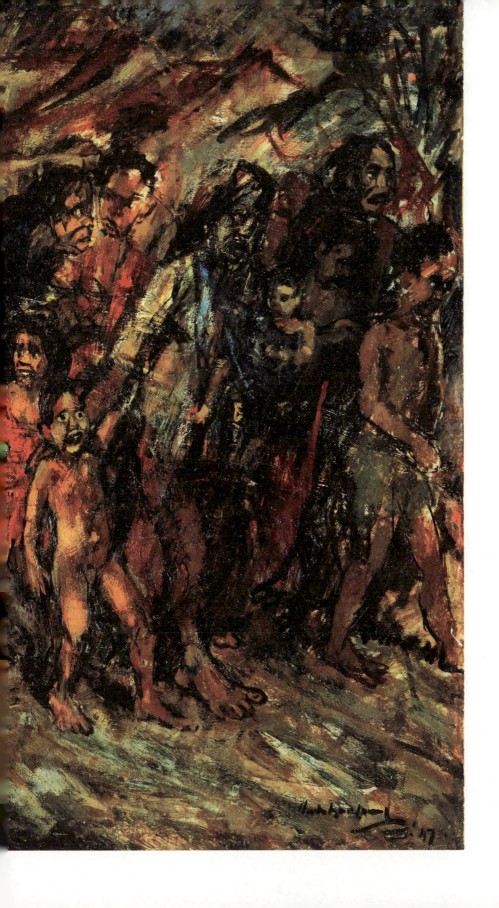

[8]　The lead Republican and Dutch negotiators in Linggajati, 11–13 November 1946

[9]　Mohammad Hatta and Huib van Mook during the negotiations in Linggajati, by Henk Ngantung, 11–13 November 1946

The negotiations in Linggajati, in the mountains just south of Cirebon in West Java, where from September to November 1946 the Commission-General headed by Willem Schermerhorn was in dialogue with the Republican leadership, led to an agreement that seemed to promise the imminent recognition and establishment of an independent Indonesia. This was one of the few occasions on which Dutch officials spoke to President Sukarno, whom they considered a confederate of the Japanese and a traitor. The Indonesian artist Henk Ngantung, part of the Gelanggang group, was asked by Sukarno to make drawings of the negotiations. This resulted in magnificent portraits of Sukarno and Schermerhorn [P. 172 [4]] and of Hatta and Van Mook [9].

Linggajati made it clear that there was no real basis for a political solution. The radical Republicans felt the agreement demanded too many concessions of them, while Dutch conservatives were unwilling to consent to it unless still more conditions were added. The negotiations on implementing the agreement reached a dead end, and in July 1947 this led to the offensive code-named 'Operatie Product' (Operation Product) later known in the Netherlands as the first 'police action'. This was not the first Dutch military action; since the spring of 1946, Dutch troops had been engaged in large-scale combat around Jakarta, in South Sulawesi, in Bali and elsewhere. And although the Republicans and the Dutch kept returning to the negotiating table, the fighting would not stop.

The violence was widespread, but often limited in scope. Travelling from village to village in Java, Sumatra, Sulawesi or Bali, you hear countless stories about the violent Dutch patrols and purging operations. Sometimes traces of these events can be found in the archives. In a little envelope among the papers of the Marine Brigade in the National Archives in The Hague is a small cotton ball with a piece of shrapnel in it. It comes from the body of Mbok (Mrs) Lasmo, from the village of Balongwono, just west of Mojokerto in East Java. The shard was removed by the physician Mas Hoesman, the head of the general hospital in Mojokerto. Mbok Lasmo was hit by the piece of shrapnel from a mortar shell fired from the railway by a patrol of Dutch marines. They had left Mojokerto on the morning of 4 June 1949. As they approached the village of Balongwono, they discovered that the railway tracks had been destroyed. A small group of marines entered the hamlet of Wates Lor, pillaged a few houses and shot down men at work in front of their homes or in the fields. An unexploded bomb found earlier near the railway, designed to be set off by pulling a cord, was detonated in the middle of the village. From the slope next to the railway, people were shot and grenades were thrown. One piece of shrapnel hit Mbok Lasmo.

This is a relatively minor incident in the larger story of the revolution, but one with tragic consequences for the people involved and their families. These events are still recounted in the village with great precision, and the stories are confirmed by Dutch military archives.[25] The incident never caused a scandal and was never acknowledged as an 'excess' –the Dutch legal and military term for transgressive or criminal violence. The killings in Wates Lor were never officially categorized on one side or the other of this dividing line, but the accounts of the events – including those by Dutch soldiers who participated – make it clear that unarmed men from the village were murdered in cold blood.

In their efforts to pacify the occupied territories and conduct purges of Republican soldiers, Dutch troops made little distinction between combatants and civilians, partly because the population so often supported the Republican troops [10]. People responded to the patrols with distrust and hostility, and frequently fled when they approached. Many Indonesians' strongest personal association with the revolution was their fear of the Dutch army. The tragic events in Wates Lor in June 1949 comprised just one of countless incidents in which trigger-happy Dutch troops burned down houses, stole property and shot and killed villagers – often without checking their identity or investigating the situation. There are well-known massacres such as in Rawagede, where on 9 December 1947 a company of Dutch soldiers shot down hundreds of men, or the Dutch actions in South Sulawesi a year earlier, in which Captain Raymond Westerling and his subordinates executed almost two thousand men in purges conducted over a three-month period; another few thousand victims were killed by other army divisions.[26] But much of the Dutch violence has remained almost invisible. During the war, an image was created of a vital struggle against poorly disciplined forces of revolutionary 'extremists'. This was used to justify harsh measures by Dutch forces, which were sent to 'eliminate' the enemy, inflicting the greatest possible losses. In practice, this often meant that they shot at anything that moved, or whenever there was the slightest suspicion of resistance. They also engaged in violent reprisals and torture.[27] Even after all these years, it is still not clear how many people lost their lives in these Dutch military actions.[28] But every town, village and region in the war zones in Java, Sumatra, Bali and Sulawesi has its own memories of this brutality.

On the Dutch side, there was little opposition to the use of large-scale violence. Most civilian officials and members of the military firmly believed in the necessity of rigorous measures to restore order.[29] In their eyes, that was an essential first step towards good, responsible administration. Many officials seem to have had misgivings about the use of extreme force, but then again, they also witnessed the abduction and murder of Indonesian local officials by pro-Republican groups. The violent acts committed by Dutch forces arose from a deep conviction of the legitimacy of the colonial system and a sense of responsibility. There was growing opposition in some Dutch circles, especially when the guerrilla war flared up after the second major Dutch offensive – 'Operatie Kraai' (Operation Crow), in December 1948, which was launched in order to break through the diplomatic impasse and eliminate the Republic. Soldiers wrote horrified letters, clergy members protested and Dutch parliamentarians began to ask questions. The army in Indonesia kept manipulating the information about the use of force. Whistle-blowers were silenced.[30]

[10] *Pembersihan Desa* (Purge of the Village), by Soerono, 1949

[11]　　　Hizbullah march, Islamic armed forces, presumably Yogyakarta, 1946/1947

Of course, Indonesian fighters were also guilty of large-scale, murderous violence. In Indonesia, this topic has not received much attention from the authorities or from historians. Although the leaders of the Republic endeavoured to rein in the violence, they had to acknowledge that they did not have all the militias and military leaders under control. Some were fairly autonomous in their activities and strove for a different kind of Indonesia; such groups include Hizbullah and Sabilillah, who fought for an Islamist Indonesia [11].

At times the struggle degenerated into murder and plunder, which gave the impression that a more criminal motivation was involved. Yet most of the violence had political motives. For instance, it is striking that in the first few weeks after the Japanese capitulation in August 1945, there was not yet any large-scale violence against Dutch or Eurasian individuals. Only after the first British troops landed, and especially after Dutch soldiers appeared on the scene and it became clear that a colonial reoccupation was in progress, did the various groups of fighters erupt into violence. It was especially in the first months after the arrival of Dutch troops that they carried out numerous acts of often sadistic violence. The number of victims in the Dutch and Eurasian population is unknown, but a realistic estimate would be around 5,500.[31]

This violence illustrates that the spirit of revolution sometimes took on sinister forms. In Dutch circles, this period is known as the *Bersiap*, after the battle cry of the groups of Indonesian fighters, but the term has never caught on in Indonesia.[32] From the Dutch perspective, the Bersiap ended in early 1946, when British and Dutch military units were able to keep the peace by force in the major cities and most Dutch individuals were either in those cities or confined in Republican internment camps. But Dutch and Eurasian individuals were not the only targets of violence; other groups associated with the colonial regime were also among the victims, such as the Chinese, the Ambonese and the former governing aristocracy. Where central authority was absent, irregular troops had an especially free hand.

Violence also broke out in the areas occupied by the Dutch during their military actions. The Dutch troops there were often confronted with fierce guerrilla warfare, which had the support of the general population. In such areas, local officials who worked for the Dutch were threatened, kidnapped, and not infrequently murdered. Intimidation of 'collaborators' was often instigated by the central military authorities. In the last year of the war, when the guerrilla fighting was at its peak, some six hundred officials – mostly *lurah* (village chiefs), *juru tulis* (village secretaries) and *wedana* (district chiefs) died in this manner. This campaign of intimidation and terror had a profound impact, because many officials no longer dared to work with the Dutch and instead fled or went into hiding.

On all sides of the conflict, terrible suffering was inflicted. The Dutch were guilty of excessive, systematic violence on a massive scale, but so were the Indonesians. We often see these two observations in a single sentence, as if one explains, excuses or neutralizes the other. There is a human tendency to invoke the principle of an eye for an eye, in an attempt to justify one's own conduct. Yet the motives, the numbers of victims and the rationales for the murderous violence differ too greatly between the two sides for any objective calculation of relative guilt. Resistance against domination is not the same thing as a colonial war of reoccupation. The violence of irregular military groups acting independently of any central authority is distinct from the murderous reprisals of a state military force. Violence cannot be weighed in the balance.

VOICES

In war and violent conflict, all sense of nuance tends to get lost. The blinding light of the struggle overwhelms all subtle shades of grey. Yet the Indonesian revolution cannot be reduced to a conflict between two parties, the Republic and the Netherlands. When Indonesians have looked back on their history, incongruous and idiosyncratic voices have often been smothered or relegated to the margins. In both Indonesia and the Netherlands, the history of the war has mainly been told from a national perspective shaped by the dominant political interpretation of the war. Of course the primary conflict was about who would decide the future of Indonesia. But the perspectives on and experiences in that conflict were dizzyingly varied. For example, the Dutch, with the help of regional elites, set up states that would together form a future United States of Indonesia and provide a counterweight to the Republic in Java and Sumatra. But there were also ethnic communities, ideologically and religiously inspired movements, and the various experiences of men and women, villagers and city dwellers. All this made the revolution chaotic, confusing, fluid and self-contradictory.

To understand anything about the Indonesian revolution, we must make room for polyphony, for the whole wide range of diverse, chaotic, contradictory voices. Personal stories are a vital means of illustrating the complexity of history in the Netherlands. Indo-Dutch, Moluccans and Papuas, as well as conscientious objectors and communists, have fought for years to bring attention to their memories and perspectives, often unsuccessfully. In Indonesia, likewise, there has been little openness – at least in the national public sphere – to the boundless variety of experiences and perspectives. Strikingly, it is novelists who have been able to reach beyond the standard narratives, such as Y.B. Mangunwijaya, and more recently Iksaka Banu.[33] Of course, no account of the revolution can ever encompass every single point of view. But a polyphonic approach shows that national interpretations, or those of dominant ethnic groups, are limited in value, from the perspective of the individuals involved in the conflict.

The revolution was not a war between two free nations. From the Dutch perspective, it was a war to defend colonial interests overseas and control the process of decolonization. For the Indonesians, it was a war of independence, but Indonesia was a package for which the contents still had to be found. In other words, it was not only a war against the Netherlands, but also a war over who would decide Indonesia's future.

At the time of the proclamation of independence, Indonesia was still just an intention, and was mainly the preoccupation of a small intellectual and political elite. Many people had yet to learn the idea of the nation. For example, Minarsih Wiranatakusuma only began writing her diary in Indonesian on 1 January 1945. Others did not begin thinking about politics until much later. Many Indonesians went on working for the Dutch, some out of loyalty, others in the conviction that the Netherlands was best able to maintain law and order, and still others simply because they needed the income. This group included a large number of local government officials who went on working for the colonial administration after the Dutch reoccupation. Was this collaboration? Yes, in the eyes of the guerrilla leaders. Hundreds of these officials paid for their services with their lives. Others fled, preferring a life full of uncertainties to a position in the employ of the Dutch.

There were also Indonesians working in the central colonial administration. The best-known of them may be Abdulkadir Widjojoatmodjo, one of Van Mook's main advisers and the leader of the Dutch delegation that negotiated with the Republic. Was he a bad nationalist? He believed in an orderly transition and a Netherlands-led path to independence. The same is true of the lawyer Oerip Kartodirdjo, who was the procurator-general – the senior official for legal matters in the colonial regime – in the final months of the Dutch occupation. In that role, he was responsible for prosecuting the crimes of soldiers in the Dutch army, a process that never got off the ground. Some Indonesians changed sides. Nico Palar, a member of the Dutch parliament – one of three 'Indonesians' ever to serve in that institution – resigned from the Dutch Labour Party, gave up his seat in parliament and joined the Republic on the afternoon of 21 July 1947, when the Dutch military offensive known as Operation Product began. He was immediately sent to New York to influence international opinion as a representative of the Republic there.

The revolution created a new political reality, in which the old elites had to find their way. There were deep divisions among the Balinese nobility about what road to take. Some backed the Republic; others opposed it. The primary concern of many was to safeguard their own authority. For example, Ide Anak Agung Gde Agung, the raja of Gianyar, used his position to become president of Negara Indonesia Timur (NIT, State of East Indonesia), the first federal state established by the Dutch.[34] On Bali and in South Sulawesi, the struggle became tangled up with conflicts between the different princely and aristocratic houses. Although it is hard to generalize, many old rulers and princes chose the Dutch side because they believed the former colonial power could offer the strongest guarantees of their continued authority. In summary, there was nothing like a united struggle of the entire Indonesian nation against the Netherlands.

Minorities often had divided loyalties. To some extent, that even applied to the Eurasians, some of whom certainly supported the Republic. Similar mixed feelings could be found among the Chinese Indonesians. In many parts of Sumatra and Java, leading members of the Chinese community set up the Pao An Tui, a local force dedicated to protecting the Chinese community from Republican violence. In Bagan Siapiapi, a large fish-producing town in Central Sumatra, there were even a few battles between Republican troops and armed Chinese groups, which managed to retain control of the city for some time. Because of their wealth and the image of them as accomplices of the colonial regime, the Chinese were targets of violence in many places. Thousands of them were killed, and others were driven out of their homes. But there were also pro-Republican Chinese individuals, especially in Java. A large number of cities had *pemuda* organizations whose members were of Chinese descent.[35]

The revolution set countless people in motion who fought for their own vision of the future. Many Indonesians had communist ideals, although the number of actual communists was probably far lower than the Dutch authorities wanted people to believe. In September 1948, communist rebels under Musso, who had just returned from Moscow, attempted to form an alternative state in East Java. They were crushed by the Republican army. Thousands of communists and suspected communists were killed in the affair, including the former prime minister Amir Sjarifuddin.

There were also groups that sought an Islamic state. These were especially successful in Aceh, North Sumatra. In 1948, the Republican Sekarmadji Maridjan Kartosoewirjo in Java began to champion the cause of an Islamic state, Darul Islam. There were thus three or four groups jockeying for power in West Java: the federal state of Pasundan, supported by the Dutch, the Republic and Darul Islam.

This shows how innumerable the contrasting visions of Indonesia's future were. Some could be accommodated within the Republican political system, while others conflicted with the Republic's values and ambitions and drove their supporters to found alternative states, none of which survived. There were far too many perspectives and voices for any history of the revolution to include them all. We can never entirely do justice to this polyphony. But even just sampling a few of these voices reveals the crude and schematic nature of national perspectives on this chapter in history.

THE ARCHIVE OF THE REVOLUTION

One of the most impressive images from the revolutionary period is that of Sukarno's triumphal entry into Jakarta on 28 December 1949. At an undramatic gathering the day before, Tony Lovink, the Dutch High Commissioner of the Crown, had handed over the reins of power to Sultan Hamengkubuwono IX, who represented the Republik Indonesia Serikat (RIS, Republic of the United States of Indonesia). Afterwards, they had watched the changing of the flag outside the palace and Lovink had boarded his aircraft. President Sukarno had not been in attendance. He arrived from Yogyakarta the next day in a KLM aeroplane that had hurriedly been painted in the colours of Garuda Indonesia Airways. At Kemayoran Airport in Jakarta, an open car was waiting for him, a fabulous maroon Packard Convertible borrowed from the businessman Agus Musin Dasaad. Hundreds of thousands of people had rushed to Ikada Square, which Sukarno would very soon rename Medan Merdeka (Freedom Square).[36] Sukarno was driven through the cheering crowd at walking speed and stepped out of the car at the steps of the palace. Before long, the throng burst through the cordon and surrounded their president. If the Dutch had ever doubted the popularity of the self-appointed president among the masses, here was the proof. The famous French photographer Henri Cartier-Bresson – who was married to a Jakartan woman and had in the previous weeks already been photographing the Indonesian spirit of independence [12] – attended and took magnificent photos of the celebration.[37]

The president stood on the steps of the former palace of the Dutch governor-general, which had now become the presidential palace. There he spoke about the four-year period when he had been separated from the people of Jakarta, saying it had felt to him like forty years. The crowd chanted 'Merdeka!' The president asked, rhetorically, what had made it possible to raise the bicolour flag on the lawn in front of the palace. He answered his own question: 'It is because no one other than the people of Indonesia, all seventy million of them, risking their own lives, fought to make it possible.' And he concluded with the words, 'Now we must work, work and work for the reconstruction of our country.'[38]

Sukarno knew that this was not the end, but the beginning of an arduous struggle for Indonesia. The departure of the Dutch was one thing, but building a thriving, united nation was quite another. The country had been damaged by the war and the trade boycott, and groups of rebels and criminals remained active in many places. As the hostilities between the Republic and the Netherlands had dragged on, the Indonesian military had risen to an extraordinary powerful position, which after the conflict it would never really relinquish. Furthermore, colonialism and the war of independence had left deep scars. After the transfer of sovereignty in late 1949 many political issues remained unresolved, such as the status of the Papuans and the dominance of Dutch companies in the private sector. The change of regime had also created new problems, such as demands for autonomy in the provinces.[39] Indonesia was still not much more than an intention. Also for the Dutch, decolonization was not completed by the transfer of sovereignty. Decolonization proved an exceedingly difficult process, for the legacy of colonial experiences are far-reaching and persistent.

Indonesia and the Netherlands each have their own ways of talking about the revolution, narratives that did not come about by chance. The history of the revolution presented by Sukarno was crystal clear: the independence struggle was the struggle for a single, inevitable nation. Not surprisingly, this story is enshrined in the rituals of state, especially the annual celebration of independence on 17 August. The fundamental message of these rituals is that freedom is worth celebrating and that it took strength and courage to fight for it. But this narrative leaves out the complexities, the alternative

[12] Enthusiastic crowd in Yogyakarta in the period around Sukarno's inauguration as president of the Republik Indonesia Serikat (RIS, Republic of the United States of Indonesia), photo by Henri Cartier-Bresson (Magnum), 1949

futures, the internecine violence and the many haunting ghosts of the revolution. As the Irish-British-American historian Benedict Anderson once wrote, the formation of a national identity relies on the act of forgetting.[40]

The Dutch have an entirely different mode of dealing with the legacies of the conflict. In the Netherlands, the historical narrative of the war revolved around its legal basis – and still does. This manifests in many different ways – above all, in the legal construction of Indonesian independence, which was not formalized until December 1949. Only much later, in 2005, did Dutch foreign minister Ben Bot declare while visiting Indonesia that the Netherlands accepts 17 August 1945 as the start of Indonesian independence, 'in a political and moral sense'. In other words, not in a legal sense. Likewise, the approach to Dutch violence in the war with Indonesia is dominated by the legal approach. This has its roots in the war itself, when the responsible parties applied legal standards to their acts of violence, drawing distinctions between what was 'permissible' and what was 'excessive', and often talked about the revolutionaries in legal terms – for example, referring to them as 'terrorists' and 'criminals' who were 'disturbing the peace' and fighting the 'legitimate' authorities. The primacy of legal thinking is rooted in the conviction of colonial justification.

A second characteristic of the Dutch attitude towards the war in Indonesia is that the topic of discussion is always the political disputes in the Netherlands and, more recently, the Dutch acts of violence. Indonesia itself rarely excites much interest. That too perpetuates the colonial gaze: only the actions of the Dutch are seen as worth discussing, not the lives or arguments of the Indonesians. The war in Indonesia – which, of course, could never be called a war – was an internal Dutch political problem, and the Netherlands responded mainly by trying to avoid scandals and control information.[41] The main question under discussion in the Netherlands was how the end of the colonial empire in Indonesia could have led to such political chaos, soiling its reputation as a benevolent colonial power. The question of what the war had been like for Indonesians did not receive any attention then, and hardly does today.

Both the legal discourse and the dominant issue of domestic political responsibility have prevented the Netherlands from paying serious attention to Indonesian views. There has been much less interest in Indonesian historical writing in the Netherlands than vice versa. Many Dutch historical works have been translated into Indonesian; even General Abdul Haris Nasution's monumental study was based in many respects on Dutch studies and archival documents.[42] Conversely, we find little interest in Indonesian sources and studies among Dutch historical writers.[43]

The archive of the revolution does not exist. No collection can encompass the experiences of the revolution. There are also very practical barriers to creating such an archive. For one, historical writing is made difficult by the scarcity of source materials. Large portions of the Republican archives are in the Netherlands, having been confiscated and plundered by the army and placed in the archives of the Netherlands Forces Intelligence Service (NEFIS) [13].[44] Hardly any local archives from this period exist in Indonesia. Much has been lost, or perhaps was seized by the army in later years. In any case, local government archives are consistently absent until 1965. One result is that the history of the conflict has been easily hijacked by the dominant narrative of collective struggle; another is that oral history has flourished. Where no written documents are available, historians in recent decades have collected oral eyewitness accounts of local history.

The archives determine our preoccupations, aided by the deep gulf created by decolonization and the persistence of colonial worldviews that have led the Dutch to focus mainly on their own role. In many respects, the Netherlands has never undergone decolonization. In Indonesia, on the other hand, the story of the united revolution has been perpetuated. This semblance of unity underpins the legitimacy of the postcolonial state. Only in local history is there some room for variations on the narrative of a unified revolution and accounts of internecine violence. It is also, in a fundamental way, equally true of Indonesia that it has never been decolonized. The legacy of colonialism takes countless forms, but its full extent is rarely acknowledged or made explicit.

In *Revolusi!*, the different stories and registers are allowed to coexist in all their contradictions. The myths of the revolution are presented alongside the chaos of individual testimonies. Propaganda stands opposite authentic images. The Indonesians stand opposite the Dutch. But if you look and read carefully, you will see the spaces and the connections between them. History resists facile schematization, and it does so by juxtaposing different perspectives and narratives.

[13] An Indonesian kneels surrounded by Dutch marines. A propaganda poster is seized, c. 1946–1949

PROKLAMASI

INDEPENDENCE CAPTURED

YUDHI SOERJOATMODJO

REVOLUSI!

In the night and early morning of 17 August 1945, intense preparations were underway for the *Proklamasi*, the declaration of independence of Indonesia. At the house where, according to plan, the proclamation would be read out, *pemuda* (young freedom fighters) of the Barisan Pelopor (Vanguard Corps) stood ready. Alongside this provisionally armed Indonesian paramilitary brigade, soldiers from the Indonesian volunteer army Pembela Tanah Air (PETA, Defenders of the Homeland) and scouts from Kepanduan Bangsa Indonesia (KBI), Indonesia's scouting movement, were also present. They were there to prevent the Japanese military disrupting the independence declaration. Also on the spot early was photojournalist Soemarto Frans Mendur, from the newspaper *Asia Raya*, to record the events of the day. The most important participants – Sukarno and Mohammad Hatta – had yet to arrive. The two older leaders had been kidnapped the previous day by several young revolutionaries in an attempt to force them to proclaim the independence of Indonesia that very day, 16 August, over the radio. Ultimately this plan was abandoned, but, again under pressure from the youths, the various parties agreed to have the independence declaration take place on 17 August.

What follows is an account of the actions of the various people involved on that day – from three o'clock to ten-thirty in the morning – culminating in the proclamation of the independent Republic of Indonesia, a historic event immortalized in eighteen photos by Frans Mendur.

05:00–08:00 A.M. DAWN MANOEUVRES

They had waited since before daybreak. The boy scouts in their khaki shorts, guarding the front garden of the house at Jalan Pegangsaan Timur 56. The handful of young men from the Barisan Pelopor paramilitary brigade watching the main roads, gripping their long rattan defensive staves in nervous silence.[1] And the armed platoon of Defenders of the Homeland who had rushed in soon after with their carbine rifles. Some of them quickly took positions out front while their *shodan-cho* (lieutenant), Arifin Abdurachman, stationed himself beside the house telephone – requisitioning the owner's office as the field command centre of operations.[2] The rest dashed to the rear where, camouflaged in their battle fatigues, they took cover behind the train embankments running along the back of the building.[3]

This was what they had been recruited for when in October 1943 the Japanese Occupation Government first set up the homeland defence volunteer force – later renamed Pembela Tanah Air (PETA) – as auxiliaries to its own army.[4] This was the culmination of those rain-soaked midnight manoeuvres – and the humiliating slaps, canings and verbal abuse they had endured – that would soon prove their mettle as revolutionary guerrilla infantry units.[5] Except that they would not be shooting at the Americans, British or the returning Dutch. Instead they would face the Japanese Imperial Army, which had trained them in the first place.

Daidan-cho Abdul Latief Hendraningrat's instructions as PETA's acting battalion commander had been clear that morning: open fire on seeing any Japanese soldiers approaching the site. His plan was to incite the Barisan Pelopor militias to join in the attack while awaiting the arrival of more reinforcements that were still being held at their barracks, some ten minutes' drive away. With nearly three quarters of its soldiers redeployed to the Burma (now Myanmar), Sumatra, Timor and Guadalcanal fronts, the Japanese army in Java had been reduced to only two garrisons and eight battalions of about 15,000 men. Yet it was still a formidable force that had swiftly and brutally struck down previous PETA rebellions – even beheading some of the insurrectionists' leaders – in half a dozen cities and regencies across the island between September 1944 and June 1945.[6]

Thus, Hendraningrat's initial plan was to completely barricade all streets north, west and south leading to the house – with an additional platoon hidden among the residential buildings to flank the Japanese assault. He knew the Barisan Pelopor, who mostly trained with wooden rifles, rattan staves and sharpened bamboo spears, could not long survive an assault by the better-armed Japanese soldiers. He and his men had been up all night – taking advantage of the Ramadan dawn meal while their Japanese superiors were still fast asleep – and looted the battalion's armoury, most of which were weapons taken from captured or killed Koninklijk Nederlandsch-Indisch Leger (KNIL, Royal Netherlands East Indies Army) forces defending Java in 1942: rifles; water-cooled Vickers machine guns, which the Japanese called *zukikanju*; *keikikanju* (light machine guns); and hand grenades, though, alas, no *kugekihos* (trench mortars).[7] All were loaded onto trucks and ready to go under the guise of an urban warfare exercise. All seemed fine, except for the one thing he had failed to predict: the Japanese military instructor who insisted on coming along. That would have given the game away; they would have been swiftly overrun by Japanese troops before they could organize themselves. There would be no proclamation, then. No independence. Only a bloodbath.

Hendraningrat had quickly ordered the trucks and his men to be on standby at the barracks – one of whom was instructed to sit at all times beside the battalion staff office's telephone, waiting for that call from the *shodan-cho* he had dispatched earlier to Sukarno's house. A single ring from the lieutenant to the garrison was to mean only one thing: send reinforcements – the Japanese are attacking. He then somehow got the instructor's permission to reconnoitre the locations for their morning's exercise, using the opportunity to rush to the house where that morning he and his men would make history safeguarding their country's independence.

05:00–09:00 A.M. THE GATHERING

Soemarto Frans Mendur had observed all these comings and goings since he arrived at the house at Jalan Pegangsaan Timur 56 in the early morning gloom [1]. He had noted the change in atmosphere from the front garden, the house with its still-empty veranda and shuttered windows, and the scouts and young men of the Barisan Pelopor quietly but anxiously readying themselves.[8] The photojournalist was joined by his brother Alex, six years his senior, who had mentored him in his

[1] Soemarto Frans Mendur (left) with Indonesian police officers, probably Yogyakarta, 1946

profession. After receiving a tip-off from one of his colleagues at Domei, the Japanese news agency where he served as chief of photography, Alex had arrived at the scene from his house at Jalan Batoe Toelis around the same time as Frans.[9] Yet at first Frans had seen nothing – no scribbled announcement, no flags flying from the two steel poles in the front garden, no one who could tell them what exactly would happen that day – to appease the doubts that had been gnawing at his heart since the sympathetic Japanese editor at the *Asia Raya* newspaper where he worked told him, sometime after three in the morning, the urgent news: 'Independence. Today.'

He had become agitated, and before daybreak he left the Unie building, with its cavernous printing floor and the rows of windows that had once overlooked the editorial offices of his and his brother's former employers, the *Java Bode* daily and the *Wereldnieuws en sport in beeld* (World News and Sport) picture magazine, Batavia's (as Jakarta was called under Dutch colonial rule) most popular publications. The Japanese had replaced them with *Asia Raya* and the *Djawa Baroe* periodical after the fall of Java in 1942.[10] Frans had brought along his own Leica camera, but he had to use all his wiles and his position – both as photographer and union member of the printing shop – to sneak a couple rolls of film from the storeroom. In the last few days Japanese supervisors overseeing the local press had resorted to hiding all photographic and cinematic equipment and supplies under lock and key, reflecting the increasingly puzzling realities of the occupation.[11]

On 14 August, Indonesia's two leading politicians – Sukarno and Mohammad Hatta – returned to Jakarta bearing the Japanese gift of independence. In Dalat, in the central province of former French Indochina (now Vietnam), they had met Field Marshal Terauchi Hisaichi.[12] To the welcoming Japanese and Indonesian dignitaries in Jakarta, Sukarno had confidently announced that Indonesia would be free before the corn stalk flowered – unaware that Emperor Hirohito at that very moment had officially capitulated to the Allies.[13] By the dying hours of 16 August 1945 confusion was rife among Indonesian intellectuals, journalists and revolutionaries. That the Japanese were reneging on their earlier promise – part of the terms of their surrender was to return the country as a Dutch colony – and had threatened to deploy their army to punish anyone trying to contravene. That, at that very moment, Sukarno and Hatta were drafting the proclamation at the house of Tadashi Maeda, Rear-Admiral of the Japanese Imperial Navy, who was known to be sympathetic to the Indonesians and supportive of independence.

Frans's dawn tip-off had been the result of his long efforts to befriend his Japanese colleagues and chiefs, although, he would later admit, the news had still caught him by surprise. But not only had the Japanese editor confirmed that Sukarno and Hatta were going to proclaim Indonesia's independence at Sukarno's house that very morning, he had even handed Frans the keys to his car to get there. Frans had brought along his colleague Dal Bassa Pulungan, *Asia Raya*'s city editor, who had been at the office with him that morning – both facing their journey with heavy scepticism but also desperate hope.[14] Many things would feed their anxieties as they sped on their fifteen-minute drive towards their destination on the Molenvliet Oost road built alongside the 300-year-old canal.

There had been signs that the war was not going well for the Japanese: increasing blackouts; unexplained explosions; food shortages; rumours of starving people dying on roadsides; corpses piling up in morgues. On some days the tropical heat carried the smell into people's homes, up to half a kilometre away.[15] Lately, they had also observed the listless faces and the loss of discipline among the Japanese military and civilians.[16] But there were also many grim reminders of Japanese resoluteness and brutality, such as the dozens of internment camps across the city for captured Allied and KNIL soldiers as well as for European civilians – with women and children held in special containments. The most populated camps, at Cideng, were just minutes' walk away from Frans's own home – as were the Kempeitai (Japanese military police) jails at the former Rechtshogeschool building where prisoners were tortured.[17]

Once Frans and Pulungan had passed the PETA barracks (where, unbeknown to them, Hendraningrat's men must have just finished loading their stolen weapons onto trucks) they would have also witnessed some of the 300 or 500 bayonet-wielding Kempeitai soldiers at the Hosokyoku radio station – dispatched there after Rear-Admiral Maeda got wind of the young revolutionaries' kidnapping of Sukarno and Hatta on the previous day and the *pemuda*'s subsequent plan to take over the radio station to broadcast Indonesia's independence.[18]

The threat of violence must have weighed heavily on the minds of the Mendur brothers and Pulungan as much as the PETA, Barisan Pelopor young men and KBI scouts – though somehow it did not deter the streams of people they saw coming into the front garden from various directions as the tropical sky swiftly turned from translucent grey to bright and clear.

Among them was Etty Abdul Rachman, a young secretary from the office that provided translations and consultations to the Kaigun (Japanese Navy). She had been told about the special event by her boss and uncle, the law scholar Achmad Subardjo, who was nowhere to be seen. Finding herself one of the first arrivals, she had quietly chosen her spot under the garden's twilight crape myrtle tree – its purple flowers in full bloom.[19] There were the students from the nearby Ika Daigaku (medical school) who had driven from their dorms in their automobiles, twenty to a car.[20]

And then came S.K. Trimurti, the very picture of a traditional Javanese in her sarong and *kebaya* (blouse), belying the fierce journalist and women's rights activist underneath, who had suffered jail under the Dutch East Indies Politieke Inlichtingendienst (PID, Political Intelligence Service) in 1936 and 1939, as well as torture by the Kempeitai in 1942.[21]

She had had little sleep after having spent the previous night of 16 August being directed to a house in the city by her contacts in the resistance, where she had met a group of machete-carrying brawlers from Banten and young toughs from North Sulawesi with a pre-war reputation for winning bar-fights against Dutch soldiers and sailors.[22] All were waiting for the call to attack the radio station and start the revolution.[23] Thankfully, that midnight folly – hastily planned in the space of a two-hour get-together at the billiard hall of the City Zoo – had been aborted some time before three in the morning; the result of the young revolutionaries' own overconfidence and ineptitude at organizing all the manpower, weaponry and logistics that would have been required to assault the extensive Japanese encampments and Japanese-controlled installations in the city.[24]

Trimurti had quickly returned home to prepare breakfast for her six- and three-year-old sons before heading out for the planned proclamation at Sukarno's house. There she would be reunited with her former comrade-in-arms (with whom she co-published the monthly *Pesat* in 1938) and Sukarno's new private secretary, Sayuti Melik – her husband, whom she had last seen nearly twelve hours ago.

Sayuti Melik had spent the night until the early morning at the residence of Rear-Admiral Maeda, witnessing the historic moment when Hatta dictated to Sukarno the draft of the proclamation. He had been given the honour to transcribe it, even correcting the original Japanese Imperial date of 2605 to 1945, on a typewriter borrowed at the last minute from the German Kriegsmarine (Navy) office.[25]

By now, the crowd of these revolutionaries was starting to spill out into the street with the arrival of 800 men and women armed with sharpened bamboos and cleavers. These fighters from Tangerang, Klender, Balaraja and Mauk in the western hinterland and coastal regions of Banten must have been a sight to behold, with their death stares, long hair, black trousers, blood-red lips from chewing betel leaves, and amulets that reputedly made them impervious to bullets.[26]

When Commander Hendraningrat's car entered the driveway, 15 minutes before 10, that crowd would also have included many who had simply come out of curiosity – friends tagging along or passers-by like the young Mangoendihardjo, who that morning had decided to visit his girlfriend. Not finding her at home, he had forlornly walked by Pegangsaan Timur and, on a whim, decided to join the line of brave-looking PETA soldiers out front.[27]

And yet, many would also miss the historic event. Some by accident – such as Etty's patron, Subardjo, Indonesia's future foreign minister. He was fast asleep at home, exhausted after having spent the previous day negotiating the release of Sukarno and Hatta whom young revolutionaries had hidden in Rengasdengklok, two hours away from Jakarta, before taking them to Maeda, who had contravened the direct order of his superiors by providing his residence for their midnight deliberation of the proclamation. Some by design – such as Sutan Sjahrir, who on the afternoon of 14 August had been the first to inform Sukarno and Hatta of Japan's surrender. The anti-fascist politician had even prepared his own 300-word version of the independence bill, which he insisted Sukarno announce that very evening via the radio station his followers were planning to seize. He and his followers were distancing themselves from what they perceived as a Japanese-sponsored event.[28] Some out of ignorance – like the crowd of people who since morning had come to Ikada Square on foot and by bicycle, carrying sharpened bamboo sticks and the Indonesian red-and-white flags while noisily singing Indonesian folk songs. They were unaware that for security reasons, and on the advice of Rear-Admiral Maeda, Sukarno and Hatta had agreed to move the site of the proclamation to Sukarno's house minutes before bidding their host farewell at 3 a.m.[29]

Burhanuddin Mohammad Diah, *Asia Raya*'s editor, was also at Ikada Square – though he had spent the preceding night with Sukarno and Hatta at Maeda's mansion. He had witnessed their debates with the young revolutionaries; had stood behind Sayuti Melik when he retyped the proclamation; and had impulsively pocketed Sukarno's original handwritten draft that had been left forgotten on the desk [2].[30] The last thing he heard before leaving the house, just before 3 a.m., was Hatta's instruction to him to distribute flyers announcing the proclamation of independence that was to be held at Ikada Square at 10 a.m. that morning – which he promptly did, racing to an all-night print shop, where, in his hurry, he had carelessly drafted the wording on the back of Sukarno's historic handwritten proclamation for the printing assistant to copy. Diah had then spent the rest of the morning travelling around the city, pasting up the freshly printed bills. When he finally arrived at the square, around 9 a.m., the Japanese army had brought in their panzers and troops to trap everyone inside the perimeter.[31]

03:00–09:52 A.M. CHAOS AND CONFUSION

We can only speculate what had been on the minds of Sukarno and Hatta as they rode home from Maeda's mansion through leafy Showa Dori, the pre-war Oranje Boulevard, shortly after 3 a.m. Sukarno pedalling up front with the devout Hatta hitching at the back.[32]

That ten-minute ride might have felt like a short reprieve in contrast to the torrid seventy-two hours following their triumphant return from Dalat. Not only had the Japanese broken their earlier promise of Indonesia's independence, Hatta and Sukarno had also been threatened with a bloodbath by their own young revolutionaries for refusing to proclaim it without first consulting the official – though Japanese-sanctioned – Panitia Persiapan Kemerdekaan Indonesia (PPKI, Preparatory Committee for Indonesian Independence).

In a final effort to put pressure on the two leaders, at three in the morning of 16 August 1945 a group of *pemuda* from the Barisan Pelopor, and PETA soldiers, roused Sukarno and Hatta to be taken away – along with Sukarno's wife and nine-month-old son – to Rengasdengklok, sixty kilometres from Jakarta. There, they claimed, Sukarno and Hatta could safely broadcast Indonesia's independence, free from Japanese dictates or threats, as 15,000 citizen-soldiers launched the revolution.[33] In reality, the four had been forced to wait the whole day, resting on plain mats in the wooden hut serving as billet for the local PETA soldiers, before being moved to supposedly bigger and more comfortable accommodation: the house of a local Chinese farmer, whose front yard was littered with pig droppings.[34] Sukarno's hungry son had soiled Hatta's trousers while being pacified and Hatta had been unable to perform his prayers.

Subardjo finally came and with great difficulty negotiated their release from the hostile PETA soldiers and their leaders, convincing them that Sukarno and Hatta would proclaim independence the next morning, on 17 August 1945. By then, the promised radio with which they were

Proklamasi.

Kami bangsa Indonesia dengan ini menjatakan kemerdekaan Indonesia.

Hal² jang mengenai pemindahan kekoeasaan d.l.l., diselenggarakan dengan tjara saksama dan dalam tempoh jang sesingkat-singkatnja.

Djakarta, 17-8-'05
Wakil² bangsa Indonesia

The draft of the *Proklamasi*, written by Sukarno, 17 August 1945

supposed to make the announcement had yet to arrive, as was the people's revolution they had been bragging about. The only flames they had seen, as they soberly drove back to Jakarta, were those of the dried rice husks a local farmer was burning on the roadside at sunset.[35]

Whatever they had been thinking on that dawn ride home – twenty-four hours after their kidnapping and eight hours after their safe return to Jakarta – it had not been the organization of that day's historic event. Sukarno himself would later boast that it had been without protocol. He had not assigned Hendraningrat to knock on the door to his room, to remind him of the time for the proclamation, nor told him to station the steadfast *shodan-cho* beside the phone.[36] No one had assigned Sudiro of the Barisan Pelopor to instruct young Soehoed to cut a piece of bamboo,[37] which Riwu Ga, Sukarno's manservant, would then stick into the ground in front of the veranda – later serving as the simple mast for the red-and-white national flag to which Sukarno's wife, Fatmawati, had been making some final touches that morning. No one had even told Hendraningrat he would later be tasked with flying it.

The hired men wiring-in the veranda had no idea that only minutes later their home-made microphone and speakers – concocted out of the magnet from a disused bicycle dynamo and some cigarette foil – would amplify the words that set their country free.[38] They had been as clueless as those passengers on the 10 o'clock Jatinegara-bound train, gaping at the mobs at the rear of Sukarno's house.[39] Similarly, no one had told the spirited medical students at Jalan Prapatan 10 to prepare a parallel ceremony. Despite their disdain for what they perceived as a lack of fervour in the proclamation bill (and for having been drafted in sight of a Japanese official) they had sent one of their own to relay the ceremony via the telephone at Sukarno's house, ensuring the proclamation would still be broadcast even if the Japanese had tried to disrupt it.[40] And clearly, no one had thought to invite any journalists to record the event for posterity – although Sukarno and Hatta had always had an easy and warm relationship with the press. There had only been Pulungan and Suroto, a Domei reporter, at the house.[41] The Mendur brothers, who had diligently covered the independence preparatory meetings with Sukarno and Hatta since June, would be the only photographers present.[42]

When many of the actual witnesses decided to write down their memories of the day they would provide conflicting accounts. When Sukarno and Hatta finally emerged from the house, at two or three minutes before 10, some, like Frans Mendur, had clearly heard jubilant shouts of 'Merdeka!' (freedom!).[43] Others, like Etty, merely remembered people gently and politely clapping their hands – still fearful of the Japanese retaliation that could have come at any moment.[44] Pulungan later wrote that it had only been the sight of Sukarno and Hatta stepping out onto the veranda to meet the increasingly anxious crowd that had appeased his all-consuming doubts: that Indonesia's independence was finally to become a reality.[45]

10:00–10:30 A.M. THE PHOTOGRAPHER AND THE PHOTOGRAPHS

That sense of precariousness was one that Frans had intimate knowledge of, ever since he first joined Dr Soetomo's Persatuan Bangsa Indonesia (PBI, National Unity Organization) in 1930. He was just seventeen then – like so many of his compatriots, young enough to be swept up by the fervour of national awakening; yet old enough to have experienced the painful consequences of Governor-General Bonifacius Cornelis de Jonge's iron-fist regime (1931–1936). Combative, asinine and blunt-speaking,[46] the Dutch East Indies' 64th governor-general was a deeply conservative aristocrat who quickly abandoned his predecessor's pro-ethical and relatively liberal policies, unleashing the full force of his main security agency, upon those increasingly daring anti-colonial intellectuals and political organizations among the country's Indigenous population.[47]

His new reign of *Rust en Orde* (Peace and Order) soon metastasized into a police state. De Jonge's (not-so) secret agents took copious notes during political and cultural gatherings. They sat at the back of theatres, scrutinizing dialogue and gestures for the least signs of sedition. They muzzled the press and orchestrated show trials against nationalist leaders such as Sukarno, Hatta and Sjahrir, sentencing them to exile on malaria-infested islands. While organizations led by Dr Soetomo did not have a reputation for radicalism, like many of his peers Frans somehow got into the cross-hairs of the politicalintelligence service PID. He had never disclosed the true reason for this, but judging by his later activities during the Japanese occupation, the revolution and in the 1960s, it might have involved the distribution of pam-phlets or publications which authorities would have found subversive.[48] And simply being suspected of something in that period would have been enough to destroy one's prospects. Frans had to abandon a perfectly respectable job as a scribe in the public works office at Klungkung (in the south-eastern part of the island of Bali). Escaping to the sweltering port city of Surabaya, East Java, he found anonymity among the small traders, lowly porters and burly thugs and hustlers swarming its market.[49]

It was a time of economic depression and he was forced to work on the street selling *kretek* (clove cigarettes).[50] But he was a hard worker and had a knack for befriending locals – an innate talent which many friends such as the journalist Rosihan Anwar and Des Alwi remembered him for. He was adopted by an elderly and childless salt-merchant couple who gave him his Javanese name, Soemarto, which was used by his neighbours and relatives in place of his original Christian name.[51]

Converting to Islam, he – a descendant of pig farmers and faith healers from a small hamlet at the foot of Mount Tondano in North Sulawesi – appeared to complete his transformation.[52] Until that fortuitous day in 1933, when his eldest brother, Alex, finally located him in Surabaya and took him to Jakarta (then called Batavia). He rebuilt his life in the capital city, working his way up from paperboy to full-time employment at the Unie printing press.[53] Meanwhile, he was acquiring new skills as photographic assistant to his brother Alex, a freelancer for the publisher's most important periodicals: the *Java Bode* and the *Wereldnieuws en sport in beeld*. Safely integrated within the proverbial lion's den,

Frans even gravitated towards his old passion for political activism: joining the Partai Serikat Celebes (Celebes Federation Party) in 1934, and Partai Indonesia Raya (Parindra, Great Indonesia Party) and the youth organization Surya Wirawan (Valiant Sun) the year after.

Most importantly, he had got himself elected as Head of the Unie Union Workers, which would soon prove key the day the Japanese Imperial Army entered the city.[54] On 6 March 1942, he alerted troops from the Sato Detachment, then personally went back to Molenvliet Oost 8 to help them prevent his Dutch bosses from their final desperate scorched-earth tactic to burn down the printing-shop machines and valuable paper stocks.

The grateful new conqueror had given him a medal for his role and he even retained his position in the union (renamed Djawa Shimbun Sha). Equally significant, in Frans and Alex they saw skilled and seasoned locals who were not only co-operative but could also replace the Dutch professionals they were starting to lock up in camps. Frans was soon appointed photographer at *Asia Raya*; Alex, chief of photography at the Domei news bureau. A newly recruited member at that agency later reminisced about being in awe of the senior reporters milling about the Domei office in Postweg Noord. Professionals who had earned their credentials as anti-colonial journalist-activists. 'I was experiencing life among the leading newsmen of the time', gushed the young typist Pramoedya Ananta Toer. Among those he mentioned in particular was 'F. Mendur, persfotograf [press photographer]'.[55]

Likewise, it might have been a similar sense of dignity and respect that Soemarto Frans Mendur had tried to capture in the photographs he made on the morning of 17 August: the formal, even austere, quality of his compositions seemingly stripping away all trace of any previous discord, division and disorganization to show the image of a young nation, willing itself to construct a new yet still unknown future, soberly and collectively.

This unity was already evident from what could well be the first in the set of eighteen photographs taken by Mendur that we currently have of that day: of the *kopiah*-wearing Dr Moewardi, head of the Barisan Pelopor – who just the day before had been one of the co-conspirators abducting Sukarno and Hatta from their homes – rallying his columns of troops in their Japanese-style field caps and shorts to show their deference to the two leaders. Shot from within the veranda, it provided a patriotic vista of the mass of people in the front garden who had by then spilled into the main road, and a glimpse of part of Sukarno's torso (also from behind). It also captured – to the front left of the image – the solitary figure of a *kebaya*-clad woman, whose slightly dishevelled yet striking appearance seems to mirror that of the unvarnished and undecorated cut-bamboo mast [3].

Frans's second image is probably the one showing Sukarno and Hatta more prominently – though still photographed from behind. Both half-raise their hands in acknowledgment of the crowds' various forms of respect – many bowing in the Japanese style, some giving the military salute – reminding us not only of the event's lack of protocol but also of its singular time and the diverse backgrounds of the day's participants [4].

What could be the third photo in the series – still made from the veranda but slightly to the left – provides a more startling image and evidence of the vast number of people who were present at Jalan Pegangsaan Timur. The crowd is dominated by a large group of young men – probably Barisan Pelopor – who had somehow managed to escape or avoid the Japanese encirclement at Ikada Square. This particular photograph also presents us with our first sighting, standing on the right side of the veranda, of acting PETA *daidan-cho* Hendraningrat [5]. Though the Japanese Imperial Army had frugally patched his uniform out of some old KNIL cloth – the *katana* (Japanese military long-sword) is merely a cheap knock-off manufactured in Java or Singapore – his commanding presence nonetheless impressed many that day.[56] Yet, as he recollected later, that morning he was anything but calm and collected as he kept his eyes on the street beyond, alert for any sudden movements – half expecting the Japanese to rush in and break up the gathering at any moment; listening intently for the first volley of shots that would signal that his platoon had done what he had instructed them to do that morning: to defend the proclamation and everyone taking part in it at all cost. Luckily, the Japanese army was still too busy containing the huge mass of young and old who had gathered at Ikada Square, the original site for the proclamation – perhaps too distracted with securing the Governor-General's Palace and radio station, located just a stone's throw away. We can only imagine how differently that day's history would have turned out had soldiers been instructed to immediately seek out Sukarno and Hatta.

Instead, the next sound everyone would hear was the voice of Suwiryo, deputy mayor of Jakarta during the Japanese occupation (and soon the capital city's first mayor in independent Indonesia), whose bespectacled and solemn face is nearly bleached out by the sun's rays in Frans's fourth and fifth photographs. By this time the photographer had somehow sneaked himself out into the garden, turning the lens of his Leica back onto the people inside the veranda. The first shot from this new vantage point gives an overview of the other participants on that historic day: Fatmawati Sukarno, in her sarong and *selendang* (head covering) to the right of Suwiryo, surrounded by what were probably members of the Independence Committee – while to their left her husband Sukarno stands contemplating something far off; his right hand gripping the corner of a paper with the terse yet resolute proclamation that would forever change history. Mohammad Hatta next to him, invariably impassive and imperturbable, had always been a study of contrast to the impeccable but impassioned lion of the podium that was Sukarno – which Frans captured perfectly that day [6, 7].

The sixth photograph shows Sukarno, resplendent in white, at the microphone, raising the piece of paper that he had been holding in his hand, about to read his brief speech – the one that had kept him up through early morning, drafting and redrafting, until the malaria fever had finally driven him back to bed – the gist of which had been to dispel once and for all the notion of Japanese support or sanction of that day's proclamation. Then, under the watchful eyes of the revolutionary soldiers equipped with second-hand KNIL boots and garters, Sukarno – his voice rasping from exhaustion – finally uttered into the home-made transmitter the now immortal proclamation that seven hours ago he and Hatta had drafted and then transcribed on the Nazi typewriter in the mansion of a high-ranking Japanese officer:

> We, the people of Indonesia, hereby declare Indonesia's independence. Matters concerning the transfer of power and other matters will be executed in an orderly manner and in the shortest possible time.

Soemarto Frans Mendur clicked on his small camera and thus, shortly after ten o'clock in the morning of 17 August 1945, the Christian-born pig-farmer's son turned political fugitive, Javanese Muslim convert and decorated union hero captured the birth of his nation and thereby completed his final metamorphosis as Indonesia's first photojournalist [8, 9].

That highly charged moment seemed to have made the subsequent minutes rush by in a haze since – as Frans recounted in the *IPPHOS Report*, seventeen years after the event – the sole image he remembered taking following Sukarno's proclamation was the raising of the flag, a ceremony that had so moved him to tears he nearly forgot to document it except, 'just the one shot before it reached the top of the mast that leaned onto the house wall'. Frans's recollection seems to have contradicted the evidence of his own handiwork since we have several more images which he probably documented between these iconic moments – two of which were of Sukarno from slightly different angles, hands raised in a prayer of thanks, as Dr Moewardi and Hendraningrat, who had since removed his PETA cap, stand with their heads bowed in piety [10, 11]. The third depicts Hatta at the microphone, his hands held behind his back as he did throughout most of the ceremony, while Sukarno stands at the rear [12]. Curiously, no one – including Hatta himself – recalled this singular moment in their memoirs. (It is known that Hatta did give a speech but that had been much later, when he addressed a troop of Barisan Pelopor that had arrived too late for the ceremony, standing in for Sukarno who by now had retreated to his room with a fever.)

Frans had in fact shot not one but at least six other pictures of the flag-raising ceremony that followed. The first in this sequence – the eleventh in the set of eighteen pictures – was photographed from the steps to the left of the veranda, revealing the figure of Fatmawati, who had since descended onto the garden to stand near S.K. Trimurti, both solemn and subdued in their traditional costumes, alongside another group of men and young women [13].

The photographer must then have quickly and quietly positioned himself in between the proud column of Barisan Pelopor youths (from his third picture) and just behind the two eminent women, blending in with the crowd to capture the two shots of Sukarno and Hatta on the steps of the veranda, their white suits gleaming in the sun, standing to attention for the flag ceremony [14, 15]. This was the moment when Hendraningrat and Soehoed, who had earlier cut the bamboo mast, pulled on the simple flax rope to raise the red-and-white flag up the relatively short (though not at all tilted) pole – the moment when the naive Mangoendihardjo finally realized he had not been participating in a *flauwekul* (nonsensical)

[3] Photo 1: Sukarno (left) and Dr Moewardi (right) on the veranda of Sukarno's house in front of the Barisan Pelopor troops and other participants at the start of the proclamation, photo by Soemarto Frans Mendur (IPPHOS)

[4] Photo 2: Mohammad Hatta, Sukarno and Dr Moewardi (left to right) on the veranda of Sukarno's house greeting the Barisan Pelopor and other participants at the start of the proclamation, photo by Soemarto Frans Mendur (IPPHOS)

[5] Photo 3: Sukarno (left), guarded by Abdul Latief Hendraningrat (right), on the veranda of his house, facing the Barisan Pelopor and other participants at the start of the proclamation, photo by Soemarto Frans Mendur (IPPHOS)

[6, 7] Photos 4 and 5: Suwiryo (centre) giving his speech at the start of the proclamation while Fatmawati Sukarno (back left) and Sukarno and Hatta (right) listen on the veranda, photos by Soemarto Frans Mendur (IPPHOS)

[8, 9]   Photos 6 and 7: Sukarno reading the text of the proclamation from the veranda of his house, watched by Fatmawati Sukarno (back left), Abdul Latief Hendraningrat (left) and Mohammad Hatta (right), photos by Soemarto Frans Mendur (IPPHOS)

[10, 11] Photos 8 and 9: Sukarno conducting prayers on the veranda of his house after the proclamation, with Abdul Latief Hendraningrat (far left) and Dr Moewardi (left), photos by Soemarto Frans Mendur (IPPHOS)

[12] Photo 10: Mohammad Hatta giving a short speech on the veranda of Sukarno's house following Sukarno's proclamation. Abdul Latief Hendraningrat (far left), Dr Moewardi (left) and Sukarno (back right) listen, photo by Soemarto Frans Mendur (IPPHOS)

[13] Photo 11: S.K. Trimurti (left) and Fatmawati Sukarno (right) with other participants waiting for the flag ceremony in the front garden of Sukarno's house, photo by Soemarto Frans Mendur (IPPHOS)

meeting, as many Indonesians jokingly referred to the numerous patriotic ceremonies organized by the Japanese, but a truly historic moment.[57]

By the next photograph – shot from the steps of the veranda – the flag had billowed to nearly its full length as it rose higher up the pole while someone, hidden by the figure of Fatmawati, held on to one of its ends. It also showed how the young men from Frans's earlier pictures – and most remarkably a dozen young women who had been standing at the back – had since surged forward protectively around the simple ceremony [16]. As the flag finally reached the top of the mast – of which we sadly only have a very blurry image that most probably had been, in contrast to the rest of the series, reproduced and cropped into a portrait format – Frans had again moved to a different position: returning to the original spot where he had made the first of his images, on the veranda and behind Sukarno and Hatta, who were still standing on the steps [17].

And there he remained to document the last sequence of the flag ceremony as well as the one picture in the series that stood out in stark contrast to the seventeen others he had made that day. This was the stirring moment after everyone had just sung the *Indonesia Raya* national anthem, when the fear and uncertainty – which for the past fifteen minutes or so had forced everyone to restrain themselves – finally erupted into a groundswell of emotions. This time there had been no confusing protocol, no jumble of expressions, as everyone – those on the veranda and in the garden – raised their hands in unison, in unity, and perhaps also in relief, and jubilantly shouted 'Merdeka!', again and again [18].[58]

FRANS MENDUR'S REVOLUSI PHOTOGRAPHS IN DUTCH COLLECTIONS

As with the proclamation, no one had planned for a post-ceremony reception. Sukarno had quickly retired to his room following the onset of another fever – but only after having sent Riwu and a young driver to announce the proclamation all over town, instructing his trusty servant to wave the red-and-white flag at passers-by.[59] Others, like Hatta, had stayed a while to sit and chat in the garden – as had Frans – when the late arrivals came. These included *de ouwe heers* (elder statesmen), Indonesia's senior politicians and members of the Preparatory Committee for Indonesian Independence: Dr Radjiman Wediodiningrat, Teuku Muhammad Hasan and Dr Sam Ratulangi – as well as the group of Barisan Pelopor from Penjaringan in North Jakarta who had arrived drenched in their own sweat, after having run the last half kilometre to Jalan Pegangsaan Timur. They had demanded Sukarno repeat the proclamation, which he flatly refused. Luckily, the affable Hatta was willing to say a word or two while Frans took their pictures, completing the last two of the eighteen images we have today [19, 20]. The photographer then had time to observe people enlisting for Dr Radjiman's suicide troops before he too finally left the house – just ahead of the arrival of the Japanese officers who had been sent there to stop the proclamation.[60]

His colleague, Pulungan, had gone straight to Molenvliet Oost 8 – 'wrestling' with his emotions and typewriter to produce a report in time for *Asia Raya*'s 13:30 printing deadline.[61] Likewise, Alex returned to

[14, 15] Photos 12 and 13: Abdul Latief Hendraningrat (centre) and Soehoed of the Barisan Pelopor (centre) preparing to raise the Indonesian flag in the front garden of Sukarno's house, while Sukarno (far left), Hatta (left), Fatmawati Sukarno (front left) and S.K. Trimurti (front right) sing the national anthem, photos by Soemarto Frans Mendur (IPPHOS)

[16] Photo 14: The flag-raising ceremony following the proclamation, viewed from the veranda. Abdul Latief Hendraningrat (far left) and Soehoed of the Barisan Pelopor (left) unfurl the Indonesian flag while Fatmawati Sukarno (right) and other participants sing the national anthem, photo by Soemarto Frans Mendur (IPPHOS)

[17] Photo 15: Abdul Latief Hendraningrat (centre) raising the Indonesian flag as Hatta (front left) and Sukarno (front right) watch from the steps of the veranda, photo by Soemarto Frans Mendur (IPPHOS)

[18] Photo 16: Following the flag-raising ceremony, Sukarno (centre) and other dignitaries on the veranda raise their arms and shout 'Merdeka!' (Freedom), photo by Soemarto Frans Mendur (IPPHOS)

his office in Noord Postweg 53. Both were futile attempts. The Military Authority had quickly banned all news about the proclamation. At Domei, Alex's Japanese supervisor had even destroyed all his negatives as these were still drying in the photo laboratory.[62]

It is not clear today where Frans had been at this time except that after having received news from his brother, he had entrusted his two rolls of film to his father-in-law and wife, who promptly placed them inside an old kerosene can, which they buried under a clump of banana trees in their back garden, safely hidden from the Japanese censors who came to the house soon after (as the photographer had feared).[63]

Those photographs are the only visual documentation of the historic proclamation we have today. For generations of Indonesians (a selection of) these images became part of the country's most important iconography – a collection of perhaps two dozen images of the *revolusi*. Frans, Alex and their colleagues would create a total of 23,005 pictures of the Indonesian struggle for independence at the legendary Indonesia Press Photo Service (IPPHOS) they co-founded on 1 October 1946.[64]

Most people had only ever seen just a handful of the eighteen photographs shown here – including the two photographs that the Indonesian public first saw headlining the *Merdeka* newspaper of 19 and 20 February 1946 respectively (one showing Sukarno reading the proclamation; the other of Hendraningrat raising the unfurled flag).[65] The *Semangat '45 Dalam Rekaman Gambar IPPHOS* in 1985, edited by the eminent historian A.B. Lapian, managed to compile and print two further images,[66] although when the Galeri Foto Jurnalistik Antara conducted its historic survey of the IPPHOS collection in 1997–1998, their team could only find three 35-mm original negatives that had remained from Frans's reportage of that day.[67]

Over time, this paucity of images in Indonesia's popular media, school books and academic publications had led to the perpetuation of a particular myth: that Frans Mendur had only managed to make three images of the historic event,[68] an argument that was given traction by Hendraningrat's recollection in his 2011 memoir of having seen Frans Mendur on the day of the proclamation equipped with just an 'ancient' plate camera and two sheet films.[69]

It was not until seventy years later – in the trio of exhibitions, *70th Histori Masa Depan*, *13 untuk 17 Agustus* and *24 Jam 17 Agustus*, organized by the Galeri Foto Jurnalistik Antara in 2015 – that the Indonesian public would finally see the largest-ever set of images of the proclamation, thirteen in all, which the curators had borrowed for the occasion from the Yayasan Bung Karno foundation in Jakarta.[70] Dr Rushdy Hoesein, senior member of the foundation's Photography Research and Bibliography Team, explained later that they had spent many years tracking down their collection of thirteen images – a few that had been purchased from IPPHOS and other unknown sources.[71] The other half they got from various archives in the Netherlands. These included reproductions of the three original prints – with the IPPHOS stamp at the back – formerly owned by the Dutch journalist and politician Frans Goedhart (inv. no. 52 B), as well as the four photographs (inv. no. 7267, two of which are similar to Goedhart's) that were part of the nine albums confiscated from unknown

[19, 20] Photos 17 and 18: Members of the Preparatory Committee for Indonesian Independence (PPKI): Teuku Muhammad Hasan (left), Dr Radjiman Wediodiningrat (centre) and Dr Sam Ratulangi (right), with troops of the Barisan Pelopor who arrived late for the proclamation at Sukarno's house, photos by Soemarto Frans Mendur (IPPHOS)

sources by the Netherlands Forces Intelligence Service (NEFIS). Consequently, the eighteen photographs we have today comprise the largest set of images found thus far: six from the Yayasan Bung Karno collection and the others from the Nederlands Instituut voor Militaire Historie (NIMH, The Hague) and the aforementioned albums and collection (Goedhart) currently kept in the National Archives in The Hague. It is still unclear what happened to the original negatives in the IPPHOS archive – which, sadly, was sold following the economic crisis of 1998 – or if there existed more images that Frans had made that day.[72] This still needs proper investigation. What is undeniably clear is the importance of the images found in the Dutch archives, the majority of which had been hidden for seventy years. We can now belatedly reconstruct – frame by frame – the urgency, solemnity and the coming together that finally brought about Indonesia's independence.

FREEDOM THE GLORY OF ANY NATION

REVOLUTION IN THE STREETS AND ON PAPER

HARM STEVENS
BONNIE TRIYANA

REVOLUSI!

For a glimpse of how the Indonesian revolution appeared in Jakarta in the first few weeks after 17 August 1945, when Sukarno proclaimed the country's independence, we can look through the lens of second lieutenant Duncan MacTavish. A cameraman with the British Army Film and Photographic Unit, MacTavish must have arrived in Java on 29 September, along with the first British troops to enter Jakarta to oversee the retreat of the Japanese army after its surrender and to make it possible for European internees and prisoners of war in the Japanese camps to return home. That day MacTavish filmed the battalion of Seaforth Highlanders (eight hundred men) disembarking and marching off the ship in Tanjung Priok, Jakarta's port. Later, the military cameraman filmed the Allied forces in Jakarta taking over the watch from the defeated Japanese troops. British army vehicles arrive and depart under the watchful eyes of a few Indonesian onlookers.

Not until 'McTavish Roll 3' (as indicated in a shot inserted in the film) does MacTavish show the Indonesian revolution in the streets of Jakarta: serene black-and-white images without sound. A shot of an Indonesian flag gently waving in the wind is followed by language that clearly expresses Indonesia's yearning for freedom. Large letters on the Art Deco front of the pre-war Hotel des Galeries, presumably in the same red-and-white colours as the flag, spell out the message, 'Freedom the glory of any nation' [1]. MacTavish's camera pans from left to right as if reading the giant slogan on the wall of the hotel, which accommodated British soldiers and the small group of international journalists who tagged along. The hotel, which had suffered from wartime neglect, had been transformed by the young Republik Indonesia's informal yet sophisticated propaganda machine into an English-speaking billboard for 'Indonesia Merdeka!' (Indonesia Free!).

INDONESIA MERDEKA

This slogan, too, was clearly visible to passers-by on the hotel's plaster wall. High above an entrance is a large banner bearing the word 'Merdeka' [2]. A poster next to the same entrance states, in capital letters, 'Indonesia Merdeka', with an image of a man above the words. MacTavish's camera lingers on this poster for a full fourteen seconds, as if he was pleased that after dutifully filming all the revolutionary slogans on the wall – which sent a clear message but eventually started to seem a little perfunctory – he had found a potent image of the Indonesian revolution at last: an Indonesian with broken chains dangling from his wrists, carrying an Indonesian flag on a pole on his shoulder, his hair blowing in the wind and his mouth wide open and shouting [3].

This was a picture that told a story, and it would grow into an icon of the Indonesian revolution, just as French painter Eugène Delacroix's Marianne in the painting *La Liberté guidant la peuple* (*Liberty Leading the People*, 1830) had become the icon of the French Revolution. In other words, the Indonesian freedom fighter with the flag on the poster had his feet firmly planted in art history. In practical terms, the creation of this image could be traced to the Indonesian artist Affandi [5], who is said to have received a telephone call from Sukarno soon after the *Proklamasi*

[1] Slogan on the wall of the Hotel des Galeries in Jakarta, film stills from *British Troops Arrive in Batavia*, captured by Duncan MacTavish, September 1945

[2] Banner on the wall of the Hotel des Galeries in Jakarta, film still from *British Troops Arrive in Batavia*, captured by Duncan MacTavish, September 1945

[3] Poster on the wall of the Hotel des Galeries in Jakarta, film still from *British Troops Arrive in Batavia*, captured by Duncan MacTavish, September 1945

(independence proclamation) requesting posters for the national revolution. The result was this dynamic design, which Affandi made in collaboration with his fellow painter Sudjojono, another artist in Sukarno's inner circle [4]. The best-known version of this prototypical poster for the Indonesian revolution bore the words of encouragement 'Boeng, Ajo Boeng' (Brother, Come on, Brother). This slogan, devised by the poet Chairil Anwar, not only echoed the amicable, non-hierarchical idiom of the revolution ('Boeng' or 'Bung' is also the Indonesian equivalent of 'comrade'), but was in fact inspired by the words used by streetwalkers in urban back alleys to draw in clients. Multiple versions of this poster were in circulation, probably because the motif of a shouting man with flag was also used by other artists in the provisional poster workshop in Affandi's house.[1]

From the start of the Indonesian revolution, the revolutionary slogans in the streets of Jakarta were part of the visual canon of the new Republic, as demonstrated by the documentary photo series published by the American magazine *Life* on 12 November 1945 under the title 'The Javanese revolt against their Dutch rulers'. In one of the photographs a group of Indonesian nationalists are carrying large versions of the poster Affandi had designed, probably printed on canvas, with the slogan 'Boeng, Ajo Boeng' [6].

Alongside the reporting by the British army, Indonesia set up its own official news service in the weeks immediately following the *Proklamasi*. Berita Film Indonesia (BFI, Indonesian News Films) was off to a flying start, using the inventory of the former Japanese studio Nippon Eiga Sha and the expertise of the Indonesian film professionals trained there to make a series of newsreels, which, like the film made by the British army, include the revolutionary slogans. BFI film no. 3 displays, under the title card 'Napsoe Meloeap' (Boundless Desire), images of the pre-war Van Heutsz Monument in the south of Jakarta. In 1932 the city (then known as Batavia) had unveiled this towering monument in honour of J.B. van Heutsz, governor-general of the Dutch East Indies (1904–1909) and, prior to that, general in the Koninklijk Nederlandsch-Indisch Leger (KNIL, Royal Netherlands East Indies Army). Van Heutsz, a national hero in the Netherlands, was known as the 'pacifier of Aceh', the province in North Sumatra where the Netherlands had waged a bitter colonial war that cost many lives. To Indonesian nationalists, he was a colonial oppressor with blood on his hands. The Indonesian cameraman shows how the statue of the Dutch general was covered with a wooden box by the Japanese to conceal it from view; the only part still visible is the feet. But most important of all are the words on the monument: 'Indonesia never again the life-blood of any nation!', written in black tar on the hard stone of the Dutch colonial memorial [7].

The BFI cameraman and the Indonesians who saw these nationalist exts in tarred letters must have been acutely aware that in those weeks, on that historic spot, world history was being written, or better yet: *re*-written. The obsolete, arrogant colonial inscription carved into the stone – 'J.B. van Heutsz ... established order, peace and prosperity' – had been superseded by a new claim to 'The right of self-determination', written on the central pillar of the monument. This phrase is a reference to the

[4]　　　Sudjojono, 1951

[5]　　　Affandi, 1949

[6] Indonesian nationalists ride through the streets of Surabaya with the 'Boeng, Ajo Boeng' poster, photo published in *Life*, 12 November 1945

[7] The monument in Jakarta to J.B. van Heutsz, Governor-General of the Dutch East Indies, painted in revolutionary slogans, October 1945

Atlantic Charter signed by the United States and Great Britain in 1941, which states in its third clause that all peoples have the right to self-government. The Indonesian nationalists issued a forceful reminder to the world of this Western promise: the creation of a new world order that had no place for colonialism.

The slogan on the monument's large protruding block – 'We are a free nation conceived in liberty and dedicated to the proposition that all men are created equal' – could also be traced back to historical roots. This was based on the exact wording of the Gettysburg Address made by United States president Abraham Lincoln in 1863, aside from the word 'free', which replaced the original word 'new'. The sentence above the American-inspired text was also important: 'Respect our constitution of Aug. 18-'45', alluding to the constitution of the Republic of Indonesia, proclaimed on 18 August 1945 by the Panitia Persiapan Kemerdekaan Indonesia (PPKI, Preparatory Committee for Indonesian Independence). By these simple means, the supremely colonial Van Heutsz Monument was transformed into an eloquent tribute to Indonesian self-determination.

By marking public buildings with 'Milik Republik Indonesia' (Property of the Republic of Indonesia), the young Indonesian members of the Angkatan Pemuda Indonesia (API, Indonesia's Young Generation) conducted a campaign of taking over public services in Jakarta, such as the railway, the trams and the telephone company.² The city tram not only offered free transport to the people of Indonesia for weeks (to the frustration of the service's managers) but, as it rattled down Jakarta's main thoroughfares, also served as a propaganda machine. The above-mentioned BFI film shows a tram car with a message in Indonesian: 'V. Mook + Plas, Djanganlah mengoesik keamanan rakjat!' (Van Mook and Plas, don't you dare threaten the safety of the people). This is a reference to Huib van Mook and Charles van der Plas, two high-ranking civil servants sent to Java by the Netherlands in September and October to pave the way for the reoccupation of the former colony. In the early weeks of the revolution, when it was almost impossible to print daily newspapers because of the extreme scarcity of paper, the gap was filled by the alternative medium of the city tram, which provided both news (the arrival of Van Mook and Van der Plas) and outspoken opinions [8].

The slogans on the streets of Jakarta (and other cities) were a novelty; never before in history had Indonesian nationalism been expressed so publicly, in such bold capital letters. Furthermore, the campaign proved to be exceptionally mediagenic, widely covered by the few photographers, camera operators and reporters on the scene. It sent a powerful image around the world about the new Republic's political aspirations, not only demonstrating spontaneous activism with brushes and pots of paint – for instance, through the spontaneous chemistry among artists and poets in Affandi's house – but also expressing, through slogans, a carefully conceived political programme that extended far beyond the borders of the new Republic and no longer saw any place for Dutch colonial authority: 'V. Mook watcha doin' here', read one of the slogans, an echo of brazen American street talk. The allusions to the United States in the repertoire of Indonesian slogans reflected an accurate perception of the new balance of power in the post-war world, and the use of English was a cosmopolitan appeal to a global community in which the Americans and the British – the latter of which already had headquarters in Jakarta by this time – would call the shots.

YOUNG FREEDOM FIGHTERS

Spontaneous, refined, saturated with a consciousness of world history, larded with Yankee slang and the colloquial language of Jakarta's dark alleyways and informed by a systematic political programme, the spirit of the Indonesian Revolution in Jakarta's streets was, from the outset, difficult to pin down. Just who were the real authors of the graffiti in *Kiblik*-Jakarta? (*Kiblik* is a vernacular term for 'Republic'.) The answer is not easy to give, but has something to do with two youth groups, each named after the address of its informal headquarters: student house Asrama Menteng 31 and student house Jalan Prapatan 10. Both were semi-underground hotbeds of revolutionary activity; the house in Menteng was the more radical of the two.[3] Prapatan 10 was home to students from the medical faculty, who advocated a more moderate course in the highly volatile political climate of those first weeks of independence.[4] This did not prevent Prapatan 10 being a hub for revolutionary activism. According to eyewitness Sidik Kertapati, a *pemuda* (young freedom fighter) born in Bali and active in the workers' movement, a meeting took place in the student house on the day of the *Proklamasi*, at which it was decided to set up a small, flexible revolutionary unit, called Dajal,[5] which was to engage in sabotage against the Dutch and the dissemination of news about Indonesian independence. Ultimately they concentrated on putting revolutionary slogans on the city's walls.[6]

Both of these youth and student groups immediately cast a critical eye on the leaders of the Republic: Sukarno, Mohammad Hatta and the government formed in October. That government was made up of representatives of the old political elite, the first wave of Indonesian nationalists; many had impressive records of service, but in the eyes of the youth, they were tainted because they had collaborated with the Japanese occupiers, whether to a greater or a lesser degree. The student activists also accused this older generation of being unable to perceive the full momentum of the Indonesian revolution. For instance, Sukarno's *Proklamasi* had been a direct outcome of ongoing pressure from several leaders of the Menteng 31 *pemuda*, who had been impatient for revolution.

The youthful revolutionaries in Jakarta felt the strongest political affinity with two other major Indonesian nationalists who had been active before the war, had considerable intellectual stature, had gone underground (at least in part) during the Japanese occupation and were critical of the political leaders of the new Republic of Indonesia. The elder of these two prominent politicians was Tan Malaka, born in West Sumatra in 1896 [9]. From mid-August 1945 onwards, Ibrahim Gelar Datuk Tan Malaka was in close communication with his young comrades at Asrama Menteng 31. Another important inspiration was Sutan Sjahrir, also born in Sumatra (in 1909), who at the age of thirty-six was an important, inspirational role model thanks to his youthful charisma. Sjahrir was

[8] Slogan on a city tram in Java: 'Van Mook and Plas cause a Rebellion in Indonesia', photo by H. Ripassa, 1945

[9] Photos of Tan Malaka from various periods, taken from his personal file in the archives of the NEFIS military intelligence service

especially popular among the students in Prapatan 10. In the early weeks of the Indonesian revolution, these two political heavyweights distanced themselves somewhat from the first Sukarno government. Unlike that government, Tan Malaka and Sjahrir had spotless records of opposition to the Japanese, and that was precisely why they were taken up as shining examples by the critical activist youth groups.

These two inspiring Indonesian nationalists merit a closer look, especially because Tan Malaka and Sjahrir each independently, in the early stages of their nation's independence, published an important series of writings that grounded the Indonesian revolution in political theory and a historical perspective. The contrasting political views of Tan Malaka and Sjahrir, as expressed in their extraordinarily urgent treatises, encapsulate the opposing forces that would determine the course of the Indonesian revolution: negotiation and diplomacy versus struggle and the pursuit of '100% merdeka'.

POLITICS, ECONOMIC PLANNING AND TACTICS

Approximately a week after 17 August 1945, when Indonesian independence was declared, Tan Malaka surfaced in Jakarta, at the home of Achmad Subardjo Djoyoadisuryo, an acquaintance from his years as a student in Amsterdam. Before the war, Subardjo had studied law in Leiden, where he had served as president of the Indonesian student association Perhimpunan Indonesia and gravitated towards the political left, even paying a brief visit to the Soviet Union. On that day in August 1945, Subardjo could not believe his eyes when he saw his old friend standing in front of him: 'I thought you were dead. First I read that you'd died in a revolt in Burma, and right after that came news that you'd gone to Jerusalem and been killed during an uprising in Israel.' Tan Malaka smiled and responded with an old Dutch saying: 'Weeds never perish.'[7]

Tan Malaka's unexpected return to the Indonesian political scene had been preceded by a difficult career. This resistance fighter had been compelled by circumstances to become a man of the world. Born into the Minangkabau aristocracy in West Sumatra, young Tan Malaka received an elite education in Bukittinggi (then Fort de Kock). When he went on to study in the Netherlands, he suffered from loneliness but discovered Marxism. In December 1921, after returning to the Dutch East Indies, he became president of the Partai Komunis Indonesia (PKI), the recently founded Communist party. A few months later Tan Malaka fell into the clutches of the colonial administration's powerful machine of repression and was banned from the Dutch East Indies. A career in the Dutch Communist party, in which he came close to winning a seat in parliament, was nipped in the bud, and he spent the next two decades wandering the globe. As a representative of the Communist International (Comintern), he visited Moscow, Canton (Guangzhou), Bangkok and Manila. After a few years when the draconian framework of the Communist party began to chafe at him, and he had no one to depend on but himself, he returned from Singapore by way of Medan to Jakarta in July 1942, during the Japanese occupation. There he lived an anonymous life in dire poverty, like his neighbours in the south of the city. From 1943 onwards, he worked as a clerk for the mining company in the neighbouring port of Banten, where he was witness to the inhumane treatment of the *rōmusha*, Indonesians performing forced labour for the Japanese. In the days surrounding Japan's surrender on 15 August 1945 and the *Proklamasi*, which followed two days later, Tan Malaka moved unobserved through Jakarta under a pseudonym.[8]

His reunion with his old friend Subardjo in August 1945 was Tan Malaka's first reappearance in public under his own name. 'Until today, I have lived underground, incognito. Now that Indonesia is independent, I want to live above ground, officially. I wish to meet the leaders of Indonesia', Tan Malaka is said to have told Subardjo.[9] During the Japanese occupation, he had forged clandestine ties with young people in Banten under the *nom de guerre* of Iljas Hussein. On 9 August 1945, he attended a youth meeting in Rangkasbitung, where 'Iljas Hussein' was made the young people's delegate and sent to Jakarta with a message for Sukarno and Hatta: 'now that Japan faces certain defeat, announce Indonesia's independence as soon as possible'.[10] During these days of excitement and uncertainty, Tan Malaka made contact with young people in the student house Asrama Menteng 31. There he met two prominent youth leaders: first, on 14 August, Sukarni, who would become Tan Malaka's faithful follower, and later Chaerul Saleh.

Tan Malaka was not only an inspiration to the revolutionary youth and perhaps the spiritual father of at least some of the street slogans;[11] he was also a man with a vision for the fledgling Republic's future. This vision found expression in a series of writings he wrote in November and December 1945 under the titles *Politik*, *Rentjana Ekonomi* and *Moeslihat* (Politics, Economic Planning and Tactics) [10].

Tan Malaka wrote these three works in the form of dialogues with five fictional characters: Mr Apal, Toke, Denmas, Pacul and Godam. These characters, Tan Malaka explains, stand for different social classes: Mr Apal is an intellectual, Toke a merchant, Denmas an aristocrat and Pacul and Godam represent labourers in agriculture and manufacturing.[12] *Politik* expounds the basic meaning of independence, the form of a nation, the way an independent country is governed and the separation of powers, which is rooted in popular sovereignty. *Rentjana Ekonomi* discusses the main causes of economic problems such as capitalism, lays out Karl Marx's critique of capitalism, explains how capitalist production leads to 'surplus value', sketches the inevitable crisis of capitalism and warns that an anarchic mode of production leads to the threat of war and imperialist expansion. At the end of the dialogue, Tan Malaka argues that an economy of struggle is the right path to a socialist society in Indonesia.

In *Moeslihat*, Tan Malaka describes the tactics of that struggle, 'in as much depth and detail as possible'.[13] He sheds light on the struggle against recolonization by the Netherlands and its allies. In the final months of 1945, this was a timely discussion for the people of Indonesia. He provides persuasive arguments for the potential power of the Indonesian people during the revolution, pointing out Indonesia's large population and the momentum behind the demands for freedom, which were clearly more insistent than they had been under Dutch colonial rule or Japanese occupation. According to Tan Malaka, this new mentality gave the people greater courage and motivation to oppose the occupying forces with all their might.

From his perspective, diplomacy was not the most promising path to freedom. He contended that Indonesia should not enter into negotiations that would be entirely to the advantage of the Netherlands and its allies, that independent Indonesia should not pursue a diplomacy of begging and receiving: 'The diplomacy of struggle and conquest; that is our diplomacy!'[14]

Moeslihat was published on 2 December 1945. Until a week and a half before that date, Tan Malaka stayed in Surabaya, the city that was the focal point of the fighting between British troops and Indonesian nationalists. He was deeply impressed by the courage displayed by young Indonesians in this unequal military conflict. Despite all the limitations they had to grapple with, their daring exhibited the true spirit of freedom. The Indonesian forces had a shortage of arms, but the young fighters had other weapons, Tan Malaka declared: 'Truth! Justice! And finally, the Proletariat.'[15] He did not mind the fact that the young people's spirit of resistance carried traces of Japanese fascism. On the contrary, he saw this legacy as instrumental in overturning Dutch imperialism and reaching the ultimate goal: '100% merdeka'.

But Tan Malaka could not hold his own in the often highly polarized environment of revolutionary Indonesia. He was arrested on suspicion of involvement in a planned coup and spent more than two years as a political prisoner, from July 1946 to his release in September 1948. On 21 February 1949, Tan Malaka was executed by Suradi Tekebek on the orders of second lieutenant Sukotjo of the Sikatan Battalion in Selopanggung, Kediri, in East Java.[16] He was the victim of internecine struggle within the Republic – a tragic end to a wildly eventful revolutionary career.

OUR STRUGGLE

Sjahrir [12], like Tan Malaka, rejected the idea of working with the Japanese. From his sister's country house in Tjipanas, near the city of Bogor, he built up an underground network. In 1944, Sjahrir rented a house in Jakarta and began to expand his network among the students in the capital. In the Asramas set up by the Japanese, student houses that served as political centres, revulsion against the Japanese occupier was rapidly growing. Here Sjahrir met young people who were striving for Indonesian freedom.[17] Sjahrir's disgust towards Indonesian politicians who had collaborated with the Japanese was such that at first he resolutely turned down Sukarno's invitation to become part of the first government. Many of the Indonesian politicians who had emerged into the spotlight – Sukarno and Hatta not excepted – were too closely linked to the former occupying power, Sjahrir believed. He was later compelled to rethink his opinion of Sukarno; after travelling around Java to determine the mood of the masses, he concluded that Sukarno was seen as the incontestable leader.[18]

In the early months of the Indonesian revolution, Sjahrir established an international reputation as the author of an influential

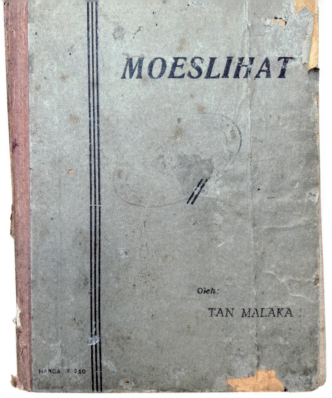

[10] *Moeslihat*, Tan Malaka, 1945

[11] *Onze strijd*, Sjahrir, 1946

manifesto expounding his vision for Indonesia's future. *Perdjoeangan Kita* (Our Struggle) was the title of the thin booklet in which, unlike Tan Malaka in his post-war writings, Sjahrir fiercely opposed the remnants of the fascist spirit ignited by the Japanese among the Indonesian people.[19] *Perdjoeangan Kita* was also published in Dutch in January 1946 by the Amsterdam publishing house of Vrij Nederland, under the auspices of the Indonesian student association in the Netherlands, Perhimpunan Indonesia, to which Sjahrir had belonged [11]. The publication of this translation demonstrated Sjahrir's popularity in progressive Dutch circles and was a highly effective way of promoting the Indonesian cause in the Netherlands. On the cover of the Dutch translation was a well-chosen quotation from the book: 'Our power must consist in arousing feelings of justice and humanity. Only a nationalism founded on these feelings can carry us forward in world history.'[20] These words resonate with a universalist humanism and the desire for inclusion in the march of progress, sentiments also found in some revolutionary slogans.

Sjahrir had been politically active since secondary school in Bandung, and he continued his political activism during his time in the Netherlands, where he studied law, first at the University of Amsterdam and later in Leiden. In Amsterdam, he befriended Salomon Tas, the president of the Social Democratic Students Club in which the young Indonesian was also active. Sjahrir, like Mohammad Hatta, who had begun his studies in the Netherlands earlier, was a member of the aforementioned Perhimpunan Indonesia; his membership came to an end in the autumn of 1931 when the association became increasingly explicitly infiltrated by the Comintern, an organization directed from Moscow.[21] In March 1934, soon after his return to Indonesia, Sjahrir was locked up by the colonial administration in a prison for convicted criminals in Java. The reason for his arrest was the nationalist publications with which Sjahrir was associated and his membership of a movement that strove for Indonesia's independence. Without a conviction or a sentence or an end date for his confinement, Sjahrir was banished a year after his arrest to Boven-Digoel in the interior of New Guinea (Papua). In 1927, the Dutch had established a settlement there that served as an 'isolation colony' – in other words, a concentration camp for political prisoners. In early 1936 Sjahrir and his fellow prisoner Hatta were transferred to the island of Banda Neira in the Maluku Islands(then known as the Moluccas), where he was forced to remain in exile for more than six years.

After his release by the Japanese occupying regime in 1942, Sjahrir decided to go underground and follow world events by secretly listening to international radio news. In October 1945, Sjahrir wrote *Perdjoeangan Kita*, published in Jakarta on 10 November. That was three weeks before Tan Malaka's *Moeslihat* was published in Surabaya, where the fighting with British troops was heaviest.[22] Rosihan Anwar, who lived through these events, says that *Perdjoeangan Kita* had a mixed reception from young people and intellectuals.[23] The reason may be that Sjahrir expressed deep concern about the revolution's violent nature in those early months, unlike Tan Malaka, who embraced the nationalist spirit and the young people's struggle. According to Sjahrir, the cause of this unbridled aggression was the fascist spirit that had infected some of the country's youth. This had, in his eyes, turned nationalism into a narrow-minded, dangerous ideology.

Perdjoeangan Kita addresses several central problems arising from the legacy of the Japanese occupation: corruption, violence, forced labour, the requirement to pay a monetary tribute to the authorities, a militaristic, fascistic attitude and racist acts targeting citizens who were Eurasian (part European, part Asian), ethnically Chinese, Ambonese or Menadonese (Minahasan), who were often seen as accomplices of the Dutch colonial administration. Sjahrir also discusses the development of Indonesian society under Dutch colonial rule and the Japanese occupation, as well as the influence of that history on the nature of the Indonesian revolution.

According to Sjahrir, modernity hardly took hold in the Dutch East Indies; most of the colonized society remained caught up in feudal ways of thinking. The Dutch regime was built on this traditional feudalism, Sjahrir argues, and therefore stood in the way of progress for 'our people'; the Indonesian officials in the Dutch civil service were vestiges of feudalism and tools of the Dutch oppressors.

'Dutch rule', Sjahrir wrote in his pamphlet, 'gained its power from uniting modern rationality with Indonesian feudalism and thus became the first model of fascism in the world. This colonialism preceded Hitler's or Mussolini's fascism.' And he added, 'long before Hitler established Buchenwald or Belsen concentration camps, Boven-Digoel already existed.'[24]

The Japanese occupation toppled the Netherlands from its role as colonial power. During the Japanese period, much of the legacy of Dutch colonialism was abolished. For instance, the Japanese government made the use of the Indonesian language mandatory and prohibited the use of Dutch. Many new organizations for young people emphasized nationalism and patriotism. As a result, the sense of national pride grew stronger than it had ever been in the centuries of Dutch colonialism.

In Sjahrir's eyes, when Dutch colonialism had ended, the underlying feudalism had remained, and that feudalist spirit was still alive and well in the popular mindset, overlaid by the even stronger influence of fascism inculcated by Japanese schooling. Sjahrir hinted that populism and a nationalistic and national spirit, if not accompanied by democratic principles, would place Indonesia's future at risk. Sjahrir's criticism also specifically targeted the Republic's first government, formed on 4 September 1945. He believed that the composition of this government, as noted above, still showed too much Japanese influence. Sjahrir's assessment of some members of government was sharply critical: he said they were not 'strong figures'. And he continued:

> Most of them had bowed down *too* often and run *too* fast for Japan and for the Netherlands; they were fence-sitters, who did not dare to take action or assume responsibility. Secondly, many among them felt morally indebted to the Japanese, because they believed the latter had paved the way for the birth of free Indonesia. Finally, they believed they had risen to power precisely *because* they had collaborated with Japan.[25]

[12] Sjahrir, in Cas Oorthuys, *Een staat in wording*, 1947

Sjahrir suggested that if Indonesia wanted to build a democratic way of life, its revolution had to be cleansed of the remnants of the influence of Japanese fascism and of the patterns stemming from Dutch and Japanese occupation. Only then, he argued, would the Indonesian national revolution be capable of elevating the human dignity of a colonized people to the level of an independent people, liberated from a feudal mentality.

Sjahrir's role in the Indonesian struggle for independence was not limited to that of commentator from the sidelines, as soon became clear. On 15 November 1945, five days after the publication of *Perdjoeangan Kita*, a new government was formed, with Sjahrir as prime minister and foreign minister. At the age of thirty-six, Sjahrir was the youngest prime minister in the world. He was also one of the most threatened statesmen in the world. During the Christmas holidays in 1945, after Sjahrir was arrested in the street by Dutch KNIL soldiers, he wrote rather laconically to his Dutch wife about the mortal dangers he faced:

> Yesterday I happened to escape death. The situation is now such that I might be shot dead here in Jakarta at any moment. You might ask why I stay. It is because we are determined to hold on to the last here. As far as I am concerned, I sometimes do not much care whether they shoot me dead. The people do not seem to have learned much from the war. On all sides here, they are beastly. On our side too, but definitely not just our side.[26]

In spite of these bitter experiences, *diplomasi*, negotiation with the Netherlands and the international community, remained an important part of Sjahrir's policy. From January 1946, the Sjahrir government had a formidable political adversary: Persatuan Perdjoeangan (Struggle Union), a broad coalition of representatives of left-wing parties, Islamic parties and military circles who collectively rejected all forms of diplomacy. In the rough-and-tumble of the political arena, Sjahrir learned from experience to stay on his feet at the Republic of Indonesia's political centre. From November 1945 to July 1947, he served as prime minister of three governments. After that, this internationally oriented social democrat no longer played a leading role, but he continued to serve the interests of the Republic as a diplomat.

THE SIGNAL TO RISE UP

MENACE AND VIOLENCE AT THE START OF THE REVOLUTION

HARM STEVENS
MARION ANKER

REVOLUSI!

In 1945, Laetitia Kwee was part of the population of 150,000 Chinese living in Jakarta, a city totalling more than 800,000 inhabitants [1]. Laetitia lived with her family in a house in the city centre, not far from the central canal that the Dutch called Molenvliet. Laetitia also had a Chinese name, Lim Him Nio, but she was called Letty at home and by her friends. Like her husband Kwee Thian Yoe, who also went by the Dutch name Jan, Letty had had a European education before the Dutch East Indies were occupied by Japan. She had trained at a vocational school to become a teacher. Jan had completed secondary school in Malang. The Kwee family was part of the elite of Peranakan Chinese, who had been established in Indonesia for generations and often maintained strong ties with the colonial European elite. Dutch was spoken in the Kwee home.

On Sunday 12 August 1945, Letty gave birth to her second child, a daughter. The girl was named Tjoe by her grandfather, meaning 'meek'. Three days after she was born, on 15 August, the capitulation of Japan to the Allied forces brought an end to the Second World War in Southeast Asia. Another two days later, on Friday 17 August, less than three kilometres from the Kwee family home, Sukarno declared the independence of Indonesia.

BABY YEARS IN THE INDIES

No hint of these world events appears in the baby book compiled by Letty Kwee. 'Baby-jaren in Indië' (Baby Years in the Indies) is printed on the book's title page, a 'publication of the association of housewives in Batavia', which opens with a saccharine picture of a blue-eyed baby bursting with health. A baby book is not a genre that lends itself to reflection on the turbulence of the outside world. Tranquillity, purity and regularity set the tone of this baby book compiled at a time of revolution. Tjoe grows, catches a mild cold in the Jakarta drizzle and eats her first *pisang* (banana) with her two grandmothers. Photos are taken behind the house: mother dressed in a sarong and *kebaya* (blouse) with her daughter in her arms and, kneeling and crouching at her side, three Indonesian women who are part of the domestic staff [2]. Beyond this, Letty also made brief notes about several family events. On 19 August, for example, her husband held a *'kambing* bash' for his friends in honour of his daughter, with *sate kambing* (goat meat) and *kambing* soup.

Had the news about the declaration of Indonesian independence two days earlier filtered through into the life of the Kwee family, and was it a topic of conversation among the father's friends? The mother's diligent notes in the baby book provide no conclusive evidence. On Sunday 26 August, the mother went out for the first time 'for a treat' in Glodok, the Chinese quarter in the older section of Jakarta, while Aunt Corrie looked after the baby. And on Wednesday 12 September, the first outing with the baby takes place: a pleasant drive in the Buick Light, the American automobile belonging to Letty's father, who had run a brokerage firm with a Dutch partner before the war. Such a car was an ostentatious possession in a city where most inhabitants had been left in dire poverty by war and Japanese occupation.[1]

From the end of September 1945 Jakarta became a highly dangerous city in the throes of a deadly spiral of street violence from all sides: terror waged by Indonesian revolutionaries, Dutchmen and others loyal to the old colonial regime, the former Japanese occupying forces and soldiers of the newly arrived British army alternated at an irregular and chaotic pace. Jakarta had been declared 'Milik Republik Indonesia' (Property of the Republic of Indonesia) by Indonesian revolutionaries in the weeks following the *Proklamasi* (independance proclamation) and Indonesians considered it the capital of independent Indonesia, but the state authority of the new Republic was still insufficiently established. The landing of British troops in the city on 29 September, with in their wake a battalion of two hundred men from the Koninklijk Nederlandsch-Indisch Leger (KNIL, Royal Netherlands East Indies Army) and a number of military attachés from the Netherlands Indies Civil Administration (NICA), threw oil on the fire of revolution. The return to the city of Dutch who left the Japanese internment camps, against the orders of the Allies, contributed to rising tensions. Trigger-happy soldiers from the 10th Battalion of the KNIL, stationed in barracks on the Waterlooplein (now Lapangan Banteng), made the streets unsafe: Indonesians who went out wearing red-and-white displays of Republican loyalty were shot at random from army trucks.[2]

Countering this open violence was the more hidden, but certainly no less terrifying, violence of the *badan perjuangan*, Indonesian guerrilla groups formed by an amalgam of revolutionary *pemuda* (young freedom fighters), seasoned criminals and opportunists who operated autonomously, outside any authority. The weeks of terror unleashed by these guerrillas from the back streets and *kampongs* (villages) were aimed at preventing the Dutch from resuming their normal lives in the city. Looting, plunder, kidnappings and massacres were the order of the day in the last months of 1945.[3] The violence was visible in broad daylight in the centre of Jakarta, as shown by footage of the Molenvliet canal most likely filmed during those months by an unidentified cameraman, not far from the Kwee family home. A man's corpse floats by, carried by the canal's slow current. The camera then swings upwards towards the quay, where passers-by, mostly young boys, observe the gruesome scene. Many bystanders are holding handkerchiefs to their noses against the stench.[4]

The Kwee family must have felt the menace of violence in their city. The Kwees were part of an ethnic minority that was a frequently selected target of revolutionary (and criminal) violence. The Kwee family enjoyed relative economic wealth in a city in which the vast majority of the population was dirt-poor in 1945; they had occupied a privileged position in the pre-war Dutch East Indies, and had resumed their Dutch orientation with the return of the Dutch, something that could easily be interpreted as enmity towards the Republic. All of this made the Kwee family and many other Chinese suspect in the eyes of the militant Indonesian activists. Throughout the struggle for independence, Chinese communities fell victim on a vast scale to violence perpetrated by autonomous guerrillas and by certain groups within the Republic's army. In the aftermath of large-scale Dutch military campaigns in 1947 and 1948/1949 especially, when troops of the Tentara Nasional Indonesia

(TNI, Indonesian National Armed Forces) carried out 'scorched earth' tactics as they retreated, Chinese communities found themselves and their property in grave danger.[5] It is estimated that between 1945 and 1949 there were 10,000 Chinese fatalities in Java.[6] Violence against the Chinese was not exclusively attributable to Indonesian groups. Soldiers serving under the Dutch flag were also responsible. This was reported to the Dutch authorities by Chinese committees from early 1946 onward.[7]

Caution was therefore crucial for the Kwee family in the last months of 1945. At times this meant seeking cover. In the note made by Letty Kwee on New Year's Day 1946 – in the first person on behalf of her young daughter, then four and a half months old – the gunfire in Jakarta invades the otherwise so-placid baby book for the first time, albeit in the form of celebratory shots fired into the air, but that made it no less frightening:

> Around midnight or twelve-thirty I was woken up and then put under the baby table (on a mattress), for Pappy, Mok and Aunt Corrie were afraid of bullets. It was New Year's Eve, after all, and the 'people' like to greet the new year! The bullets were the fireworks, after all, the way they welcomed new years before the war – that was how the old year that so many had spent in misery came to an end. Let us hope that 1946 will bring peace and quiet.

OPERATION POUNCE

For the Kwee family, what 1946 brought was exile from Indonesia, the country where they were born and raised. The father eagerly accepted a Dutch grant to train as a mathematics teacher in Amsterdam and left for the Netherlands aboard a cargo ship in mid-1946. As hoped by Letty Kwee, who for now remained in Jakarta with her family, 1946 did indeed bring more peace and quiet to the city. Thanks to a ruthless intervention by British troops, 'Operation Pounce', the chaos and the violence that had defined the final months of 1945 came to an end. On 27 December 1945 the army began by blocking the access roads in and out of Jakarta. In the ten days that followed, houses and citizens were searched. The British investigation troops, made up partly of soldiers from India, were assisted in this by Indonesian police officers and interpreters. Indonesian freedom slogans and anti-colonial graffiti were also stripped from buildings and trams throughout the city. The operation led to the arrest of about seven hundred *pemuda*, criminals and Republican police officers. Sutan Sjahrir, who became prime minister of the Republic in November, had called on the people of Jakarta, at the insistent demand of the British (who out of practical considerations engaged in dialogue with the Republic's political leadership from the outset) to cooperate with the cleansing campaign. In addition, on 19 November, in the run-up to the British strike, Sjahrir had ordered the Republican Tentara Keamanan Rakjat (TKR, People's Security Army: a forerunner to the TNI) and the irregular troops to leave the city.[8]

Despite the restoration of relative safety in their city, the future of the young Kwee family lay elsewhere. On 15 November 1946, Letty

[1] Letty Kwee, Jakarta, August 1945

[2] Letty Kwee with daughter Tjoe and domestic servants, Jakarta, August 1945

[3]   Mateni, the Javanese domestic, hand in hand with
      Tjoe on the Joos Banckersweg, Amsterdam, 1948

[4]   The Kwee family. Tjoe sits next to her youngest brother,
      Tjoe Houw, and her elder brother Tjoe Liong, Amsterdam, 1949

travelled with her two children (a third was on the way) and the Javanese domestic servant Mateni to join Jan in Holland, aboard the *Oranje*. Letty continued to update Tjoe's baby book faithfully. On 4 December 1946, the day of arrival in the port of Amsterdam and at their new residence in the Bos en Lommer borough of the city, she noted: 'Around 12:30 at Joos Banckersweg 19 II, after riding around Amsterdam on the bus for at least two hours. ... How cold it is in Holland' [3, 4].

'NOT WELCOME'

That cold in Holland is inextricably linked with the cold reception accorded to the sizable stream of migrants that reached the Netherlands from Indonesia beginning in early 1946. A significant group consisted of Dutch people who had been held in Japanese internment camps. The first of these repatriates, some 100,000, began making the journey to the Netherlands in 1946.[9] Was this a temporary stay, to recover from the ordeal of the camps, or was it forever? Only the future would tell. Jeanne van Leur-de Loos was one of these repatriates [5]. In order to rebuild her strength after years of internment, and chaotic months in the city where it was increasingly clear she was no longer welcome, she left on 25 January 1946, along with more than a thousand other Dutch people, aboard the *Johan de Witt* from Tanjung Priok, the harbour of the city that most of the passengers probably called Batavia rather than Jakarta. A little less than a month later, Jeanne, called Peu by her friends and family, set foot ashore in Amsterdam. In her luggage was an item of clothing that bore in a very particular way the traces of her final months in the country where she had spent her life: a house dress made of silk maps [6].

Such silk (topographic) maps were originally intended to be taken by crews of British Royal Air Force planes on their flights over various countries in Southeast Asia. They were also called escape maps, because they could serve for orientation in the event of a crash landing. Peu's gown was composed of maps of the countries 'Burma', 'French Indo China', 'Siam', 'China' and 'India'. The escape maps may have found their way, probably via British soldiers, to one of the many *passars* (markets) in Jakarta. Peu, possibly with the help of a middleman, must have bought a stack of them there. Perhaps the silk maps came from the black market that Peu described in one of the letters to her parents in the Netherlands: 'a thieves' *passar* several kilometres long has sprung up on Noordwijk from the Huisbrugstraat to the Harmonie, where colourful rags flutter in the wind, dresses, children's clothes, buttons, notepads, etc., all looted and thus brought to the people.' Later in the letter, an addition follows that reveals something of the hostility that Europeans faced in those days: 'Westerners have not been welcome in *tokos* and *passars* for quite some time.'[10] That 'not welcome' was probably somewhat euphemistically phrased in order to avoid worrying her concerned parents in Holland about the situation in Jakarta any more than necessary. Out of fear of reprisals by militant nationalists, Indonesians refused to work for Europeans. Even the sale of food to Europeans in the market was seen as an act of colonial collaboration. Employees who were suspected of bringing food to the Menteng quarter, where many Europeans resided, were interrogated by nationalist street activists.[11] Eurasian families in particular, who lived outside the relative safety of the Japanese camps, fell victim to street boycotts and terror in September and October.

Peu must have considered it a great stroke of luck that she had managed, in spite of these difficult circumstances, not to mention at a time of great textile scarcity, to become the proud owner of several metres of silk fabric. Using a Singer sewing machine, she was able to turn them into a decent house dress. According to the family story, that sewing machine was one of the rare possessions that Peu recovered after her time in the camp. The machine had apparently been hidden during the war by someone from the household staff, to prevent it being confiscated by the Japanese, and was later returned honestly to Peu. After the deprivations of the Japanese internment camp, a garment like this was more than just an article of clothing: made with great care at the trusty, humming sewing machine, it was quite reminiscent of the dresses that Peu wore before the war (as can be seen in a photo from 1940).

'Liberation' on 18 September 1945 from the women's camp of Kampong Makassar, located south of Jakarta, had brought an end to a period of more than two years of Japanese internment for Peu (which had begun on 31 August 1943 in the Tjideng camp in Jakarta). Peu's husband, the progressive administration official and Indologist Job van Leur, had been killed at the Battle of the Java Sea in 1942. Before the war they had lived at Parkweg 7 in Bogor (then called Buitenzorg), situated further inland. After the war she wrote a brief sentence to her parents about it: 'Everything is gone.'[12]

As a thirty-five-year-old widow, Peu must have found her way from the camp back to Jakarta, where she had worked until 1943 as a curator at the Oud-Batavia museum, located on was then the Stadhuisplein in the old city. When she returned, Peu had endeavoured, along with several other Dutch museum colleagues, to resume the antiquarian work of the museum as best they could. The imposing culture temple had been run by the Bataviaasch Genootschap (Batavian Society) until the war. During the war the building had been painted in black-and-green camouflage colours by order of the Japanese occupying regime. Since sometime in September 1945 the museum had been under Republican management, which did not prevent the Oud-Batavia museum, now housed in a building on the Koningsplein, falling prey to large-scale looting in December 1945.[13]

MURDERED

The fate that the Eurasian family Uhlenbusch met on 11 October 1945 is blood-curdling. On that day, the father, Wilhelm Friedrich Uhlenbusch, his wife, Christina, and their twenty-five-year-old daughter, Anna Sofia, were murdered along with two other families in the town of Balapulang, situated in the interior, south of the port city of Tegal on the north coast of Central Java.[14] The massacre took place in the local sugar factory, which had lain dormant since the economic crisis of the mid-1930s. The deadly violence was part of a series of murders committed between 10 and 12 October 1945 by Indonesian militants in various locations in this region, which had traditionally featured a large concentration of

[5] Jeanne (Peu) van Leur-de Loos after her return from Indonesia, c. 1946

[6] House dress of silk maps, made by Jeanne (Peu) van Leur-de Loos, Jakarta, 1945

Personen, die te Tegal tussen 10-12 October 1945 door Indon. zijn vermoord.

3603

TEGAL.
1. L.F. Koster (55 jr.)
2. Heer Humans (55 jr.)
3. Mevr. Humans (45 jr.)
4. Eddy Humans (20 jr.)
5. Johnny Humans (25 jr.)
6. Jeane Wegman (3 jr.)
7. Heer Wegman (45 jr.)
8. Zoon Wegman (20 jr.)

POENGKOERAN.
1. J.W. Buman (55 jr.)
2. D. Buman (14 jr.)
3. Gomis (35 jr.)
4. R. Rongkes (60 jr.)
5. De Lacambre (35 jr.)
6. Jan Manuhutu (25 jr.)

SLAWI.
1. Heer Frederiks (60 jr.)
2. Mevr. Frederiks (50 jr.)
3. Willy Frederiks (25 jr.)
4. Betsie Frederiks (-
5. Noes Frederiks -
6. Heer Deighton (60 jr.)
7. Mevr. Deighton (55 jr.)
8. Heer Mac Gillavry (40 jr.)
9. Mevr. Mac Gillavry (35 jr.)
10. Zoon Mac Gillavry -
11. Dochter Mac Gillavry -
12. Dochter Mac Gillavry -
13. Karel Plantinga -

DOEKOEWERINGIN.
1. Zuster Risahotta
2. Heer Anahotta
3. Heer Sinambella
4. Heer Pannei.

PANGKAH.
1. Heer Gill
2. Heer Adriaan.
3. Heer Masokko
4. Heer Masokko.
5. Heer Masokko.

DJATIBARANG.
1. N. Isaak
2. Heer Bloemhard
3. E. Bloemhard
4. F. Borgen
5. Heer Pitraroia
6. Heer v. Erp
7. Heer Westbroek
8. D. Westbroek
9. J. Nikijuluw
10. J. Nikijuluw
11. Heer Kakaloe
12. Heer Kakaloe
13. Heer Kakaloe
14. R.A. Matulessia
15. E. Tupamahu
16. R. Soffner

PROEPOEK.
1. Fam. Schwab
2. W. de Jonker

DJATIBARANG (vervolg)
17. Havelaar.
18. "
19. "
20. "
21. "
22. "
23. "
24. "
25. "
26. "
27. "
28. "
29. "
30. "
31. N. Pieters
32. Pieters.

S.F. BANDJARATMO.
1. J. Riedyk
2. E. Meeng (Jr.)
3. E. v. Someren
4. A.M. Hercules
5. Heer Mulder
6. Zoon Mulder
7. Heer Koster
8. Zoon Koster
9. Senduuk (Menadonees) in Slawi vermoord.
10. Lapi (Ambonnees).

BREBES.
1. Heer Verarie.
2. Zoon Verarie
3. Van Manen

DOERENSAWIT.
1. Heer Kruisboom
2. Mevr. Kruisboom
3. J.E.F. Godschalk
4. S. Godschalk
5. P. Godschalk
6. H. Godschalk
7. Zuster Harting

BODJONG.
1. Heer Angelbeek
2. Mevrouw Angelbeek
3. Heer v.d. Huis

BALAPOELANG.
1. Mevr. Ulenbusch
2. Annie Ulenbusch
3. Heer Galwitz
4. Mevr. Galwitz
5. Heer Lapré
6. Mevr. Lapré
7. Dochter Lapré
8. Dochter Lapré
9. E. Wyck
10. J. Wyck
11. B. Wyck
12. R. Wyck
13. C. Wyck
14. Ch. Wyck
15. Heer Bart
16. De La Fontaine

BOEMIAJOE.
1. Frederiks
2. Borgen
3. Rudolph.
4. P. Jacobs
5. Fam. Colmus

sugar factories. The sugar factory was seen as a symbol of the unjust colonial economy since Javanese workers worked in harsh conditions. The violence seemed primarily directed towards staff that had been privileged during the colonial period, and may therefore have been rooted in resentment bottled up among the populace. In total, more than one hundred Eurasians (people of mixed European and Indonesian origin), Ambonese, Menadonese and others who were suspected by the Indonesian perpetrators of being pro-Dutch fell victim to this extreme Indonesian brutality.[15] In Dutch sources, the incident was referred to at the time as 'the mass murder in Tegal'.[16] In the Netherlands, the period from October 1945 to early 1946 is known as the *Bersiap* (a reference to the word *siap*, which means 'be ready' and was shouted by Indonesian revolutionaries).[17] The term is mainly reserved for anti-Dutch violence during this period.[18]

The Indonesian revolutionary avant-garde considered Eurasians, as well as other groups who had shown themselves to be allies of the colonial Dutch in the past, to be a fifth column of the Netherlands Indies Civil Administration (NICA), an organization consisting of Dutch administration officials and military, which had begun its recolonization campaign rather haphazardly in September. Eurasians, often without personal confirmation, were considered accomplices of the Dutch colonial power in their attempt to regain control of the 'rebellious colony'. The Eurasians, Ambonese and Menadonese who lived in and around Tegal had to be killed in retribution for the 'NICA terrorism in Jakarta', violence perpetrated against innocent Indonesian women and children in the capital. This was claimed by the Republican radio broadcasts that reached the guerrillas in Tegal from Jakarta.[19]

The names of the dozens of victims were typed in a list headed 'People murdered by Indonesians in Tegal between 10 and 12 October 1945', a document probably compiled by the Opsporingsdienst overledenen (ODO, Investigation Service for the Deceased), which was active in Dutch-controlled territory beginning in December 1945 [7]. The European names must have largely been those of the many Eurasian victims. There are also a few Moluccan names – 'Jan Manuhutu (25 years old)', 'Lapi (Ambonese)' – and 'Senduuk (Menadonese)'. We can put faces to the names of the Uhlenbusch family, which also featured in the typed list, thanks to two surviving family photos. These images are part of a collection that otherwise consists primarily of gruesome images of exhumed corpses and must have been compiled a year after the events as a sort of evidence exhibit, possibly directed by the ODO. One of the photos shows the Uhlenbusch family in happier times, probably before the war. In the other picture (actually a photo of a photo) the four young sisters pose [8]. '[T]he four happy daughters of Mr Uhlenbusch', reads part of the caption on the back of the photo. Anna Sofia Uhlenbusch must be in this photo, but we do not know which one of these four Eurasian teenagers she is.

[8] The Uhlenbusch sisters, before 1942

SURABAYA

One testimony of the violence of the first months of the Indonesian revolution of a different order from the business-like list of 'people murdered by Indonesians' and the black-and-white family photos is the colourful literary story *Surabaja*, published in 1946 or 1947 by the Indonesian writer Idrus. *Surabaja* has been described as a satire, but it is also the account of an eyewitness to the beginning of the Indonesian revolution.

Idrus, a Minangkabau born in Padang (Sumatra), spent the last months of 1945 in Surabaya, when the large port city in East Java became the scene of steadily escalating street fighting between Indonesian youth, Japanese soldiers and returning Dutch civilians and military beginning in September [10]. When British-Indian troops landed in Surabaya on 20 October, violence in the city and its environs only increased in scale. The cause was a series of British measures intended to disarm the Indonesian fighters, and the unsolved death of the British Brigadier A.W.S. Mallaby, on 30 October, after an attempt at negotiations. Was he murdered by Indonesians? Or was Mallaby the victim of a bullet from his own troops? The British had come to Surabaya to evacuate the thousands of former prisoners out of the Japanese internment camps in the region, but they encountered distrust among the Indonesians, who saw the arrival of the Allies as nothing more than a colonial invasion. An important mobilizing effect was triggered by the fatwa proclaimed on 22 October 1945 by the Nahdlatul Ulama (Council of Islamic Scholars), which said 'The Islamic community, especially followers of Nahdlatul Ulama, is required to raise arms to oppose the Dutch and their accomplices who wish to re-colonize Indonesia. This requirement is a "jihad" that becomes mandatory for every Muslim who is within a radius of 94 km'.[20]

What became known as the Battle of Surabaya entered a new phase when the British issued an ultimatum: the Indonesian leaders were to turn over their weapons within twenty-four hours. When the local Indonesian leaders refused to surrender, the conflict broke out in all its intensity in the early morning of 10 November 1945 with a British bombardment of the city. Idrus poignantly described the effects of the Allied shelling: 'The air smelled of gunpowder, of human and animal corpses and the hospitals smelled of ether and rose oil. ... The rainwater contained black and filthy ash, which hurt eyes and hearts.'[21] Only at the end of November, after weeks of ferocious street fighting, did the city fall into Allied hands.

Even though the Indonesians were defeated militarily, the Battle of Surabaya was a feat of unprecedented symbolic significance for the Indonesian struggle. The large-scale fighting became world news, putting the Indonesian struggle for independence on the international map. 'Surabaya' was seen as a crucible of Indonesian revolutionary fervour. Not for nothing did Idrus devote the first paragraph of his short story to a description of this spirit:

> The people were caught up in a victory trance. Like a serpent out of the undergrowth, their courage darted into the open. Their self-confidence and patriotism bubbled like beer foaming over the top of a glass. They no longer used their reason; they followed their

instincts like animals, and the result was astonishing. No one believed in God any more. A new God had arrived and he had all sorts of names: bomb, machine gun, mortar.[22]

A voice like a machine gun: this was a feature of the twenty-six-year-old *pemuda* leader Sutomo, born in the *kampung* of Blauran in the centre of Surabaya, who had returned to his hometown in mid-October from the *Proklamasi* city of Jakarta as a dedicated revolutionary [9]. In the weeks that followed, Bung Tomo (Brother Tomo), as he was called in comradely fashion by his compatriots and fellow fighters, played a role as effective as it was loud in mobilizing the masses during the Battle of Surabaya. At the microphone of Radio Pemberontakan (Radio Uprising), which he had founded, the former journalist, but as of 1945 first and foremost a '100% merdeka' nationalist, exhorted his fellow city residents to persevere in the struggle against the British interlopers and to defend the independence of the Republic of Indonesia by any means necessary. While the old power structures of Surabaya had collapsed, the inhabitants of the besieged city found in the passionate voice of Bung Tomo a beacon audible to all, which sharpened the vibrant revolutionary spirit of Indonesians like a bamboo spear. The distribution of radios among the populace had begun to some extent under Japanese occupation, and Radio Pemberontakan could be heard in sitting rooms and through loudspeakers in the streets. Street vendors, *becak* (pedicab) drivers, clerks and schoolchildren listened together to the pep talk of their fellow city resident, which always began and ended with the call: 'Allahuakbar!'[23]

On 24 October 1945, the following words, spoken by Bung Tomo, rang out from the loudspeakers:

> We extremists and the masses cannot now trust sweet talk. We distrust every movement [they make] as long as the independence of the Republic goes unrecognized! We still shoot to kill, we still spill the blood of all who stand in our way! If we are not given independence, we will destroy the imperialists' buildings and factories with the hand grenades and dynamite we have, and we will give the signal to revolt, to tear the guts out of any living creature that tries to colonize us again! It is the masses in their thousands, starved, stripped, and shamed by the colonialists, who will rise to carry out this revolt. We extremists, we who revolt with a full revolutionary spirit, together with the Indonesian masses, who have experienced the oppression of colonialism, would rather see Indonesia drowned in blood and sunk in the bottom of the sea than colonized once more! Allahuakbar! Allahuakbar! Merdeka![24]

Bung Tomo also figures in the literary story by Idrus, not as a radio man but as a speaker at a mass gathering in Malang. 'His voice', wrote Idrus, 'was hard and snappy; he himself was short and kind. His eyes flashed like the light of a lighthouse by the sea.' Yet the incisive observer Idrus's *Surabaja* is not the story of individual heroes, who are seldom mentioned by name. Instead, Idrus devoted a remarkable amount of attention to the anonymous masses, the ordinary city dwellers who were crushed in the

[9]   Sutomo (Bung Tomo), 1946

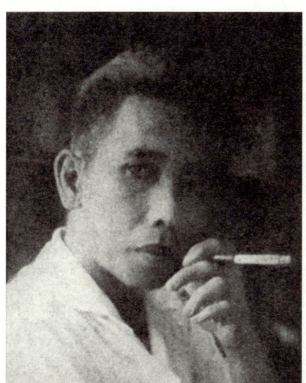

[10]   Idrus, 1948

[11]   Tony Rafty, c. 1944

[12]   Battle of Surabaya, by Tony Rafty, 14 November 1945

violence of war, the stream of refugees prompted by the fighting. Idrus describes the heroic struggle that the war in Surabaya may have been for the Indonesian guerrillas in a remarkably distant tone, as the metaphor of the 'beer foaming over the top of a glass' shows. The struggle engendered mainly a humanitarian disaster, which affected large groups of civilians, Indonesians and Indo-Dutch. The intended evacuation of European women, men and children from the Japanese camps in the hinterland was partially blocked by the war, but there were also successes on the humanitarian front: tens of thousands of Indo-Dutch owed their evacuation and their lives to the British-Indian military. In the meantime, large groups of Indo-Dutch were transferred to Republican camps in the vicinity of the city, where they were later used as hostages of the negotiations by the Republic.[25] Indonesian city dwellers had to leave their homes as a result of the fighting and bombardments. About this large group of displaced people, Idrus wrote:

> The roads outside the city were filled with people, most of them women. They looked exhausted and drained by their long march. They were leaving behind smoke, fire, cowboys and bandits, and everything they held dear: their husbands, their burned-out houses, their European chickens, their children and their steel beds. As they walked they wept like little children, they sighed, and a few women gave birth.[26]

'NOBODY KNOWS WHO IS FIGHTING WHO'

The Australian artist-reporter Tony Rafty was witness to this evacuation on 14 November 1945 [11]. He must have smelled the gun powder, the black ash must have rained down on him, and he saw the smoke, the fire, and heard the weeping and sighing. Rafty made rapid sketches out in the streets. The result was a snapshot in pen and ink of a procession of passing evacuees [12]. Behind them the burning city is visible. The fleeing men, women and children, dressed in tattered clothes, are carrying bags with their possessions. They are accompanied by two young men holding up a flag, probably to indicate that these are refugees. In the left foreground, two British soldiers unroll wire (electrical or barbed) from a spool. Behind them, an Indonesian is being searched by a compatriot. At back right, more evacuees are coming.

Tony Rafty had served as an artist correspondent in the Australian army during the war, including in Kalimantan (Borneo) (when he was still a soldier) and in New Guinea. In September 1945 he was dispatched to Java by the Australian newspaper *The Sun*. The editors had given him a specific assignment: find out who Sukarno is. Who is the man who declared Indonesian independence? How is he getting the Indonesian people to support him?

Rafty must have been a smooth-talking man with a certain swagger, who found it easy to gain access to many places. Shortly after arriving in Jakarta, the Australian had reported to Jalan Pegangsaan Timur 56, the address of Sukarno, whose home had become the unofficial headquarters of the government of the Republic of Indonesia in a matter

[13]   Evacuation of the Muntilan camp on Java, by Tony Rafty, 1945

[14]   'Dutch soldier fully armed at the elert [alert] throughout the streets', by Tony Rafty, 1945

[15]   An Indonesian policeman in Jakarta, by Tony Rafty, 1945

of weeks. Rafty had been received with open arms by Sukarno, who from the outset, as a mediagenic statesmen, knew how to conduct his public relations via foreign journalists with great success. The good relationship between the president and the correspondent, fuelled in part by shared artistic interests, meant that on 29 October Rafty was able to secure a seat on board the British Dakota plane that brought Sukarno to Surabaya, to sign a truce between the British and Indonesian freedom fighters. The visit by Sukarno and other high representatives of the Republic – Vice President Hatta and minister Amir Sjarifuddin also came along – was meant to calm the revolutionary sentiments and subdue the intense street fighting that raged against everyone and anyone who stood in the way of the Republic. This at least was the hope of the British authorities, who had insisted on Sukarno's coming, in the process acknowledging the authority of the president (to the chagrin of the Dutch). Rafty experienced the plane, carrying the entire leadership of the Republic and the British commander in chief, Major General Douglas Hawthorn, being shot at from the city shortly before landing. But he also saw how that hostility suddenly turned into enthusiasm when the president, amid loud cries of 'Merdeka! Merdeka! Merdeka!', set foot on the East-Javan soil.

    A day after the landing, the conflict had reignited once more with the death of the aforementioned Brigadier Mallaby, whose portrait Rafty had drawn from life just the day before. The war had now fully broken out in Surabaya. Tony Rafty was there from the end of October until well into November with his sketchpad, pen and ink. He saw the street fighting, the British bombardment, the roadblocks, the British tanks fighting the Indonesian (formerly Japanese) tanks and the battered population of the city on the run. By observing and making sketches, he put together a small oeuvre that presents a fascinating sampling of scenes as well as people in the first weeks of the Indonesian revolution in Java. There are quick-fire portraits of the Indonesian Republican leaders and of the British commanders. He depicted the evacuation of Europeans, mainly women and children, from the Japanese internment camp of Muntilan, undertaken under the protection of British-Indian troops [13]. But Rafty also had an eye for the Indian military policeman (captured in a colourful watercolour) who was attached to the British army, or for the Nepalese Gurkha who was part of the large contingent of troops from India that comprised the British army dispatched to Java. Rafty scribbled a short text on a drawing of an Indonesian police officer in Jakarta: 'The Indonesian Police were a peace time Force. Although followers of the Indonesian uprising they co-operated with the British to maintain law and order' [15]. It was a motley crew of army and police troops that Rafty had pose for him or drew in passing on his sketchpad, in Jakarta, Surabaya and Semarang (where Rafty recorded a Japanese patrol saluting a British patrol). On 2 November Rafty wrote from the conflict zone of Surabaya: 'Nobody knows who is fighting who, for if they do it is a good guess'.

    What the Indonesians envisioned becomes clear from a somewhat smaller drawing that Rafty must have made behind the back of – according to the caption – a fully armed Dutch soldier, if we assume that this street scene was drawn from life [14]. An Indonesian family, alert to the danger, trudges past the soldier. In the background, Rafty drew a banner – or is it supposed to be a large billboard? – bearing the words: 'We want our Independence'. In a rather cartoonish way (Rafty was often seen more as a cartoonist than as an artist), the sketch makes it clear that dark clouds had gathered over the Indonesian desire for independence in the final months of 1945. The actual violence, the human suffering, the menace, the fear, insecurity and the poverty of those months are difficult to capture in images.

PROPAGANDA FOR THE REPUBLIC

AT THE FOREFRONT OF THE INFORMATION WAR

AMIR SIDHARTA
HARM STEVENS

REVOLUSI!

Dutch photographer Cas Oorthuys was thirty-eight years old when he arrived in Java in early January 1947. In his luggage he carried the distinctive Rolleiflex reflex camera, an ingenious photographic device with two lenses that could be hung from the neck by a leather strap. To take a photo, you looked into it from above. A short-sleeved white shirt and khaki shorts completed Oorthuys's tropics outfit [1]. This is how the photographer, stepped resolutely into the arena of the Indonesian revolution. The Dutch-Indonesian conflict that followed Sukarno's declaration of independence on 17 August 1945 had abated somewhat in the weeks preceding Oorthuys's arrival, at least in Java, thanks to constructive diplomatic exchanges. That promise of detente was precisely why ABC Press Service, an Amsterdam-based photo agency that supplied Dutch newspapers with images of world news, along with the Contact publishing house, also based in Amsterdam, considered it a good moment to commission from Oorthuys a photo reportage in Indonesia.

Negotiations between the Republic of Indonesia and representatives of the Dutch government had resulted in a fragile truce in October 1946. In addition, an agreement had been struck in the mountain village of Linggajati, West Java, in November 1946, calling for a federal Indonesia and a permanent union between the Netherlands and the United States of Indonesia. Alongside the Republic, which held de facto authority over Java, Madura and Sumatra, these states encompassed Negara Indonesia Timur (NIT, State of East Indonesia: all islands east of Java in the Indonesian archipelago) and Kalimantan (Borneo). A certain optimism reigned, although conflicting interpretations of the draft agreement by the Dutch administration on the one hand and the Republic on the other were gathering like dark clouds over the peace process.

Oorthuys was familiar with photo-reportage commissions: his photo book *Landbouw* (Agriculture), for example, had been published in 1946, commissioned by the Agrarisch Fonds (Netherlands Agrarian Fund). His Indonesian photo-journalism expedition in Java, with a short excursion to Kalimantan, would last until late March. On the 25th of that month, Dutch and Republican delegations ratified a more detailed version of the Linggajati Agreement at Rijswijk Palace in Jakarta. Oorthuys returned to the Netherlands in early April 1947 with hundreds of rolls of film containing more than 2,500 photos.

A NASCENT STATE

Over the preceding twelve weeks, Oorthuys had worked feverishly on a reportage in which he looked beyond the view of the Republic of Indonesia that prevailed in the Netherlands, which was that of a problem, an illegitimate Japanese concoction that had plunged the country into chaos. Oorthuys saw Indonesia in 1947 in a more positive way, the results of which became his photo book with the constructive title *Een staat in wording* (A Nascent State) [2]. He handled its design himself, immediately upon his return. The educationalist Albert de la Court contributed the sometimes biblical-sounding captions ('and tranquillity returns to the land'), lending the publication a somewhat patronizing tone redolent of Dutch colonialism. The book was published shortly before the first large-

[1] Cas Oorthuys in Indonesia, January 1947

scale Dutch military offensive in July 1947: 'Operatie Product' (Operation Product). After that the optimism of the Linggajati Agreement of over six months before definitively evaporated. Following violations of the treaty provisions on both sides, the Netherlands took up arms. War was on in Indonesia once more. While this did not diminish the conciliatory strength of *Een staat in wording*, sales of the photo book, produced in a large print run, were extremely disappointing.

Nevertheless, *Een staat in wording* opened many eyes. This was because, as observed in a book review in the progressive newspaper *Het Parool* shortly after its publication: '[Indonesia] is observed for once not through a half-closed colonial eye, but through the sympathetic gaze of an unprejudiced person, who also grants the Republican his place in the sun.' Was Oorthuys really so unprejudiced? With a pre-war career with the explicitly anti-colonial Communist Party of Holland, a fine record as an anti-fascist and a member of the illegal photographers' collective De Ondergedoken Camera (The Hidden Camera) under German occupation, his role as a politically engaged leftist and humanist photographer of post-war reconstruction was merely a logical step, and his receptive gaze towards the nascent Indonesian Republic is understandable. Add to this the skilful work of Indonesian information officials, who welcomed Oorthuys and other Dutch and international press people with open arms in Republican territory, and the 'sympathetic gaze' was complete. Oorthuys was witness to a lively session of the Republican parliament, the Komite Nasional Indonesia Pusat (KNIP, Central Indonesian National Committee), which sat temporarily in the building of the quintessentially colonial society Concordia in the East Javanese city of Malang. In his photos of the occasion, the spark of the Indonesian revolution's constructive potential burns brightly [3]. This Republican charm offensive resulted in a joint declaration, issued in March 1947, by Dutch journalists 'who have gathered their own experiences in Republican territory', as the communist newspaper *De Waarheid* reported on 10 March 1947. Among other things, this declaration argued that the broad sections of the population passionately supported the national revolution. At first glance this was a rather grandiloquent assertion, but the intention, as the declaration solemnly stated, was 'to provide information about the true facts in the Republic, in order to counter the false representation of events in certain circles in the Netherlands'. One of the signatories was 'C. Oorthuys (photo reporter)'. The evidently deeply felt need to issue such a declaration makes it clear that the Indonesian Issue, as the revolution in Indonesia was known in the Netherlands, was also an information war.

The opportunity, most likely under the supervision of Indonesian information officials, to visit a workshop somewhere in Republican territory where young Indonesians were hard at work producing propaganda posters is one Oorthuys must have grabbed with both hands [4]. These little poster factories – ammunition factories in the information war – would have been a subject close to Oorthuys's heart, given his own career. In the 1930s Oorthuys had worked as a graphic designer and produced the designs for many propaganda posters: for the communists, against the Olympic Games in Berlin in 1936, against the bombardments

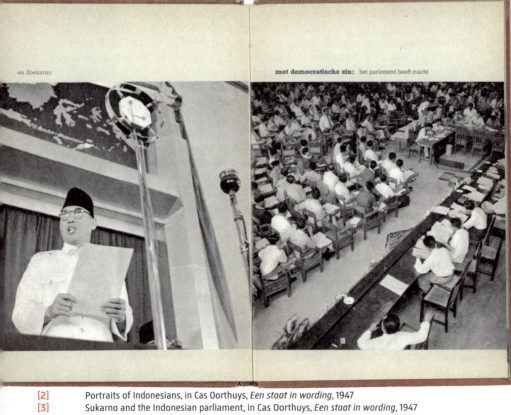

[2] Portraits of Indonesians, in Cas Oorthuys, *Een staat in wording*, 1947
[3] Sukarno and the Indonesian parliament, in Cas Oorthuys, *Een staat in wording*, 1947

[4] A poster workshop, in Cas Oorthuys, *Een staat in wording*, 1947
[5] Indonesian soldiers, in Cas Oorthuys, *Een staat in wording*, 1947

during the Spanish civil war ('This is how children are dying in Madrid') and against the wrongful conviction of seven Black men in the United States.

Whereas Oorthuys had worked with modern printing techniques and photomontage at the time, the posters in the workshops in Java were the product of simple manual DIY handicraft that anyone could perform, as shown in a series of photos taken by Oorthuys [6]. Stencils are cut on a table with a knife. Local boys operate the paint sprayer. The result is a poster of a tank and the text 'Hanja parsatoean jang memoetoesi' (only unity prevails), which can now be produced in multiple copies thanks to the reuse of the stencil [7]. Another photo shows the boys under an awning using a stamping brush. In this case a rather more complex, multi-coloured poster is being produced, which is shown being laid out on a table in another photo [8]. Above an image of a flying, demonic figure brandishing a Dutch flag and ridden by a 'colonial Dutchman' in a green uniform is the text: 'Flying Dutchman'. With his left hand the figure is setting fire to the land below. A city flying the Indonesian flag is about to go up in flames. In this way, the Indonesian propagandists attach a clear political message to the old, internationally familiar legend of the 'Flying Dutchman': the Netherlands is out to destroy the Republic of Indonesia.

It was a message that *Een staat in wording* evidently did not want to convey. '[T]he youth builds', De la Court positively preached, 'it carries out propaganda' [4] and 'it protects the republic' [5]. These latter words were illustrated in the book by a photo of the workshop showing the Flying Dutchman poster being produced. Even looking closely it is difficult to make out the image of the incendiary Dutchman. Surely that other photo, in which the young Indonesian lays out the poster on a table before the eyes and lens of the photographer, and in which the text and image are clearly visible, would have made a much stronger picture? Yet Oorthuys did not include it in his selection for the book. Was it perhaps preferable, in the presentation of 'information about the true facts in the Republic', as proclaimed in the journalists' declaration, to steer clear of the militant anti-Dutch sentiment among Republicans?

WE STRUGGLE WITH POSTERS

The demonic Flying Dutchman poster can also be found in miniature in a special album bearing the evocative title *Kami Berdjuang Dengen Poster/ We Struggle with Posters* [12]. The album consists of twenty-four pages in an oblong format with three small poster reproductions affixed on each page [9, 10, 11]. *We Struggle with Posters* provides a catalogue of Indonesian Republican visual propaganda, a sampling of the Republic's political aspirations and ambitions: internationally oriented, aiming at the unification of the islands and people of Indonesia, ready for the construction of a modern country, and fighting to defend Indonesian independence against the (mostly Dutch) forces threatening that freedom.

The foreword affixed to the inside of the cover reveals that the album was compiled and published in November 1947 in Yogyakarta, which served as the Republic's political capital at the time. According to the same foreword, the album contains examples of 'PTPI-distributed posters since the first days of our Republic of Indonesia'. The acronym PTPI stands for Pusat Tenaga Pelukis Indonesia (Powerhouse for Indonesian Painters), an artists' collective founded in September 1945 by Djajengasmoro, Sindusiswoyo, Surjosugondo, Prawito and Noor Baheramsjah. The group initially produced work commissioned by the information service in Central Java led by Dr Subandrio and was therefore explicitly linked to Republican governmental authorities.[1] Besides the design and production of posters, PTPI staged propaganda performances using cartoon figures projected onto a white screen. This kind of folk theatre found a large and enthusiastic audience in village and town squares.

The acronym PTPI also features on the cover, which is made of crocodile leather, alongside an expressive logo, a palette with two brushes and the Indonesian flag, and the title in Indonesian and English. Both languages were also used in alternation for the texts on the posters: some are in Indonesian, others in English: 'We can rule ourselves'. This was a tradition that had been initiated from the very first weeks following the *Proklamasi* (independence proclamation), for instance in English-language street slogans in Jakarta. The Republic was waging a propaganda campaign aimed at its own people, but the propaganda was also very explicitly intended for the eyes of the world. The underlying idea, as one of the poster texts in the album spelled out, was: 'A free Indonesia will contribute to the world reconstruction'. Indonesia was claiming its place in the post-war world. Stylistically, the miniature sample posters in the album also fit in with the internationally beloved comic book style, a youthful and colourful culture of superheroes that originated in the United States and became popular worldwide from the Second World War.

The contents and layout of the poster catalogue can be summed up as follows. The first section is entitled 'Proklamasi Kemerdekaan/Proclamation of Independence'. It includes posters that exhort the army and people to unite in upholding Indonesian independence. 'Perdjoangan/Struggle' is the title of the next section. Information is provided here in words and images about the tactics of the Netherlands Indies Civil Administration (NICA) and about the need to combat them. The role that women can play in the struggle is also highlighted, as part of the Red Cross or as mothers providing moral support to their fighting sons. The 'Pembangunan/Building Up' section includes poster designs that look towards the future. Practical issues like money, healthcare and education are represented here as well.

There is also a section entitled 'Naskah R.P./Linggardjati Agreement', in which the poster designs emphasize the need for unity in dealing with the outcomes of the agreement. The final section, 'Perang Kolonial/Colonialism War', once more reminds people of the stealth tactics of the Netherlands in expanding its power in Indonesia behind the backs of the Allies and later of the United Nations. There is also a call for citizens to keep secrets to themselves. The egalitarian element comes to the fore: a text on one of the posters reads 'The State has a responsibility to protect every citizen/resident, to punish criminals, no matter what their nationality/ethnicity might be'. The catalogue concludes in style

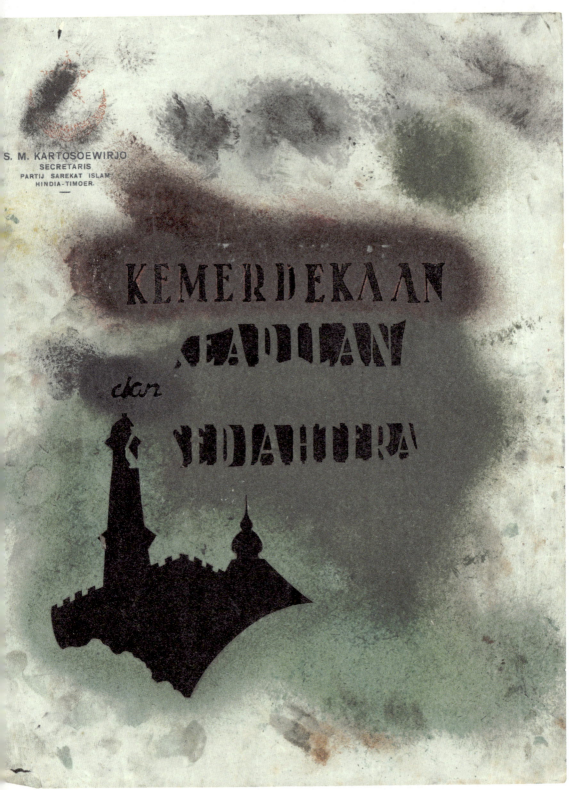

[6] Template for poster, with picture of a mosque and the text 'Freedom, justification and welfare' on letterhead of S.M. Kartosoewirjo, secretary of the Partij Sarekat Islam Hindi Timoer (PSIHT), c. 1948

[7] Production of a poster in a workshop, photo by Cas Oorthuys, 1947

[8] 'Flying Dutchman' poster in a workshop in Yogyakarta, photo by Cas Oorthuys, 1947

[9, 10, 11] Posters in the album *Kami Berdjuang Dengan Poster/We Struggle with Posters*, by PTPI, 1947

[12] Cover of the album *Kami Berdjuang Dengan Poster/We Struggle with Posters*, by PTPI, 1947

[13] Exhibition of PTPI posters in the Kedu region, Central Java, 1946/1947

with a poster depicting a flaming torch with the text: 'Api Kemerdekaan tetap menjala' (The fire of independence keeps burning).

The photos that Cas Oorthuys took of the small outdoor workshops where posters were produced with the help of local boys conjure up a picture of a truly revolutionary Atelier Populaire (people's workshop). In the case of the PTPI, besides the popular revolution character of the 'powerhouse', a network organized from above was also involved. The landmark catalogue *We Struggle with Posters* underscores this official and organized character of Republican propaganda.

A series of photos and their caption in a historical photo album shows that an exhibition of PTPI posters was coordinated by the local information service in the Kedu region of Central Java in 1946 or 1947. Albums stacked on a table, behind which stands a uniformed female information service official, are reminiscent of *We Struggle with Posters*.[2] There is no longer any hint of the DIY atmosphere captured by Oorthuys in the workshop; instead the venue in Kedu suggests the ambience of an official poster issuance office, complete with hostesses [13].

In order to achieve as wide a dissemination as possible, the PTPI worked with the Republican army Tentara Keamanan Rakjat (TKR, People's Security Army) and the Djawatan Kereta Api (Railways), which distributed the posters throughout Java. The Indonesian navy ensured that PTPI was able to fulfil poster orders from Indonesian independence fighters outside Java eager to put them up in the local streets. There was great demand in Makassar (Sulawesi), for example, for posters that registered protest against the murderous actions of Captain Raymond Westerling and his Special Forces Corps in South Sulawesi in late 1946.[3]

Besides the more or less official distribution by the army, railways and navy, all kinds of underground channels were used to disseminate the posters while keeping them out of enemy hands. The fact that the latter did not always succeed is evidenced, however, by the vast and very diverse set of posters (and pamphlets) that were seized by the Netherlands Forces Intelligence Service (NEFIS). This included four beautiful PTPI posters seized on 30 December 1946. NEFIS recorded the seizure site as 'Java Madura proa boat transport' [14-17].[4]

Another artists' collective that designed and produced propaganda posters was Seniman Indonesia Muda (SIM, Young Indonesian Artists). SIM was founded in 1946 in the East Javanese city of Madiun by Soedibio and Sudjojono. Sudjojono in particular had made a name for himself on the Indonesian art scene in the preceding years and he also maintained good relations with the Republic's political leadership. In 1947 SIM moved its activities to the Central Javanese city of Solo, and a little later to Yogyakarta, the Republic's political capital. Like the PTPI, SIM maintained direct links with the Republican authorities: the collective was made part of the art department of the secretariat of the ministry of youth and received financial support from the government. In Solo, Prime Minister Amir Sjarifuddin ensured that the young Indonesian artists had material support. This took place via the organization Pemuda Sosialis Indonesia (Pesindo, Socialist Youth of Indonesia). And the SIM posters that have survived are indeed distinguished by the quality of their printing. A set of six SIM posters, through the intervention of the Dutch communist

[14] Propaganda poster with the text 'Defend your village', by PTPI, 1946

[15] Propaganda poster with the text 'Three principles for the reorganization of welfare in the villages', by PTPI, 1946

[16] Propaganda poster with the text 'Rice for India, clothing for Indonesia', by PTPI, 1946

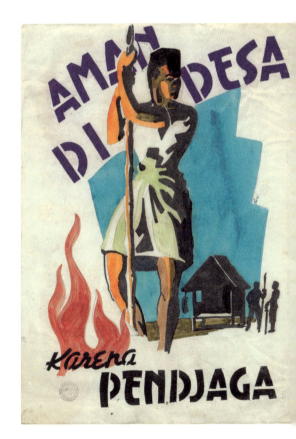

[17] Propaganda poster with the text 'Thanks to the guards it is safe in the villages', by PTPI, 1946

Joop Moriën, who was dispatched to Indonesia in 1948 as part of his military service, ended up in the collection of the International Institute for Social History in Amsterdam. Their messages emphatically mirror the policy based on diplomacy and consultation to which Prime Minister Sjarifuddin was committed. In words and images, supporters are urged to accept the draft agreement (Naskah), which probably refers to the Linggajati Agreement struck in 1946. 'The draft [agreement] is the bridge to our goal', reads the text that accompanies the image of an Indonesian about to cross a terrifyingly deep ravine, on the other side of which grows a flower in full bloom [18].

PTPI and SIM are examples of the more internationally oriented and professional centres where Republican political propaganda was produced. The educated artists who worked on the designs contributed to the programme of popular information promoted by official information services throughout the Republic. Alongside these centres, there was another kind of poster production on the Republican side, in centres that must have been attached to military units [19]. Volatility, movement and improvisation typify this guerrilla poster production. A good example is the five hand-painted posters, also bearing the handwritten 'signature' of the 'Information Service' of an army unit that was active in Sumatra: 'Penerangan Tentara. Resimen I Gadjah II. Soematera'. Although they are painted in somewhat amateur fashion, it is clear that the maker possessed some artistic talent. The crystal-clear warning on one of the posters aptly sums up the general message of the 'struggle with posters': 'Djangan Oesik Indonesia!' (Don't mess with Indonesia!) [20].

[18] Propaganda poster with the text 'The draft [of the Linggajati agreement] is the bridge to our goal', by SIM, 1946

[19] Military unit propaganda poster with the text 'Hey traitors! I've joined [the armed forces] to bring justice to people with sins like yours', 1946

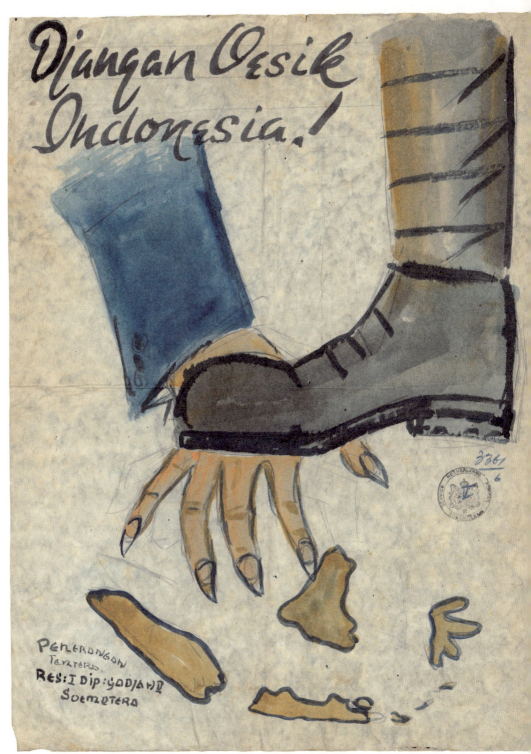

[20] Propaganda poster with the text: 'Don't mess with Indonesia', by Penerangan Tentara information service, 1945–1949

CAUGHT IN THE NET

THE DUTCH HUNT FOR INFORMATION

HARM STEVENS
BONNIE TRIYANA

REVOLUSI!

In April 1946, Rosihan Anwar's portrait photo turned up in a place where no Indonesian with a deep-rooted belief in his country's independence would want to be: the headquarters of Dutch military intelligence, known as the Netherlands Forces Intelligence Service (NEFIS). The image bears the date '29 July 1939' written in small letters, and was pasted to the first page of a classic photo album, its dark brown pages filled with photos of Rosihan Anwar's carefree school days [1].

Rosihan Anwar was born into a wealthy family in Kubang Nan Dua, West Sumatra, in 1922. His father was a district administrator. That background gave him the privilege of receiving a European education in the nearby city of Padang. In 1939, Rosihan became a student at the Algemene Middelbare School (AMS) in Yogyakarta, a six-year secondary school with Dutch teachers, which was open to Indonesians from aristocratic or wealthy backgrounds and was roughly equivalent to the Dutch secondary school curriculum. Rosihan and his fellow students – 'our gang', according to a caption under one of the photos – dressed in fashionable snow-white suits with striped ties and pocket squares in their jackets [2]. They went on enjoyable school trips, as one of the photo captions notes: 'All of us smiling for Buddha' [3]. The date is 10 September 1939, for AMS student Rosihan Anwar the day of 'our bicycle trip to Borobudur'.

But little remained of that seemingly calm world by April 1946, the month when Rosihan Anwar's carefully compiled photo album was taken into custody. The reasons it was seized remain shrouded in darkness; was it taken by Dutch soldiers who searched his house or by one of the 'informers', often Indonesian, who were paid to supply incriminating information? What we know for certain is that, through a NEFIS branch office, the album found its way to that intelligence service's Jakarta headquarters, in the stately pre-war offices of the Dutch East Indies life insurance company NILLMIJ. The building was on the Noordwijk canal, in the heart of the city's government district.

SECRET SERVICE

NEFIS had been founded in the Second World War by the Dutch East Indies government-in-exile in Australia. Its original mission was to gather intelligence about the former Dutch East Indies and pass it on to the Allied forces at war with Japan. With the move to Jakarta in late 1945 came a new activity: investigating war crimes committed by the Japanese and collaboration with the Japanese occupying regime. But the outbreak of the Indonesian revolution created an urgent new field of operations for the intelligence service, as a centre for Dutch counter-revolutionary activity and political repression in Indonesia. NEFIS thus followed in the footsteps of the notorious Politieke Inlichtingendienst (PID, Political Intelligence Service), the pre-war secret service in the Dutch East Indies, which had done a remarkably effective job of harassing and silencing Indonesian nationalist movements in the colony. The PID's ungentle methods of investigation formed the basis for the mass internment of Indonesian political prisoners, often without any form of trial, in the Boven-Digoel concentration camp. In this respect, the pre-war intelli-

[1] Rosihan Anwar, 29 July 1939, portrait photo from his photo album, seized by NEFIS in April 1946 (Jakarta)

[2] Rosihan Anwar and his classmates, 1939, photo from his photo album

[3] Rosihan Anwar and his classmates on a school trip, 10 September 1939, page from his photo album

gence service was a key component of what Prime Minister Sutan Sjahrir, in his publication *Perdjoeangan Kita* (Our Struggle) published in November 1945, described as 'Dutch colonial fascism'.[1]

Alongside its Jakarta headquarters, NEFIS also had a far-flung network of branch offices and outposts, from Ternate (North Moluccas, now North Maluku) to Medan (Sumatra), and from Parepare (near Makassar in Sulawesi) to Tanjung Priok, the port of Jakarta.[2] The activities of these offices consisted of interrogation, building a network of informants, and monitoring radio broadcasts and newspaper articles. The branch offices were in direct contact with the local Dutch civilian and military authorities.[3]

While the operational intelligence work, such as seizing documents, was performed by the offices and outposts, the Jakarta headquarters was the central hub into which all suspicious materials – seized, stolen or otherwise acquired – ultimately flowed. Such materials poured in for about four years, from late 1945 until well into 1949. The result was a record of the Indonesian revolution in hundreds of metres of paper, ranging from a complete Republican government archive, seized in Yogyakarta when the presidential palace and other government buildings were captured, to a flood of pamphlets, many fiercely anti-Dutch in tone [5]. One noteworthy set of documents is a collection of Dutch-language leaflets intended to persuade drafted Dutch soldiers that they were fighting for the wrong cause [4]. Posters with traces of plaster on the back from the walls where they were hung show that the work of NEFIS agents sometimes took them out into the streets, and they offer important evidence of how the streets and public spaces were used to spread the message of the Indonesian revolution [6]. Other items netted by NEFIS include a series of small red-and-white flags, intended for celebrating the third anniversary of Indonesian independence on 17 August 1948. Not everything in the collection is made of paper; textiles, often worn on the body itself, are also part of the intelligence agency's trove. One example is a red armband bearing the letters 'P.K.M.', short for Pemberontakan Kaoem Moeslimin (Muslim People's Revolt) [7]. Sewn to the inside of the armband is a slip of paper with mantras on it. The wearer of a *jimat*, or talisman, of this kind hoped it would make him invulnerable. One special item is a number of photo albums painstakingly compiled by the independent photo agency IPPHOS (Indonesian Press Photo Service), which provide, among other things, a visual history of Indonesian independence[8]. One of the albums contains a photographic report on the Linggajati negotiations.

Rosihan Anwar's album was among those that ended up somewhere in that whitewashed NEFIS building, under the care of Division 5, the documentation division, which also supplied translations and library services. The document had an accompanying note, just as the bureaucratic NEFIS now required. The photo album became a number: 'NEFIS document no. 01212'. The entry for 'Information regarding seizure' remained blank.[4] But whoever wrote the accompanying note did not hesitate to scribble notes in pencil on the photo album itself, providing something that was supposed to pass for intelligence. On the inside cover, the NEFIS agent drew an ominous arrow next to a photo of Rosihan Anwar:

[4] Pamphlet seized by NEFIS on 20 January 1948 (location unknown)

[5] Anti-Dutch pamphlets, seized by NEFIS on respectively: 4 October 1947 (Semarang), 15 December 1947 (Pasuruan), 8 March 1948 (Tjikampek)

[6]   Poster seized by NEFIS on 10 March 1948 (Sukaratu)

[7]   Red armband with the letters P.K.M., seized by NEFIS on 15 August 1946 (Bandung)

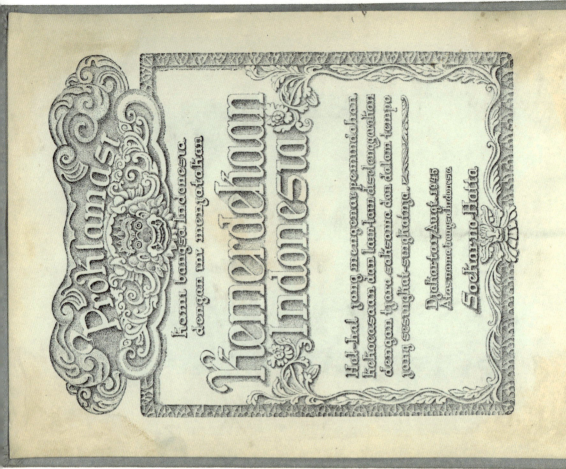

[8] Photo album about the Indonesian declaration of independence, compiled by IPPHOS (1945–1946), seized by NEFIS, date unknown

1

2

3

4

[9] Rosihan Anwar delivers a speech at the Malino Conference, July 1946

'Editor of *Merkeka*'. Underneath it, the agent wrote 'Aimant [lover] of Anna Latuasan [Laluasan], sister of A.E. Latuasan, secretary of P.K. Maluku [Maluku Communist Party]'.

STAR REPORTER

It was true that Rosihan Anwar was a journalist and, although still in his twenties, one of the driving forces behind the daily newspaper *Merdeka*, founded in Jakarta in October 1945, the mouthpiece of the Republic of Indonesia. It was incorrect, however, to claim that he was the lover of Anna Laluasan.[5] Alternative facts, conspiracy theories, rumours and gossip – NEFIS eagerly gathered all sorts of 'intelligence'. The facade of objectivity created by the document numbers, typed accompanying notes and protective dust jackets concealed a make-believe world in which the presentation of facts – so-called 'military intelligence' – was often skewed for political purposes. Accusations of communist sympathies or associations – and a relationship with the daughter of a Communist Party secretary certainly pointed in that direction – were a time-tested recipe for harassing groups and individuals.[6]

Young Rosihan Anwar clearly put his heart and soul into the cause of an independent Indonesia, but his political ideals had much less to do with communism than with the social democratic ideology of Sjahrir. A few months after the seizure of his photo album, star reporter Anwar was a prominent participant in the Malino Conference, held in the city of that name in Sulawesi. At the conference a Dutch administrator, Lieutenant Governor-General Huib van Mook, laid out his plan for the formation of a federal Republic of Indonesia composed of multiple states. An official photograph taken by the Netherlands Indies Government Information Service (NIGIS), identifying Anwar as a journalist for the Antara and Merdeka press agencies, shows the young journalist giving a speech at the closing dinner [9]. On the lapel of his light-coloured suit is an Indonesian flag pin. A few months later, in October 1946, Anwar covered the negotiations between the Republic and the Netherlands from the mountain village of Linggajati. These talks eventually resulted in the agreement of the same name, which appeared to bring the peaceful resolution of the conflict within reach.

Rosihan Anwar was always to be found wherever the political action was: in revolutionary Jakarta, as co-founder of the nationalist newspaper *Merdeka*; in Linggajati, as a leading reporter; and – much later, in 1949 – at the Round Table Conference in The Hague, where the final negotiations between the Netherlands and the Republic took place, opening the way to the transfer of sovereignty and the independence of what was then known as the Republik Indonesia Serikat (RIS, Republic of the United States of Indonesia). But Anwar had made a name for himself in Indonesian journalism long before that. His career, like those of so many Indonesian intellectuals and artists, took off under the Japanese occupation, when he had the opportunity to work as a journalist at the daily newspaper *Asia Raya*, which was under Japanese supervision. One of his outstanding journalistic and literary accomplishments for this paper was to publish an Indonesian translation of the patriotic poem 'Mi último adiós' ('My last farewell'), written by the Filipino poet and freedom fighter José Rizal in 1896. Rizal was killed by a firing squad soon after the poem's publication and became a martyr of both the Filipino and the worldwide anticolonial revolution. Anwar's translation was published on 30 December 1944, exactly forty-eight years after Rizal's execution. The day before that, he had read his Indonesian version aloud on the radio, despite the generally strict Japanese censorship. The reading had not gone unnoticed by the Indonesian people, who embraced José Rizal as a universal anticolonial hero. Indonesian soldiers recited the poem before marching into battle, to lend force to their act of self-sacrifice: 'To die to give you life, 'neath your skies to expire, / And in thy mystic land to sleep through eternity!'

The circumstances surrounding the seizure of Anwar's photo album remain somewhat unclear. The rightful owner could not later recall the house being searched in the month of April, the seizure date indicated on the accompanying note. It was a chaotic time. The *Merdeka* journalist moved to three different Jakarta addresses in quick succession. The photo album may have been in the keeping of an acquaintance when NEFIS got their hands on it.[7]

On the evening of 21 July 1947, Anwar experienced for himself what it was like to have one's house searched. Four Dutch soldiers forced their way into the house in Jalan Cianjur in the residential district of Menteng, in search of Lieutenant Sayuti or Susanto (Anwar mentioned both names in his witness statements). Rosihan Anwar said he had no idea where the lieutenant could be found. This response does not seem to have inspired much confidence; a thorough search of the house ensued. Letters and documents were checked and thrown into disarray. The floor was covered with them.

A stack of magazines entitled *Siasat* caught the eye of the soldiers. This political journal had been founded by Anwar a few months before the fateful day of the search. *Siasat* means 'tactic'; the Dutch soldiers may have concluded from this title that the magazine was connected to the Indonesian guerrilla struggle against the Dutch troops. That was how the man who, a year earlier, had given an official speech at a ceremonial dinner as part of the Malino Conference found himself in the back of a police van on the way to Bukit Duri prison in the south of Jakarta. Anwar was not alone in the back of the van, because the Dutch round-up in Jalan Cianjur that July evening had also led to the arrest of other prominent Indonesian supporters of the Republic in the district. He and three other detainees were shoved into a filthy cell measuring two square metres. The next day, after a nauseating breakfast of porridge and coffee, Anwar was released.[8]

The date of his arrest, 21 July 1947, was more than mere chance. On that day, the Netherlands launched a major military offensive, codenamed 'Operatie Product' (Operation Product) and referred to euphemistically as a 'police action'. It was a response to what the Netherlands saw as continuing violations of the Linggajati Agreement by the Republic. In Jakarta, Java's largest and most important city, this military action strongly resembled a coup. Jakarta had long had a strangely hybrid character: the institutions of the Dutch colonial administration stood side by side there with Republican institutions. In January 1946, Sukarno and Hatta left for Yogyakarta with most of the Republican government, but that did not mean the end of the Republican presence in Jakarta. More than a year and a half later, there was still an official representation of the Republic in the city; an Indonesian flag still flew proudly from some buildings, while down the street the Dutch flag was raised. But from around July 1946, the city was largely controlled by the Dutch occupiers. Prime Minister Sjahrir had remained in Jakarta, even though his life was at risk there (in December 1945, KNIL soldiers had attempted to assassinate him). He had offices at Pengangsaan Timur 56, where Sukarno had delivered the *Proklamasi* (independence proclamation). On 17 August 1946, the first anniversary of that historic event, a monumental stone obelisk was unveiled in a ceremony in the park in front of Sjahrir's office to mark the anniversary. The Indonesian organizers, a group of pro-Republican women in Jakarta, had courageously defied the prohibition of this public celebration by the Dutch occupying regime [10].

'ALL THE RED-AND-WHITE BUILDINGS WERE OCCUPIED'

Simon Admiraal, trained as a drawing instructor at the art academy in The Hague before the war, was a Dutch employee at the university library in Jakarta (then called Batavia), his birth city, on 21 July 1947, when the large-scale military purge by the Dutch army put a sudden end to the Republican presence in the city.

By then, Admiraal had five catastrophic years behind him. After three years as a prisoner of war and forced labourer, suffering under inhuman conditions during the Japanese occupation, he was confronted – even before his reunion with his wife and children, who had been detained in camps elsewhere in Indonesia – with the terrible news that his eldest son Jan was missing. In September 1946, months of uncertainty about Jan's fate came to an end when Admiraal was asked to identify his son's beheaded remains. On 12 October 1945, when revolutionary anti-Dutch violence was spreading uncontrollably in Jakarta, Jan had been murdered in the street.

In a letter of 20 September 1946, Admiraal informed his wife and his other children in the most factual terms possible, 'without sentimentality', about his dealings with the military police and the need for him to identify the body. He could not avoid the conclusion that, 'Unfortunately, however hard it is, we must give up every last shred of hope and go on with nothing but the lasting memory of what was once a son, a brother. ... The murderer, a man named Jaksa, was arrested, confessed to the crime, and was then killed.' He added, 'This must remain secret, because administering one's own justice in this manner is an unofficial practice here. Otherwise there would be no chance of achieving any results.' The lawlessness of colonial Batavia was a well-kept secret. Admiraal understandably said no more about it. He described the effect on himself of his contribution to the investigation in the same concise, truthful and factual terms: 'after returning home well after 9 o'clock, I felt so miserable that I shut myself up in the toilet and had to vomit, and cried like a little boy – I couldn't help it.' Two lines down in the letter, Admiraal had a heartfelt

[10] Series of photos taken at the unveiling of a stone monument to celebrate one year of independence, Jakarta, 17 August 1946

message for his family: 'We must put this behind us; we must, we must.' Simon Admiraal did attempt to put his life back together again, far from his wife and children, who by this time were in Holland. His work in the university library in Jakarta offered some consolation, but his greatest comfort came from his old passion for drawing and painting. He was a loyal correspondent with his wife and children, reporting in plain language on the situation in Jakarta as it developed. He advocated decolonization and saw the idea of returning to colonial politics as 'depraved'.

On 24 July 1947, Admiraal, perhaps writing from the study where he was photographed around that time, described the military offensive launched three days earlier, the same one that had resulted in the confinement of the young journalist and writer Rosihan Anwar [11]:

> It happened suddenly, so the Republicans were taken by complete surprise, at least here in Batavia. All the red-and-white buildings were already occupied on Sunday, calmly and without incident. It must have been a strange experience for the Batavians to see what had happened to their city on Monday. There was no longer a single red-and-white flag to be seen; our tricolour flew from every Republican building, guarded by Dutch soldiers. The *x-autos* (Republican vehicles) were taken into custody and are now in a row at the M.T.D. [military technical service].

Admiraal felt the military action was inevitable, due to the continuing treaty violations by the Indonesians. He had more to tell about the evening of 21 July:

> we sat in the dark until 11:30 and were not even allowed to enter the garden. The entire city was heavily patrolled. A very few shots were fired, but that was all. ... The action was swift and successful, with few losses on our side as yet. No real fighting to report, thank goodness.'[9]

The relieved tone of Admiraal's letter is understandable. The purpose of his letter was probably to reassure his family in the Netherlands. And to be sure, for 'our side' – in other words, the Dutch side – the action brought the 'calm and order in these parts' that Admiraal described. But there was also a downside, especially for the Indonesians with Republican sympathies. Rosihan Anwar may have been released after one night behind bars in Bukit Duri, as mentioned above, but hundreds, if not thousands, of Indonesians had a rather different experience. These were people who, like Anwar, were suspected, often on shaky grounds, of sympathy for the Republican cause and arrested in Jakarta by Dutch soldiers on the night of 21 July and in the days and nights that followed.[10] They were held captive in Dutch prisons for years, without trial, without evidence of their guilt, without official investigation, and without any prospect of an end to their confinement. The Dutch military authorities were shielded by section 20 of the Staat van Oorlog en Beleg (State of War and Siege Act), which authorized commanders in the Dutch territories to intern people regarded 'as a threat to public order in an area subject to Dutch rule'. In the

[11]   Simon Admiraal in his office at the university library in Jakarta, 1947

[12] Pramoedya Ananta Toer, 1951

wave of arrests in July 1947, the colonial police state flexed its muscles.[11] Between July 1947 and late 1949, tens of thousands of Indonesians were locked up in colonial prisons.[12]

'MEN WHO FIGHT FOR FREEDOM'

One such prisoner was the young author Pramoedya Ananta Toer. On Wednesday 23 July – a day about which Admiraal wrote reassuringly to his family that the cinema and theatre had reopened – Pramoedya was stopped in the street by Dutch marines because he had papers in his pocket that looked suspicious to them. A few years later, Pramoedya jotted down a telegraphic account of the ensuing events: ' Tortured by a platoon of marines, totoks, Eurasians and Ambonese. Things at home seized. Imprisoned in the naval barracks in Gunung Sahari, then in the military police barracks in Jagamonyet. Finally locked up in Bukit Duri without serious trial.'[13] Pramoedya Ananta Toer would later become the greatest Indonesian writer of the twentieth century [12].

He was twenty years old in September 1945, when he plunged into the revolutionary struggle in Jakarta. Pramoedya, previously employed as stenographer and typist by the Japanese press agency Domei, received his revolutionary trial by fire in that same month, when he took part in an attack on a Japanese marine barracks with the aim of obtaining weapons. On 19 September, he set out for Ikada Square, like thousands of other Indonesians, for the first mass gathering after the proclamation of independence, which had been made more than a month earlier. Shortly afterwards Pramoedya joined the Badan Keamanan Rakjat (BKR), the military organization for the security of the people, a forerunner of the Republican army. He was stationed in Cikampek, in the east of Jakarta, and rose to the rank of sergeant major. In mid-1946 he was promoted to second lieutenant, and after that he acted as the press and liaison officer within his division. In that capacity, he was involved in the battle with the Allied army for the city of Bekasi, to the east of Jakarta.

Pramoedya's most moving accomplishment, in those months of revolutionary struggle, was to set up a regimental library for his fellow soldiers, which consisted of his own book collection. It was around this time, probably at the front in Cikampek, that Pramoedya wrote his first short stories. The escalating internal conflict about the course of the Revolution between the official Republican army, of which Pramoedya was part, and the autonomous *laskar rakyat* (people's militias), along with widespread corruption within the Indonesian ranks, led to Pramoedya's discharge from the army at his own request in late 1946. Penniless, he returned to Jakarta in early 1947, where he found a job as an editor in the Indonesian division of The Voice of Free Indonesia, the publishing house that published an English-language magazine of the same name, with the marvellous subtitle, 'Edited by Men who Fight for Freedom, Justice, Goodwill and Understanding'. Soon afterwards his supervisor was arrested by the Dutch, and young Pramoedya, for lack of any alternative, was promoted to deputy head of the division. Despite the difficult circumstances under which he had to perform his new duties, such as a shortage of money and paper, Pramoedya also found the time for his own writing.

In that same year of 1947, The Voice of Free Indonesia published his first book, *Krandji dan Bekasi Djatoeh* (The Fall of Krandji-Bekasi).[14]

Among the 'Things at home seized' mentioned by Pramoedya in his account of his arrest was a manuscript about a few *pemuda* (young freedom fighters) in the early days of the revolution,[15] by a talented young writer who had himself been one of the first *pemuda*. NEFIS saw the manuscript as sufficiently threatening to seize it before it could be published as a book. Or did the manuscript just happen to be caught up in the NEFIS net, a mere pile of unread pages? In any case, it was never seen again.[16] As for Pramoedya, he was cast into the depths of Bukit Duri prison. Unlike Rosihan Anwar, he was not released the next day but had to get by on a concrete bed in a verminous cell until the end of the Dutch occupation.

Pramoedya was finally released in December 1949, along with eight other prisoners who were part of the very last group of political prisoners. But at least he had not vanished permanently during his detention in Bukit Duri, unlike his manuscript in the hands of NEFIS. He resisted the forced labour demanded of him on the island of Pulau Damar, off the coast near Jakarta. And he completed two novels, *Perburuan* (The Fugitive) and *Keluarga Gerilja* (Guerrilla Family). He wrote in secret, sitting on a margarine tin by day and using his concrete bed as a desk or lying under the bed by night so that the light of his little oil lamp would not be visible from the corridor.[17]

The great novel in which Pramoedya brought his fellow prisoners' stories to life was published in 1951 under the title of *Mereka Jang Dilumpuhkan* (The Paralyzed), translated into Dutch as *In de fuik* (Caught in the Net). It includes magnificent words about the moment of his release: 'And ahead of us… ahead of us we saw only one thing: almighty freedom. An almighty freedom at an elusive place and time.'[18] Pramoedya wrote the foreword to the book in March 1950, just three months after his release. In it, he addresses the reader: 'I want to show you that the world is full of people, all sorts of people. I knew many of the people in this book personally: people caught in the net, people in prison.'[19]

Pramoedya's metaphor of the net applies equally well to NEFIS headquarters. The building in the heart of Jakarta's government district, near the palace of the Dutch governor-general, was the central location for shaking out the fine-meshed net of intelligence that had been cast over the archipelago by the Dutch. Thousands of documents had been caught in this net, stolen from people, citizens, Indonesian army units and Republican institutions that were under suspicion, or else found in the street and taken into custody. After the intelligence officers had studied them at their desks, the documents were stored away in files destined for the large, ever-growing archives, which must have taken up a considerable portion of the former NILLMIJ insurance office.

'AWAY WITH KOOLOONIES'

Another foray into the archives, in search of people caught in the net. 'NEFIS document no. 2257, Inventory of documents from BK (outpost) BANDOENG... seized on 3-8-'46' offers a compelling example.[20] It is the file on A. Emoeh, twenty-three years old and a sergeant major in the Tentara Republik Indonesia (TRI), the official army of the Republic of Indonesia. His personal details can be found on a military identity card seized by Dutch soldiers in early August 1946 along with a number of other documents. The identity card includes a passport photograph; we see a young man in civilian dress with his *peci* cocked on his head [13]. The archives are full of identity cards like this one, some with photographs and others without, from both the TRI and the independent *laskar* (militias). There is also an abundance of membership cards for political parties, ranging from Islamic to socialist groups: from the militant Islamist Hizbullah (army of Allah) and Sabillilah (path of Allah) organizations to the Islamic political party Masjoemi and the militarized political movement Pemuda Sosialis Indonesia (Pesindo, Socialist Youth of Indonesia). The full breadth of the Indonesian nationalist movement and revolution was caught in NEFIS's net. The collection of documents and of files and reports compiled by the intelligence service bears witness to the fragmentation of the Indonesian independence struggle into a multitude of political and religious parties, the activities of regional splinter movements, the operations of a wide variety of militias, and the emergence of a chaotic profusion of party acronyms in the Indonesian political domain. NEFIS targeted communism in particular, especially from 1948 onwards, when protecting the world from the communist menace was described in official correspondence as 'among NEFIS's most important tasks'.[21]

A photograph of the Security Museum in Surabaya taken in June 1947 by army photographer Hugo Wilmar shows that, in any case, the intelligence service of the Dutch Marine brigade (one of the other Dutch military intelligence services operating alongside NEFIS) took the task of opposing that threat very seriously from an early stage. In the museum's exhibition about the marines, assembled with thick adhesive tape, which includes a magnificent collection of Indonesian propaganda posters [15], one wall is devoted to Indonesian communism. Among the items on display is a wooden sign from the Surabaya division of the Laskar Merah (red militia). A star, hammer and sickle complete the communist picture. The message seems to be that this sign (propped up on a washbasin in a domestic setting) reveals the true nature of the Indonesian revolution. The portrait drawings of Lenin and Stalin give global communism a face [16]. This photograph also illustrates how seized materials were used in counter-propaganda. Back in the Netherlands, the weekly magazine *De Katholieke Illustratie* echoed this anti-Republican message in a photographic report, published on 14 August 1947, about Indonesia, where, according to the magazine, 'more than one hundred thousand Dutch "boys" are now exerting themselves to establish law and order and security.' On the back of the photograph of Lenin and Stalin on the washbasin, the editor on duty made an emphatic note: 'make sure these portraits are clearly visible.'

Document 2257, in which Sergeant Major Emoeh's identity card was hidden away, never had the dubious honour of being exhibited to the public like the posters in the marine brigade's peculiar Security Museum. Yet Emoeh's notebook, also included in this file, is certainly worth a look. The first thirty pages consist of schoolroom notes in Dutch from lectures about trade ('Chapter VI: The language of the Salesman'), but halfway through the notebook, Emoeh's Indonesian freedom struggle begins: in pencil, he wrote the word 'Merdeka!' as the salutation above a note to a friend. On the last page of the notebook Emoeh drew an arm clutching a *kris* (Javanese dagger) and accompanied it with anticolonial slogans: 'Away with kooloonies, down with imperialisme' [14].

In mid-1946, Emoeh's company waged a fierce battle in the area around Garut, east of the city of Bandung, with the recently arrived Dutch army, which was trying to occupy bridgeheads in West Java and repulse the Indonesian army. One thing we learn from the notebook is that Emoeh's unit had been infiltrated by counterspies. On 26 June 1946, four were arrested by Emoeh and his fellow fighters. A day later, the suspects were executed. In those same weeks, Emoeh's company sustained a number of fatalities, the notebook tells us. On 3 July, Emoeh's company was targeted by Dutch artillery fire for an hour. Emoeh described it as follows: 'Even though we were frightened, we stayed calm and quiet.'

The notebook also contained a typed pamphlet, which was translated into Dutch at NEFIS's headquarters: 'Mr Mook and Mr van der Plas', the pamphlet read, 'Hurry up and go back home, because Indonesia does not agree to your presence here.' But it did not limit itself to addressing Van Mook and Van der Plas, who were seen by the Indonesian freedom fighters as the personification of the Dutch attempt to bring Indonesia back under colonial authority. The former regent of Garut, Karta Legawa, who had remained loyal to the Dutch, was also a target of intimidation: 'Soon your head will be chopped off. You'd better leave for Europe fast.' For the time being, the fate of Sergeant Major Emoeh, after the seizure of the pamphlet, notebook and identity card on 3 August 1946, remains unknown.

In December 1949 the archives of the Dutch intelligence service, which had been renamed in September 1948 from NEFIS to the Central Military Intelligence Service (CMI), were packed up in great haste. It is said that 130 crates were needed for the archives, which by then totalled 300 metres of paper.[22] Considering the very sensitive nature of the materials, which included not only the seized documents but also all sorts of lists of names, files on individuals, reports on the reliability of Dutch subjects, documents on communist agitation and interrogation transcripts, the Dutch authorities were determined to remove the archive from Indonesia as swiftly as possible. After all, if the contents became public, they could seriously damage relations between the Netherlands and the Republic in the days leading up to the transfer of sovereignty on 27 December 1949. The politically volatile archives – a colonial Pandora's box – were hurriedly shipped to the Netherlands, where they went into storage at the ministry for union affairs and overseas territories in The Hague. The unpacking of the crates began promptly in January 1950.[23] Rosihan Anwar's photo album and Sergeant Major Emoeh's notebook

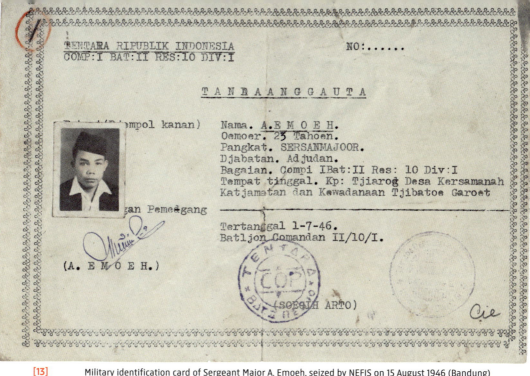

[13] Military identification card of Sergeant Major A. Emoeh, seized by NEFIS on 15 August 1946 (Bandung)

[14] Notebook of Sergeant Major Emoeh, seized by NEFIS on 15 August 1946 (Bandung)

[15] Exhibition of seized Indonesian propaganda posters at the Security Museum in Surabaya, photo by Hugo Wilmar, June 1947

[16] Portraits of Lenin and Stalin at an exhibition on Indonesian communism at the Security Museum in Surabaya, photo by Hugo Wilmar, June 1947

containing the heartfelt slogan 'Away with kooloonies' must have been handled then, along with all the other seized documents and items, which tell the big and little stories of the Indonesian Revolution. This evidence of the Indonesian struggle for independence and of the Dutch attempts to nip that struggle in the bud thus ended up, in January 1950, in the building on the Plein in The Hague known to Dutch officials in those days (and even now) as 'Colonies'.

DIPLOMASI AND AGRESI

THE UNCERTAIN PATH OF NEGOTIATION AND CONFLICT

MARION ANKER
ANNE-LOT HOEK
AMIR SIDHARTA
HARM STEVENS
BONNIE TRIYANA

REVOLUSI!

'Radio announcer', 'liaison officer', 'spy', 'collaborator', 'exotic figure', 'very well-travelled and fluent in various languages', and 'belonging to the category of dangerous women' – the Netherlands Forces Intelligence Service (NEFIS) did not seem to have enough words to describe all the faces of Tanja Dezentjé.[1] A NEFIS report from February 1946 characterized Dezentjé, its 'subject', in the typical condescending tone of the service's intelligence analysts: 'a pretty lady, very popular'.[2]

And in the ranks of the Republic of Indonesia, Dezentjé certainly was a 'very popular'. She was a member of the Komite Nasional Indonesia Pusat (KNIP, Central Indonesian National Committee), a major government advisory body, and she represented the young, independent nation in search of international recognition. In 1947, the painter Sudarso portrayed this young woman in the service of the Republic and the revolution. The latter was emphasized by her military garb [1]. This was not the first portrait of Dezentjé, as we can see from a photograph probably taken by the lawyer Piet Sanders, who headed the Dutch delegation in the negotiations [2]. Depictions such as these gradually turned her into an icon of female fighting power in revolutionary Indonesia.

A DISTINCTIVE FEMINIST VOICE

From the time of Sukarno's *Proklamasi* (independence proclamation), Tanja Dezentjé had devoted herself entirely to her country's independence struggle. In the early months of the revolution, she served that cause as a radio announcer in Yogyakarta, where according to tradition she disseminated pro-Republican messages in both Dutch and French. She also served that cause at the Republic's ministry of information, which was carefully tuned to the frequency of the international community from the very start. From 1947, she held positions at the foreign ministry and later at the Red Cross. In the struggle for Indonesian independence, Dezentjé became a distinctive feminist voice on the international stage.

She made an especially powerful case for her country's independence, which was heard far and wide: from India to Bangkok and from Singapore to Cairo. She was also the living proof that, in the conflict between the Republic and the Netherlands, individual positions were not always determined by the traditional dividing lines between ethnicities or other groups manufactured by the Dutch colonial regime. Dezentjé was born in The Hague, into a family of mixed Dutch and Indonesian descent, but returned to the Dutch East Indies before the war. When she was about twenty-eight years old, probably in 1946, she decided to adopt Indonesian citizenship (*warga-negara*).

Her good connections with the Republican political leaders opened the door to an international career in the service of the Republic. In March 1947, she was most likely part of the Indonesian delegation to the Asian Relations Conference in New Delhi, an initiative of the Indian prime minister Jawaharlal Nehru and the first conference of Asian countries that had thrown off the yoke of colonial

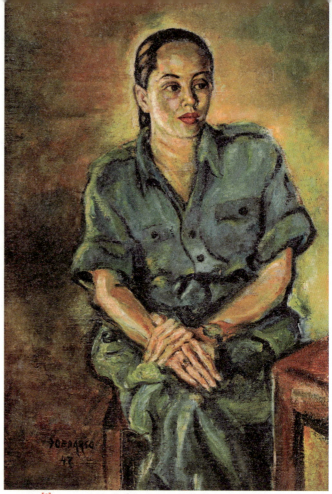

[1] Portrait of Tanja Dezentjé, by Sudarso, 1947

[2] Tanja Dezentjé with an earlier portrait of her, 1946

oppression (or were in the process of doing so). In June of that same year, she visited India again, this time as a member of the Indonesian trade commission, which managed to conclude a trade agreement between the two allied countries: Indonesia would supply India with rice in exchange for cotton. Historic photographs show the prominent place accorded to Dezentjé, dressed in a traditional Javanese batik sarong and *kebaya* (blouse), at a large prayer meeting led by Mahatma Gandhi at the Bhangi Colony in Delhi on 10 July 1947. She was seated behind Gandhi, the spiritual leader of India, and Lady Pamela Mountbatten, the daughter of the British viceroy of India, which was on the verge of independence.[3] As a member of Indonesia's diplomatic jet set, she also visited Bangkok and Singapore, where she worked in the office of the Indonesian diplomatic representative.

Her farthest journey for the Republic took her to Cairo in early 1948. As a representative of the Indonesian Red Cross, Dezentjé made a plea in Egypt for support for her country's Republican fighters. She gave talks and interviews there and published articles, informing the Egyptian public that women were serving in the provisional Indonesian parliament, in the diplomatic corps and as government ministers. It was true that women were relatively well represented in the service of the Republic: in the second Sjahrir government, installed in March 1946, Maria Ullfah, the first Indonesian woman to earn a master of laws degree (in 1933 in Leiden), was appointed as the minister for social affairs. S.K. Trimurti, who had an impressive pre-war record as an activist journalist, held the position of labour minister in the Sjarifuddin government from June 1947 onwards.

The NEFIS report quoted a somewhat shady written Egyptian source claiming that Dezentjé had said she knew 'many young women who have killed Dutch people with their bare hands'. This quotation, presented with obvious glee, fits neatly into NEFIS's attempt to portray her as a 'dangerous fanatic': '*Pemudi* [young woman] in men's clothes ... wears revolver ... behaves like a wild man.' The report paints her as a militant activist, fighting for Indonesian independence at home and abroad. A letter of 14 July 1947 from Tanja Dezentjé to her mother, intercepted by the intelligence service, reveals some of the inner struggle and self-doubt that inevitably accompanied a life dedicated to the revolution, a string of failed marriages, and single motherhood with three children. She wrote,

> I am here in India now, in a foreign country among foreign people. What tomorrow may bring, I do not know. I do not know anything. I sometimes ask myself whether I'm truly living or merely vegetating. Everything seems so devoid of value and significance. The people you like and admire leave or die, and you remain behind with an empty place in your heart in surroundings that are just as empty. Then, once more, you wonder, What am I really living for?[4]

She had made a precise calculation: when she wrote her mother in July 1947 she had had 'no time for the past 1¾ years to give any thought to my own problems, which of course was a good thing.' The revolution made you forget everything else. But now it was time for her to take on those problems, she told herself and her mother. She was especially concerned about her children's education and remarked that her teenage son, who was fighting in the Javanese interior as a *pemuda* (young freedom fighter), had become a complete stranger to her. 'The national struggle of the Indonesians, in which I felt compelled by destiny to participate, has helped me through the worst', she wrote to her mother.

We do not know what had made Dezentjé feel compelled to take part in the revolution. The sense of 'destiny' she mentioned may have stemmed from her wartime activities and the accusations (true or false) that she had collaborated with the Japanese. Yet she went on supporting the Indonesian independence struggle even after the moment of doubt that she expressed in the letter to her mother. In 1948 Dezentjé got married to an Indian diplomat. When her husband was posted to Berlin in 1949, she accompanied him and attempted to travel from the German city to the Netherlands to attend the Dutch-Indonesian Round Table Conference held in The Hague, where she hoped to find her friend Mohammad Hatta and his wife. We do not know whether she managed to make it to the Netherlands on that occasion.

IMAGES OF DIPLOMACY

The painter Henk Ngantung had made a carefully considered choice, before the war, to join the struggle for a free Indonesia. Ngantung was born in the Javanese city of Bogor (then Buitenzorg) in 1921. He spent his childhood in Tomohon, North Sulawesi, in a region with a largely Christian population. There he attended a local Dutch-language school, where his exceptional talent for drawing attracted attention. In 1937, Ngantung went to Bandung to study with the Austrian painter Rudolf Wenghart; in that modern city in West Java, he also met Indonesian artists, such as the young painter Affandi, who had gathered together a group of Indonesian painters in 1935 under the name of Kelompok Lima Bandung (the Bandung Five). This group also included Sudarso, who would paint Tanja Dezentjé's portrait in 1947.

A solo exhibition in 1939, in the famous Hotel Savoy Homann in Bandung, led to a breakthrough in Ngantung's career. From that moment on, despite his young age, Ngantung regarded himself as a fully-fledged artist. He also realized that he could use his art for social and political purposes. In that same year, he moved to Jakarta, where he met the artists of Persatuan Ahli-Ahli Gambar Indonesia (Persagi, Union of Indonesian Painters), the first Indonesian artists' association, which strove for both political and artistic independence. Like his friends in Persagi, Ngantung was able to take advantage of the opportunities for exhibiting artistic work created by the Japanese occupying regime. This brought him into contact with the nationalist leader

Sukarno, who bought Ngantung's painting *Memanah* (Archery) at an exhibition in Jakarta. The picture was displayed on the veranda of Sukarno's house, where the *Proklamasi* would be delivered on 7 August 1945.

After the proclamation of independence, Ngantung took part in an exhibition of Indonesian art at the Medische Hogeschool (medical college) in Jakarta. Even after January 1946, when the Republic's seat of government was hurriedly moved to Yogyakarta because of growing friction with the Netherlands Indies Civil Administration (NICA), Ngantung remained in Jakarta. But he did travel from Jakarta to Yogyakarta fairly regularly as a temporary member of Kebaktian Rakjat Indonesia Sulawesi (KRIS, Service of Indonesian People from Sulawesi), a militia composed largely of fighters who, like Ngantung, originally came from Sulawesi. In a photograph from 1946 or 1947, Ngantung has taken his place among a group of men and, primarily, women in military dress, members of KRIS [3].[5]

But while Ngantung was rubbing shoulders with these working-class fighters in Yogyakarta at regular intervals, he was also moving in Jakarta's artistic and intellectual circles. He became a member of the artists' collective Gelanggang Seniman Merdeka (Arena of Independent Artists) and befriended the journalist and freedom fighter Gadis Rasjid, who encouraged Ngantung to come with her to Linggajati, a mountain village in West Java, to the south of the port city of Cirebon. From 11 to 13 November 1946, it was to be the site of negotiations between representatives of the Republic and the Netherlands.

The difficult route to a peaceful resolution of the conflict had begun with the ceasefire signed by the Republic and the Netherlands on 14 October 1946. The talks that had followed this cessation of hostilities were still proceeding with great difficulty but began to make swifter progress when former Dutch prime minister Willem Schermerhorn proposed a special meeting with President Sukarno. This was a remarkable move; never before had there been an official meeting, approved by the Dutch authorities, with the man persistently rejected as unfit by the Netherlands because of his collaboration with the Japanese.

In the negotiations, Sukarno seized the initiative within the Republican delegation on the eve of Tuesday 12 November – not far from Linggajati, in the residence of the *controleur* (deputy Dutch administrator) in Kuningan, where he was staying – by giving his approval to the draft agreement negotiated by the two delegations as soon as the Dutch representatives proposed replacing the word 'free' in article 2 with 'sovereign'. This led to the following wording in the agreement: 'The Netherlands Government and the Government of the Republic shall co-operate in the rapid formation of a sovereign democratic State on a federal basis to be called the United States of Indonesia.'[6]

The key articles now stipulated Dutch recognition of the Republic's sovereignty over Java (including the island of Madura) and Sumatra, and the Republic's consent to the formation of a federation with Negara Indonesia Timur (NIT, State of East Indonesia)

[3] Henk Ngantung (third from the right) with KRIS fighters, 1946/1947

[4] Sukarno (front left), Schermerhorn and Lord Killearn seated at a table for lunch during the negotiations in Linggajati, by Henk Ngantung, 1946

all islands east of Java on the Indonesian archipelago and Kalimantan (Borneo). These territories were to be part of a union with the Netherlands headed by the Dutch monarch. On 15 November 1946, the Indonesian prime minister Sutan Sjahrir and Willem Schermerhorn, the highest-ranking representative of the Dutch government in his role as the chairman of the Commission-General, initialled the 'Draft Linggajati Agreement'. This seemed to clear the path to peaceful resolution of the conflict between the Republic and the Netherlands.

Henk Ngantung had made a visual record in pen and ink of this high-level diplomatic gathering, perhaps at Sukarno's behest. The artist's quick sketches may appear trivial, but the series is laden with political significance. The agreement between the Republic and the Netherlands had immense symbolic value for the Republic of Indonesia. Talks at the highest level between Dutch negotiators and representatives of the Republican government had taken place on Republican territory. 'Obviously, a slight shock rippled through the Dutch delegation at that moment, because we had received the fiat of the highest authority', Schermerhorn wrote in his diary once Sukarno had approved the draft.[7]

Henk Ngantung was not a witness to that moment – at the meeting in Kuningan, there were no spectators – but he had attended the buffet lunch that preceded it at the home of the Chinese Kwee family, where Sjahrir was staying. There he made a sketch of Sukarno and Schermerhorn sitting together, quite informally, at the corner of a table. Next to Schermerhorn is Lord Killearn, a British diplomat who was acting as a mediator. On the table in front of them are plates, dishes and a bunch of *pisangs* (bananas). As informal as this lunch was, it was a meaningful moment: the president of the Republic of Indonesia, which was about to be recognized by the Netherlands, and the supreme representative of the Netherlands, Schermerhorn, in conversation [4].

Ngantung's sketches captured not only the dynamics of the informal discussions and receptions but also the activities of the reporters and the Republican soldiers of the Tentara Nasional Indonesia (TNI, Indonesian National Armed Forces) who were standing guard. The series also includes portraits of the leading negotiators. A few of them signed their likenesses at the artist's request and perhaps to show their approval. The result was a modest portrait gallery of the Indonesian and Dutch politicians involved in this turning point in the history of the young Republic of Indonesia [5-9].

Although there was also opposition to the draft Linggajati agreement within the Republic, especially in the military, the political Republican elite in the government, who were still dominant in 1946 and 1947, saw the agreement as a triumph of diplomacy, an alternative to military confrontation and conflict, which the more moderate wing viewed as an unbalanced route to disaster. Prime Minister Sjahrir's Partai Sosialis Indonesia (PRI, Socialist Party of Indonesia) joined other governing socialist parties in endorsing the agreement, which was viewed as a step towards complete independence. In the short term, the agreement brought an important objective within reach:

[6] Portrait of Willem Schermerhorn, by Henk Ngantung, 1946

[5] Portrait of Sjahrir, by Henk Ngantung, 1946

[7] Portrait of Johannes Leimena, by Henk Ngantung, 1946

[8] Portrait of Hadji Agus Salim, by Henk Ngantung, 1946

[9] Portrait of Mohammad Roem, by Henk Ngantung, 1946

[10] Tjokorda Rai Pudak, 1927

[11] Tjokorda Rai Pudak's shredded army shirt

international recognition.[8] On 31 March 1947, Great Britain formally recognized the Republic, and on 17 April, the United States followed suit, as did Australia, China and India. Egypt, Syria and Iran did likewise.[9]

At the ceremonial signing of the agreement on 25 March 1947, more than four months after it had been initialled, Prime Minister Sjahrir addressed the group in attendance in the throne room of Rijswijk Palace (the predecessor of Merdeka Palace) in Jakarta, saying, 'In Indonesia we are lighting a small flame, a flame of humanity, a flame of common sense … Let us now care for this flame so it will continue to burn, and burn even brighter.'[10] Among the guests at the palace was Henk Ngantung, who made sketches at the ceremony as a way of completing his visual record.

FIGHTING LION IN BALI

Ngantung's subtle sketches form a contemporary visual testimony to an important part of the Indonesian Revolution: the way of diplomacy. A very different kind of testimony is provided by a khaki shirt worn by a prominent Indonesian freedom fighter from Bali [10].

Tjokorda Rai Pudak was forty-two years old when, on 9 October 1946, he was shot dead near the Balinese town of Ubud. His shredded army shirt makes it clear that the volley of bullets hit him at chest level [11]. The previous day, Pudak had been arrested by a local Balinese militia led by Ide Anak Agung Gde Agung, the raja of Gianyar, who saw Pudak's revolutionary struggle as a threat to his authority and to the power of his realm. The arrest took place in cooperation with a Dutch patrol. A few days later, Pudak's comrade-in-arms Tjokorda Gede Rai was also killed: 'shot dead while attempting to flee', according to the NEFIS report.[11] Today the scene of the crime, a bare roadside field, is marked with a memorial stone commemorating the two men who were executed, one soon after the other. There is also a street in Gianyar named after them.[12]

Pudak and some other members of his family had founded the pro-Republican underground resistance organization Angkatan Moeda Sosialis Fighting Lion (AMSFL, Fighting Lion Socialist Youth Organization). His son, Tjokorde Gede Dalem Pudak (who treasures his father's tattered shirt to this day), also enthusiastically joined the revolution – in 1945, at the age of thirteen. He and his classmates shouted slogans about freedom in the streets and pasted red-and-white handbills on the houses of the Japanese people still resident in Bali. Their revolutionary acts were inspired by the radio speeches of the nationalist agitator Bung Tomo.

Bali was referred to by the colonial administration as 'the last paradise'. The emphasis on the island's cultural traditions and peace-loving nature was an attempt to make its people conform to that image, a way of keeping them in line. Feudal leaders had obtained a great deal of power during the Dutch colonial occupation, while ordinary people barely had access to education. Imagine how surprised the Dutch were in 1945 when the desire for freedom proved to be alive and well even in Bali. Revolution spread from Java to Bali like wildfire.

It was the twenty-eight-year-old I Gusti Ngurah Rai, who took the lead in the struggle against the return of the colonial power to Bali from 1945 onwards. Ngurah Rai had been instructed by no one less than Sukarno to safeguard the independence of the Lesser Sunda Islands, which include Bali. Before the war, he had received thorough military officer training and gone on to serve as an officer in the local Prayoda Corps, which was an auxiliary corps of the Koninklijk Nederlandsch-Indisch Leger (KNIL, Royal Netherlands East Indies Army). In 1945, Ngurah Rai secured support and recognition for the Balinese resistance in Java from the Republic's military and political leaders, and on 4 April 1946, more than four weeks after Dutch forces landed on Bali, he returned to the island of his birth with the rank of lieutenant colonel in the Republican Tentara Keamanan Rakjat (TKR, People's Security Army). His opponents were 2,000 well-trained, armed KNIL soldiers.

The AMSFL joined the campaign for independence and coordinated the struggle in the regency of Gianyar. In that regency, the revolution was mainly being led by noble houses that had a long history of rivalry with the raja of Gianyar.[13] Tjokorda Rai Pudak and Tjokorda Gede Rai, the leaders of the AMSFL, were shot and killed about a month before the draft Linggajati agreement was initialled in Jakarta. This made it clear that the conflict for control of Indonesia was progressing along different tracks simultaneously; the encouraging, cautiously positive mood at the negotiating table stood in stark contrast to the grim warfare taking place at the same time in other parts of Indonesia.[14]

THE THUNDERBOLT REGIMENT

East Sumatra, the location of the major city of Medan, was the scene of radical social revolution, a struggle unfolded within the larger context of the Indonesian independence struggle. Socioeconomic conditions in East Sumatra were strongly influenced by the plantation economy, which had been imposed from outside by Western companies. This course of development had led to a society marked by extreme socioeconomic dichotomies. The local sultans in East Sumatra, who had settled in the coastal region long before but were of Malaysian ancestry, worked with the Dutch in the economic and political fields. There was a small European upper class and a large mass of indentured labourers from places outside the region: China, India and Java. The highlands of the interior were inhabited by Karo-Batak people.

In East Sumatra, the proclamation of independence had been supported from the very start, and on 3 March 1946, a social revolution erupted there. An assortment of local militias assailed the local sultans and their court with devastating force. They saw their foes as collaborators, colluding with the former colonial power as it plotted its return. These social tensions originated in pre-war developments such as the rise of organized modern nationalist movements in the urban area of East Sumatra and the global economic depression of the 1930s, which had hit the Karo-Batak people especially hard.[15]

In early 1946, there were confrontations between nationalist militias and the Allied occupying forces. From that time on, the Karo villages in the highlands were on the front line of the conflict. Among the Karo-Batak people, there was widespread support for the revolution. In 1947 and from late 1948 onwards, Tanah Karo, the domain of the Karo, was the target of a series of Dutch offensives, with aircraft bombing and firing on the area. Many farming families and other civilians from the area fled their homes. This was partly because of the scorched-earth tactics called for by the central Republican leadership; to prevent villages from falling into the hands of the Dutch enemy, local militias put the population under pressure to burn them down. Crops, too, were destroyed. Thousands of people became displaced, fleeing to the ever-shrinking Republican territory in the highlands of East Sumatra.[16]

Tanah Karo, far from the Javanese cities often seen as the birthplaces of the independence struggle, had its own Angkatan 45 (Generation of 1945), a group of men and women, mostly young, who dedicated themselves passionately to the defence of Indonesia's freedom. One of them was Eben Hezer Sinuraya, a Karo-Batak from the southern slope of Mount Sinabung, not very far from Berastagi, a popular destination for European holidaymakers. His father, an itinerant catechist and evangelist, had been among the earliest converts of Protestant missionaries and had given his son the biblical name of Eben Hezer.

The area around Mount Sinabung had been a rich source of recruits for the independence struggle for the first few months after the proclamation of independence, when the Indonesian nationalists were in a rush to mobilize the nation.[17] Eben Hezer, who had been teaching at a Christian school in the town of Kabanjahe, was among the enthusiastic volunteers and was soon promoted, becoming an officer in a hastily improvised militia, probably because he had been a teacher and was assumed to have served in Burma (now Myanmar) during the Japanese regime as a *heiho* soldier, an Indonesian auxiliary soldier in the Japanese force. The truth was, however, that he had evaded both service in the Japanese military and forced labour. Eben Hezer had worked in the civilian air-raid defence service, but that was as close as he came to having military experience. In May 1946, he left the Karo highlands for Medan. At that stage, he was still part of the first wave of volunteers from the Pemuda Sosialis Indonesia (Pesindo, Socialist Youth of Indonesia).[18]

For the next few years of the independence struggle, Eben Hezer was the commander of a company in the Halilintar (Thunderbolt) regiment affiliated with Nasional Pelopor Indonesia (Napindo, the National Vanguard of Indonesia), a political organization in East Sumatra linked to Sukarno's Partai Nasional Indonesia (PNI, Indonesian National Party).[19] This Halilintar regiment became part of the TNI in 1947/1948 under the name of Sektor III.[20]

[12] Eben Hezer Sinuraya (second from the right) with his fellow fighters, 1949 or later

Since late 1945, the Medan area had been a patchwork of territories defended by fairly autonomous militias against not only the common enemy but also each other. The Republican government had made several attempts, starting before the integration of the Halilintar regiment into the TNI, to place these militias under central military command, but this proved next to impossible in practice. In many areas, the militias were more dominant and influential than the civilian administration and the official Republican army.[21]

The militias fought relentlessly against the Dutch, even after the announcement in August 1947 of an official ceasefire, the result of international pressure, which was intended to put an end to the Dutch military action against the Republic. Even during negotiated ceasefires, there were ongoing confrontations between Republican and Dutch troops on the capricious front lines in the interior of Java and Sumatra.

On 7 May 1949, the very day that the Republican negotiator Mohammad Roem and his Dutch counterpart Jan Herman van Roijen hammered out an agreement to cease hostilities in the Hotel des Indes in Jakarta, Lieutenant Eben Hezer took part in a guerrilla action near Bukit Bertah. The Halilintar regiment laid an ambush, firing on a Dutch troop transport from Kabanjahe to Tiga Binanga. Information about this secret military transport had been leaked to the Indonesian guerrillas in advance by an Indonesian who worked for the Dutch as a police officer. At quarter to six that misty morning, hostilities broke out. From their hiding places on the hillsides, Eben Hezer and his men opened fire on the five-truck convoy. The hail of bullets forced the convoy to stop and turn back. In the ensuing firefight, one Indonesian commander was killed by a shot to the head. Two of his men also died in the fight. Afterwards they took stock: three Dutch trucks had been put out of commission, and the guerrilla fighters had seized a few machine guns.[22]

After the fight, Eben Hezer found a small rectangular brown leather bag on the person of a Dutch soldier who had died in combat. We know nothing about this man's identity, just as we often know little or nothing about the people whose possessions were snatched by Dutch soldiers. In the bag was a Goldy handheld box camera, 'made in France'. Eben Hezer claimed the bag and the camera as spoils of war and, in the years that followed, took many snapshots of his friends, family and comrades in arms.[23] This is how Eben Hezer and his comrades from the Karo district, striking a pose for their group portrait, ended up neatly pasted into a photo album [12]. This album was an important reminder of the time of the conflict that had caused great societal upheaval in East Sumatra, but which had also brought the Christian guerrilla commander Eben Hezer Sinuraya the prize he sought: a free Indonesia.

[13] Hans van Santen, 1945

[14] Hans van Santen, near Surabaya, 1946

[15] Funeral of Private Reint Wolf in Medan, 2 December 1946

VOLUNTARY SOLDIER

'On the battlefield', wrote the nineteen-year-old Dutch soldier Hans van Santen, in lieu of an address, in the upper left corner of a letter to his parents in The Hague [13]. The battlefield must have been in the rubber plantation area of Langkat, to the north of the city of Medan in East Sumatra, not far from the area where Eben Hezer Sinuraya and his company were presumably active at that time. Van Santen used a typewriter he had seized as spoils. In the upper right was 'The Langkat Rubber Co. Ltd.', the name of an international rubber company. Maybe the typewriter, like the letterhead, had belonged to that company. 'Today', Private Van Santen wrote to his parents, 'we entered a large rubber plantation. The first plantation to have fallen into our hands undamaged.'[24] It was the seventh day of the first major Dutch offensive, which had been launched on 21 July 1946. The Netherlands referred to this offensive as a 'police action', codenamed 'Operatie Product' (Operation Product). This name alluded to the operation's chief purpose: the conquest of economically significant areas of Java and Sumatra. The Medan area, rich in palmoil and rubber plantations, was a perfect target for the Dutch military. The efficient, business-like sound of the code name, invented in the offices of military and political leaders in The Hague and Jakarta, belied the young Hans van Santen's chaotic, disjointed, disorienting experience on the battlefield.

Van Santen, born into a family in The Hague with its roots in the Dutch East Indies, had volunteered for military service at the age of seventeen, in May 1945. His Dutch 'Generation of 1945 had several things in common with their Indonesian counterparts: youthfulness, a sense of adventure, and the heavy burden of the Second World War. When signing up for military duty, Van Santen disguised the fact that he was a minor, adding a year to his age on the form. He was assigned to the first regiment of volunteer soldiers, OVW battalion 1-1-RI. In January 1946 he boarded the ship that would take him to Indonesia. At that stage, the Allied command still did not allow the Dutch to land troops, so their only option was to dock in the British protectorate of Malacca (Melaka). When the prohibition was lifted in March 1946, Van Santen and his battalion were sent to Surabaya. In that major Javanese port, which only four months earlier had witnessed a devastating military confrontation between Indonesian fighters and British troops, Van Santen was placed on guard duty for the city and the coast. For a little while longer, the war kept its distance from that urban enclave. On 23 April 1946, he wrote to his parents that it was 'incredibly silent' at their posts near Surabaya. 'You can't even tell there's a war going on.'[25] Over the next few months – some of which he spent in hospital with malaria – that must have changed fast. In a posed photograph, Private Van Santen, with his heavy Brengun at the ready, is standing at the entrance to a small, fragile-looking village hut, probably somewhere near Surabaya [14].

In November 1946, his regiment was transferred to Medan. 'Personally, I don't mind being transferred', Van Santen informed his family in The Hague. 'At least that way you can see the world a little.'²⁶ In and around Medan, Van Santen was knee-deep in the colonial war; he and his battalion participated in combat with the TNI and local militias on various occasions; Dutch military jargon referred to these as *zuiveringsacties* (cleansing actions). They went on patrol, during which they came under fire from Indonesian troops. And they saw fellow soldiers die on the field. On 2 December 1946, Private Reint Wolf was buried in Medan. Wolf was only twenty years old when he was killed during an action in the interior. In a photograph, the 'boys' in Van Santen's battalion are standing around the grave with bowed heads and folded hands, praying for 'our friend Reint Wolf', according to the writing on the back [15]. To keep fear and danger at bay, Van Santen used the typical jargon of the Dutch troops, calling their enemies '*merdeka* rascals' and 'little extremists'. His use of diminutive forms probably served in part to reassure his family in the Netherlands.²⁷

When Operation Product began, Van Santen and his battalion entered the Medan interior, which – as his letters make clear – had fallen prey to the scorched-earth tactics of the Indonesian troops. 'Most of the *kampong*s (residential compounds) that we passed had been burned down or destroyed completely by the Red-and-Whites', Van Santen wrote.

> A few days ago we passed a Chinese *kampong* where the villains had sliced open six women's bellies and inflicted cruel injuries on many others. Yes, if that is the *merdeka* in which those gentlemen take such pride, then I pity them deeply. Such people, with such ideas and manners, now want to run a country independently. No, it is intolerable, and we must put a stop to it, for the sake of all the people who pay the price.²⁸

The enemy was invisible and the locals had fled, Van Santen wrote; some were 'working the land again, like complete innocents, and crying out "Long live the Dutch!" again. What a country this is, let me tell you. I no longer understand the first thing about it.'²⁹

The Linggajati Agreement was a dead letter. That became clear as soon as the Dutch began their offensive in Java and Sumatra on 21 July 1947. The spirit of diplomacy that had been roused at the negotiating tables had gradually been smothered by irreconcilable differences in the interpretation of the agreement's vague wording by the Republic and the Netherlands, by die-hard groups in the Republic (radical left-wing parties and the army) and in the Netherlands (right-wing parties and military leaders), and by persistent violations of its terms. The two countries' distrust of each other's underlying intentions grew ever deeper. The federal solution advocated by the Dutch was seen by Republican political leaders as a divide-and-conquer strategy. Meanwhile, the Dutch did not believe the Republic was capable of enforcing law and order and creating a suitable climate for international business.

Ironically, it was the Dutch military action that eventually sent the two parties back to the negotiating table. The Netherlands received a stern reprimand from the United Nations. Its colonial war, which it had thought it could wage freely, was roundly condemned by the rest of the world. Quite quickly, by 4 August, the Netherlands and the Republic were put under enormous pressure to negotiate an armistice. The United Nations sent a Good Offices Committee (UNGOC) to Indonesia, with members from the United States, Australia and Belgium, to help the parties to the conflict resolve it peacefully. It became clear that thanks to its special emissary Sjahrir, who had delivered an impressive speech at the meeting of the UN Security Council in New York on 14 August 1947, the Republic had been stunningly successful at persuading the international community to recognize and respect it as a peer. The Netherlands was confronted with the hard facts: the 'Indonesian issue', as the Dutch liked to call the decolonization of Indonesia, was no longer a purely domestic affair but would from then on take place on the international stage.

The conflict's international dimension is illustrated by the fact that the next agreement between the Republic and the Netherlands, in January 1948, was negotiated and signed on board the United States attack transport ship USS *Renville*. This signalled the growing influence of the United States over the process of decolonization in Indonesia. The USS *Renville* was anchored in the stifling heat of Tanjung Priok, the harbour near Jakarta. But even this Renville Agreement, which essentially returned to some of the central provisions of the Linggajati Agreement, was unsuccessful. When the negotiations foundered, despite the UNGOC's help, on the political disagreements between the two countries, the stubborn Dutch government, swimming against the current of international opinion, once again sought a military solution.

This second large-scale military offensive also led to a furious international response. It began on 19 December 1948 with a great show of force and was once again referred to by Dutch military and political leaders as a 'police action', this time codenamed 'Operatie Kraai' (Operation Crow) in Java and 'Operatie Ekster' (Operation Magpie) in Sumatra. The UN Security Council was convened for an emergency session and, at the initiative of the United States, issued Resolution 63, which called upon the Netherlands 'to cease hostilities forthwith'. The Dutch had no choice but to comply, and the 'police action' ended on 31 December 1948. But in the weeks that followed, they launched a number of devastating attacks, supported by Dutch warplanes. On 5 January 1949, some 180 paratroopers from the Korps Speciale Troepen (Special Troops Corps) in Rengat massacred the local population, murdering an estimated 400 to 1,000 civilians.[30]

Against a backdrop of international disapproval, this second offensive had calamitous international political consequences for the Netherlands. But in military terms, it seemed at first to be a spectacular success, capturing the major cities in Republican-held territory at a furious pace. The Republican capital of Yogyakarta fell into Dutch hands just a few hours after an airborne landing by 350 parachutists. The objective of completely crushing the Republic seemed within arm's reach. The Republic's leaders were taken into custody and sent into exile. Sukarno and Sjahrir were imprisoned in Sumatra; Mohammad Hatta and Mohammad Roem, a diplomat, negotiator and prominent member of the Indonesian Muslim party Masyumi, were banished to the island of Bangka. But although the Republic's political leaders fell into the clutches of the Netherlands, the Republican military forces beat a rapid retreat to their hideouts in the interior. From there, they unleashed a fierce guerrilla war against the Dutch troops, which were unaccustomed to the mountains, and against everyone else who stood in the way of their ideal of a free Indonesia.

CHILD REPORTER

But what did the Dutch attack on Yogyakarta, which descended from the skies with sudden menace in the small hours of 19 December, signify to Mohammad Toha, an eleven-year-old boy who lived with his family in the proud Republican capital [16]? His inner feelings and those of all the city's people – their anger, perhaps, their worries about the future and their likely hatred of the Dutch soldiers – remain shrouded in uncertainty. But Mohammad Toha must have been an eyewitness to the attack on his city and the following months of military occupation. We know that thanks to the dozens of small watercolour paintings the talented Toha made during the occupation in 1949.

In late 1947, the famous socially engaged realist painter Dullah had taken the initiative to train five young pupils. Alongside Mohammad Toha, the other four were Muhammad Affandi (12 years old), Sardjito (14), Sri Suwarno (14) and F.X. Supono Siswosuharto (15). He taught them to make quick watercolour sketches. Dullah's plan was for the teenagers, who also sold cigarettes in the streets, to use their paintings to document the situation in the city. He hoped there would not be an attack and occupation by Dutch troops, but he had decided to prepare for the possibility. When the time came and Dullah was among the many who fled, the work of documenting life in the occupied city turned out to be extremely risky for the child reporters. They operated in secret, but two of them met with great misfortune. Sardjito was arrested by Dutch soldiers in 1949 and sent to a children's prison in Tangerang, where he died. And Sri Suwarno painted events closely following the Dutch attack, but afterwards he vanished, never to return.

How much risk Mohammad Toha was running by making miniature watercolours is unclear. Maybe he was painting from life, out in the streets, disguised as a cigarette vendor, his box of paints concealed beneath his wares, as he later claimed. But it is also possible that he made some paintings a little later or that he first made quick sketches outdoors and then produced the finished works in a safer setting. In any event, the images of the attack and occupation created by this very young painter of the *revolusi* appear true to life. The details are accurate: the uniforms, the insignia on cars, the weapons and the Dutch aircraft in the tropical sky [17, 18, 20]. Mohammad Toha was a keen observer.

[16]   Mohammad Toha and his mother, date unknown

[17] A squadron of Dutch bombers over Yogyakarta at sunrise, by Mohammad Toha, 1948
[18] Dutch soldiers forcing Indonesian civilians together, by Mohammad Toha, 1948–1949

[19] Dutch soldiers searching Mohammad Toha's home, by Mohammad Toha, 1949
[20] Dutch troops surrounding the city forcing the Indonesians to hand over their weapons, by Mohammad Toha, 1948–1949

[21] Republican troops returning to Yogyakarta, by Mohammad Toha, June 1949

He depicted his own father being taken prisoner in Lempuyangan Market and his family home being searched by Dutch soldiers who hoped to find Mohammad's brother, a suspected guerrilla fighter [19]. Mohammad was ordered to sit quietly in a corner, but as soon as the soldiers left, he documented the intimidating event in a small painting. He also depicted the celebration of the victory of the Indonesian forces, which very briefly recaptured Yogyakarta from the Dutch on 1 March 1949 [21].

According to Dutch statistics, the second *agresi* (the Indonesian term for the second Dutch military offensive) resulted in the deaths of more than 4,300 Republican TNI soldiers. In the following eight months of continuous guerrilla war, there were more than 46,000 fatalities in the Indonesian military.[31] By comparison, the Netherlands Institute for Military History has calculated that the number of Dutch soldiers who died in combat or in accidents from August 1945 to December 1949 was 5,281.[32] The total number of Indonesian fatalities over the entire 1945–1949 period was recently determined to be 97,421. As the researchers note, it is unclear how many of these were civilian deaths and how many were combatants.[33]

MURDER IN KALIURANG

One civilian victim was Masdoelhak Nasoetion [22], a senior Republican official and a good friend of Vice President Hatta's; a few days after the start of the attack on Yogyakarta, he was brutally assassinated by Dutch soldiers. Nasoetion belonged to the Republic's intellectual, Western-oriented elite, who inclined towards the diplomatic route to resolving the conflict with the Netherlands. He was a legal adviser and secretary to the Republican delegation, which before the Dutch attack was in diplomatic negotiation with the Netherlands and the UNGOC. One venue for these talks was Kaliurang, a mountain village about twenty-five kilometres from Yogyakarta, which had become a hub of international diplomacy in 1948. High-level Republican government officials were staying there, along with the members and staff of the UNGOC. Nasoetion's path to this mountain village, where he was dedicated to finding a diplomatic way out of the conflict between his country and the former colonial power, had been a long and international one.

Masdoelhak Nasoetion had been born into an aristocratic family in Sumatra in 1909. In 1930 he went to the Netherlands to study. There he met Adriana van der Have, and after a stay in Paris to study journalism, he married her in 1938. The couple lived in Amsterdam for a short while and later moved to Utrecht, where Nasoetion was working towards a doctoral degree, a continuation of his studies of Dutch East Indies law in Leiden. In 1943 he successfully defended a doctoral thesis in Utrecht about the role of women in Batak society. After the proclamation of Indonesian independence, Nasoetion returned to his country of birth. There he found employment as Hatta's secretary and as a judge in the military tribunal in Bukittinggi, Sumatra, where he received the titular rank of colonel in the TNI. He and his wife and three sons stayed with relatives, first in Jakarta and later in Lawang and Malang, East Java, until they found a home of their own in Kaliurang, named Air Langga (Clear Water).

On 18 December 1948, a day before the start of the second Dutch military offensive, Adriana Nasoetion-van der Have gave birth to her fourth son, Anwar, in the hospital *Onder de Bogen* in Yogyakarta. Masdoelhak just had time to visit his wife and child, before he returned from Jakarta to his other children, who had stayed behind in Kaliurang. When the Dutch air raid erupted over the city, the mother took cover from the bombing under the hospital bed with her newborn child.[34] Around the same time, Dutch soldiers were making a lightning advance on Kaliurang, which was seen as a key military target because of the many leading representatives of the Republic then present there. The Dutch troops occupied Kaliurang and proceeded, in the words of the military report, to 'cleanse' it. The UNGOC was placed under house arrest, as were the members of the Republican delegation.[35]

On 20 December 1948, the second day of the second major offensive, Nasoetion was in the back garden of his house, Air Langga, burning government documents on the instructions of Vice President Hatta so that they would not fall into Dutch hands. In the late afternoon, soldiers from the Special Troops Corps stormed the house. Nasoetion was taken to the nearby Hotel Kaliurang, where other prominent Indonesian prisoners were also brought together. His three sons were left behind in the care of his domestic staff. The next day, 21 December 1948, Nasoetion was taken to the edge of a ravine a few kilometres outside Kaliurang, where the Dutch sergeant major instructor Marinus Geelhoed shot him in the head with a jungle carbine. After this cold-blooded murder, two other Indonesian captives who had been brought to the ravine were also shot dead by Dutch soldiers.

When Adriana Nasoetion-van der Have returned to Kaliurang on 29 December, eight days after her husband's assassination, she found that her sons had been threatened and beaten by Dutch soldiers. The house had been ransacked. 'Everything gone and doors broken. No more food, no money, and all the jewellery gone up in smoke', she later wrote to Tono Maas, her former neighbour in Utrecht.[36] The Dutch soldiers ordered her to remain silent about it, so that the assassination of the high-ranking Republican Nasoetion would not become world news.[37] But Adriana refused to comply, telling the world about the murder and about the injustice suffered by the family afterwards. She first did so in her letters to Maas, whom she informed on 23 January 1949 of the horrifying events in Kaliurang:

> All the time, no matter what I am doing, I see Masdoel squatting there, and I hear his screams. I will never be able to let that go. Everything else inside me is dead; our four boys are my only reason for living. I never could have suspected that hate could be so terrible. ... I am frightened of myself. ... Do you understand, Tono, that I can never return to Holland? The feeling almost chokes me. If there ever was a God, then why is

[22] Masdoelhak Nasoetion, Kaliurang, 1948

[23] Adriana Nasoetion-van der Have and her four children at the grave of her husband Masdoelhak Nasoetion, Yogyakarta, 1949

this happening? Masdoel, who was not only the dearest person on earth to me, but was also respected by everyone who knew him for his honesty and integrity.[38]

Months later, she heard that her husband's remains had been found and reburied in the military cemetery in Yogyakarta. At Masdoelhak's grave, she had a family portrait made: her sons Soeloeng, Tigor and Paroehoem, forming a row. She held little Anwar, who was known from then on as Anwar Masdoelhak, in her arms [23].

In 1950, Adriana Nasoetion-van der Have sued the Dutch state. Three years later, the district court in The Hague found in her favour: the state was liable for her losses and suffering as a result of her husband's death. The state appealed the decision but settled for the sum of 149,000 guilders. This made Nasoetion-van der Have the first victim of Dutch military violence in Indonesia to reach a settlement with the state. But the Dutch state never accepted formal responsibility for the assassination of Masdoelhak Nasoetion.[39]

20574: DOEA NOL LIMA TOEDJOEH EMPAT

Petrus Akihary [24], born in 1908 in the village of Aboru on Haruku in the Maluku Islands, had long proved his loyalty to the same Dutch state.[40] Akihary was promoted to the rank of adjudant (warrant officer) in 1950, having served a quarter century in the Koninklijk Nederlandsch-Indisch Leger (KNIL, Royal Netherlands East Indies Army). On 12 April 1951 he and his family stepped aboard the SS *Grote Beer* in Semarang in Java. Exactly thirty days later, on 12 May, the ship moored in the Port of Amsterdam. Disembarkation followed the next morning, wherupon Akihary underwent a medical examination at the Amersfoort refugee camp and was notified that he was discharged from military service. With this discharge, suddenly and unwillingly for Akihary, came an end to years of military loyalty to the flag of the Netherlands and its royal house. The Akihary family was housed in Barrack 6 in the former Vught concentration camp, rechristened the Lunetten housing estate.

A similar fate awaited about 12,000 Moluccans in the first half of 1951, consisting of over 3,500 ex-KNIL military personnel and their families. Twelve transport ships brought these people to the Netherlands. This was intended to be a temporary stay.

As part of the Dutch recognition of the sovereignty of Indonesia on 27 December 1949, it was agreed that the KNIL should disband by 26 July 1950 at the latest. Up to that date the KNIL would be dismantled and its duties turned over to the Indonesian National Armed Forces (TNI). The native troops could opt for demobilization at a site of their own choosing or transfer to the TNI. Some Moluccan military chose the latter. The vast majority, however, wished to go to Ambon or the Maluku Islands. On 25 April 1950, the free Republic Maluku Selatan (RMS, Republic of South Maluku) was declared in Ambon in response to the dissolution of the state of East Indonesia, which included the Maluku Islands. After the proclamation of the RMS, Ambon was out of the question as a site for demobilization for Indonesia. Alternatives such as the island of Ceram or New Guinea were also rejected. Ambon was later besieged by Indonesian troops.

On 26 July 1950 almost 9,000 KNIL military personnel had still not left the service, including 4,000 Moluccans. They were assigned the provisional status of member of the Royal Netherlands Army. The Dutch Government ran out of time and wanted to force the Moluccan soldiers to demobilize in Java. In a preliminary injunction issued in the Netherlands in December 1950, further affirmed in an appeal in January 1951, the Netherlands was forbidden to discharge the Moluccan soldiers against their will in Indonesian-controlled territory. For the Dutch government, the only remaining solution was to temporarily bring the Moluccan ex-TNI military personnel and their families to the Netherlands. The assumption then was that this would last three to six months, but this temporary sojourn of the Moluccans has now lasted more than seventy years. Several later repatriated; some never saw the land of their birth again; while others were able to visit their home villages once more – as was the case with Petrus Akihary. He died in 2000 at the age of ninety-eight in Culemborg, the Netherlands.

From 1926, when the young Akihary, along with many other young men from his village, signed up for the KNIL army in Ambon, he was given the service book number 20574, *Doea nol lima toedjoeh empat* in Malay. His name and number are stamped onto a metal identity disc [25]. Akihary must have worn this body tag throughout his entire military service. His career entered a new phase when he returned from confinement as a sergeant first class, having been a prisoner of war under the Japanese, who had forced him to do hard labour on the Burma railway from 1942 to 1945. Akihary was based in Sabang, the capital of the small, strategically situated island of Weh, north of Aceh in Sumatra. There Akihary climbed to the rank of sergeant major instructor [26]. Young Dutch conscripts sent to Indonesia on special assignments were trained in Sabang by the experienced weapons specialist and instructor Akihary.

His reunion with his wife, Jacoba Nahumury, and their five children, Dominggus, Pieter Paul, Martha, Johannes and Willem Arnol, had been a long time coming. Nahumury had remained behind with the children in Magelang in Central Java during the Japanese occupation and underwent the fate that befell many Moluccans (at the time often called Ambonese) during the first months of the Indonesian revolution. There was great danger and insecurity. Not knowing the fate of their father Akihary, the family went through anxious times; no one could be trusted. Via the Red Cross, Nahumury found out that her husband was still alive, was staying in Sabang, and was looking for them. A trip was discreetly arranged. Ultimately she managed, in the course of 1946, to escape from Magelang with her family in the deepest secrecy, each of the children carrying a small bundle of clothes. They went first to Batavia (Jakarta), for them liberated territory where the Dutch were based, and the family was reunited not long afterwards in Sabang. At the end of 1947 Petrus Akihary was granted four months leave, which Petrus and Jacoba

[24]   Petrus Akihary, 1949/1950

[25]   Body tag of Petrus Akihary with service book number 20574, issued at his entry into service, 1926

No. 115407 K.N.I.L.

LEGITIMATIEBEWIJS

Houder is

Naam: Akahari
Voornamen: Petrus
Rang: S.M.I.
Alg. Stb. Nr.: 081811000

Ns De Plaats: (Mil.) Commandant,
De Ned.Pl.Mil.Tvs.Kant.Adj.

M.J. Isbrücker.
Res.Kapt.Inf.K.L.

VAN DORP 9957

Stempel gezaghebbende bevoegd tot afgifte

Handteekening van den houder:

[26] Military identity card (KNIL) of Sergeant Major Instructor Petrus Akihary, July 1950 – March 1951

spent together with their children in Aboru in the Maluku islands, the village in which they had both been born.

During the final months of 1949, Akihary was responsible for guarding Acehnese who had been taken prisoner by the KNIL, mostly young men fighting on the side of the Republic. It was a task the now forty-one-year-old sub-officer fulfilled in a humane way, strictly yet fairly. When the prisoners were transferred from Sabang to Banda Aceh on the mainland of Sumatra, where they were released, Akihary was at risk of being arrested by the local government and the Indonesian army. A return to his company and family seemed impossible, but thanks to the intervention of the prisoners, who testified to their good treatment by their *bapa* Akihary, he was able to return safely to Sabang. The end of the Indonesian war of independence brought the Akihary family a period of great insecurity. That insecurity would not cease with their departure from Indonesia in 1951.

COMRADES OF THE REVOLUTION

ARTISTS AND THE INDONESIAN REVOLUTION

AMINUDIN T.H. SIREGAR
AMIR SIDHARTA
HARM STEVENS

REVOLUSI!

It is not even one by two centimetres, a tiny red-and-white flag on a metal pin. Yet when secured to clothing, the trinket forms a powerful symbol of patriotism. 'Red stands for bravery and courage, white for purity and magnanimity', as the pro-Republican periodical *The Voice of Free Indonesia* put it.[1] The flag, along with the national anthem, had been declared the national symbol of Indonesia at the Indonesian Youth Congress in 1928. For many years, the bicolour had been outlawed by first the Dutch and then the Japanese occupiers.[2] From the proclamation of the Republic on 17 August 1945, however, the flag became more emphatically than ever the symbol of the struggle for a free Indonesia, fluttering from the top of flag-poles and as miniature versions pinned on chests. The Indonesian head of state Sukarno had set the trend. From late 1945, the presidential safari suit sported the little flag, an example many Indonesians followed [1].

In order to supply everyone with this nationalist symbol, a small metals industry must have been active at the time of the revolution. We can see how the pins were distributed in a photo taken in 1945 or 1946: a crowd of Indonesians gathers around some street vendors disseminating the red-and-white revolution among the populace from large sheets onto which are pinned a mass of little flags [3].

The mother of the Indonesian painter Trubus Soedarsono also wore such a metal pin, as a sign of loyalty to the free Republic of Indonesia. Perhaps the young artist pinned it to the lapel of her *kebaya* (blouse) when he painted her portrait in 1946. Mbah Podho Wates, as she was known to her grandchildren, is depicted facing the viewer, against a background of wooden planks [2].[3] With this detailed portrait, the painter created a modest monument to his mother. The fact that this was painted on a panel of cheap plywood says a great deal about the severe scarcity of materials with which Indonesian artists had to contend during the revolutionary period. At bottom left, Trubus wrote the word *Iboekoe* (My mother).

Trubus Soedarsono, born in 1924 in Wates, near Yogyakarta, was one of the young Indonesian artists whose artistic career was significantly influenced by the turbulent political developments in his country. During the Japanese occupation, Trubus had trained with Sudjojono and Affandi. These two artists were the driving forces, from the late 1930s, for a generation of young Indonesian artists who were searching for their own interpretation of their country and people but wanted to do this in a way that fulfilled their desire for personal artistic integrity. This tension between the political and the personal came together in Trubus's portrait of his mother in 1946: the minuscule flag made *Iboekoe* a political statement as well as an intimate portrait.

In 1946, Trubus had joined the Seniman Indonesia Muda (SIM, Young Indonesian Artists), founded that same year by Sudjojono in the city of Madiun in East Java.[4] The society operated as a revolutionary collective and specifically concentrated on the creation and production of propaganda posters, the medium through which artists in the Republic reached the people in the street. Trubus experienced first-hand how making and distributing the political propaganda of posters was also a dangerous activity when he was arrested in the street by Dutch soldiers because he was putting up an anti-Dutch poster. We do not know how long he was jailed as a result.[5]

[1] Portrait of Sukarno on Proclamation Day, by Basoeki Abdullah, 1945

[2]   *Iboekoe* (My mother), by Trubus Soedarsono, 1946

[3]　　Indonesian street vendors sell pins with the red-and-white flag, 1945/1946

CULTURAL ENLIGHTENMENT

On 26 March 1947, an article appeared in the Indonesian, pro-Republican, Dutch-language periodical *Het Inzicht* (Insight) – the name was a witty Indonesian riposte to the weekly published by the Dutch Government Information Service in Indonesia, *Uitzicht* (Outlook) – with the evocative title 'Fighting with Paint'. That fight was being waged, according to the article, by 'young people, like Sudjojono and Affandi'. Their work led the anonymous writer to cautiously conclude that 'there [is] every chance of a renaissance in painting'. According to the periodical, the Indonesian art scene, after the great nineteenth-century innovator Raden Saleh, had long wallowed in a state of decay, which could be ascribed first to the 'benign, nonchalant neglect prior to the war' and afterwards to 'misuse by Japanese propaganda'.[6]

This 'benign neglect' was an apt, though perhaps overly generous, description of Dutch cultural policy in the Dutch East Indies, or to put it a better way, of the lack thereof. And from 1942 there indeed followed, under the Japanese, a period in which Indonesian artists were primarily employed for propaganda purposes, aimed at creating a beneficent picture of the Japanese occupation of Indonesia and mobilizing the populace in preparation for the war against the Americans and British, which was eagerly and rightfully described by the leftist progressive editors of *Het Inzicht* as 'misuse'.

Yet there was also another side to the story: the Japanese occupation provided unprecedented opportunities for Indonesian artists.[7] Propaganda was an important instrument of the Japanese totalitarian regime. The objective of this aggressive public information programme was 'to attract the attention of the people' and 'to indoctrinate and tame them'.[8] The ultimate goal was the creation of the Dai Toa Kyoeiken (Greater East Asian Co-Prosperity Sphere). Within this framework, the Japanese occupier provided opportunities for Indonesians to participate in the social, political, economic and artistic life of the country. Artists were also assisted in taking a place in society, and held prominent positions in cultural organizations.

Whereas Indonesian artists had stood in the shadow of their Dutch fellows in the colonial period, under the aegis of the Japanese they were assigned a less subordinate role. Indonesian artists were given a voice in the artistic discourse and the noble task of creating an artistic consciousness among the populace. On a modest scale, a cultural infrastructure emerged that consisted of education, exhibitions and art prizes. Young painters like Trubus, Zaini, Basuki Resobowo, Oesman Effendi, Mochtar Apin, Sutiksna and many others owed their artistic training to this. Along with Japanese painters like Ono Saseo and Ohno Takashi, Affandi, Sudjojono, the brothers Agus and Otto Djaya, and Basoeki Abdullah played an active role as mentors for the next generation of Indonesian painters. Artistic activities took place within the cultural department of the Poesat Tenaga Rakjat (Poetera, Centre of the People's Power) and Keimin Bunka Shidōsho (Centre for Cultural Enlightenment). Both institutions were under the supervision of the propaganda department of the Japanese occupier, the Sendenbu. Nearly all the artists lived in

Jakarta, although Affandi commuted between the cultural centre of Jakarta and his hometown of Bandung.

While the painters did produce autonomous work, they were also actively involved as designers of propaganda material – posters, for instance – in the preparations for war and the mobilization of the Indonesian people for the Greater Asia cause. Exhibitions in Jakarta were also used as vehicles for propaganda. In November 1944, at the *Fourth Djawa Baroe* exhibition, the Keimin Bunka Shidōsho presented paintings that showed young soldiers with beaming faces fighting the enemies of Japan. At the *Fifth Djawa Baroe* exhibition, six months later, young Indonesian painters showed work as propaganda for the *rōmusha* programme that was pitilessly imposed upon the Indonesian people by the Japanese occupier. The programme, a dehumanizing system of forced labour, was depicted rather inaccurately in the paintings in the form of muscular Indonesian labourers brandishing a *pacul* (a kind of spade). More general themes like industry were also addressed. Photo reproductions were published in the newspapers *Asia Raya* and the illustrated periodical *Djawa Baroe* (New Java) to bring the arts to the attention of readers.[9]

This enabled artists to reach the masses with their art; new subjects and themes were explored artistically. In addition, as was true for the whole of social life in Indonesia during the Japanese occupation, the spirit of nationalism was stimulated among artists as well. When Indonesian independence was declared on 17 August 1945, it became crucial to put the experience accumulated during the Japanese period to use as part of a new, this time genuinely independent, artistic course. As a result, the period of Japanese occupation and the period of the Indonesian revolution, despite the political seismic shift signified by the declaration of Indonesian independence, are inextricably linked. From the moment Indonesian independence was declared, the artists were intensely involved with the revolution and the ideal of a free Indonesia.

THE REVOLUTION CALLS

'We all have the sense of entering a new age. We all realize that we must keep fighting for the independence of the nation and to preserve the state that has been proclaimed.' This is how journalist and writer Rosihan Anwar described the prevailing conviction at the last meeting in the office of the Keimin Bunka Shidōsho, a few days after the declaration of Indonesian independence. The artists present quickly agreed to disown the fascism of Japanese propaganda art in order to serve the Indonesian revolution.[10] Painters, poets, actors and musicians, all in thrall to the reconquered freedom of their country, decided to join forces in order to let the call for independence ring out everywhere, including in the most remote quarters of Jakarta.[11] This new revolutionary alliance of artists, mostly former members of the Keimin Bunka Shidōsho, was called the Seniman Merdeka (Independent Artists).[12]

The group took to the streets of Jakarta in lorries and turned their words into deeds. The artists proclaimed the independence of Indonesia and exhorted the people to resist the return of the Dutch. Battle songs were performed from the back of the lorries, remarkably, these included Japanese songs from the time of the occupation. In this period, Sudjojono, standing among the people, emerged as a leader and speaker and left a lasting impression on his fellow artists.[13] Writer Muhammad Balfas noted in 1947: 'When the fire of the revolution set Jakarta ablaze, Sudjojono left his studio and immediately ventured into the city quarters. He wrote and drew on the streets, the markets, the walls of houses. No one can forget his role during this time.'[14] The painter Dullah later noted that he himself, along with other colleagues, including Mochtar Apin, Suromo and Trubus, had also taken to the streets. And the artist Abdul Salam had expressed fierce criticism of Dutch policy in caricatures in newspapers and magazines.[15]

The activities of the Seniman Merdeka in Jakarta reached their climax in the brief, uncertain period between August and October 1945, the period in which the design for the poster bearing the words 'Boeng, Ajo Boeng' (Brother, Come on, Brother) was created, a collaboration between Affandi, Sudjojono and the poet Chairil Anwar. The image of the man breaking the colonial chains against the backdrop of the red-and-white flag formed a powerful exhortation to Indonesians to take matters into their own hands. The poster could be seen everywhere in the streets, for instance on a lorry making its rounds [PP. 82–83 [6]].

The paintings of the young artists also immediately achieved a prominent place in the representation of the young state. Sukarno's residence at Jalan Pegangsaan Timur 56 had become the political headquarters of the Republic from the moment independence was declared. The various visitors to the presidential home in the first weeks after the proclamation observed that it boasted a considerable collection of paintings by Indonesian artists. One of these visitors was the Dutch journalist Jan Bouwer. As a correspondent for United Press he had cycled to the residence on 6 September for a short interview with Sukarno. At the entrance he refused to let himself be searched by the Republican police officer on duty and the '*pemoedas* armed to the teeth'. They were nevertheless willing to let the Dutch visitor in without a search. Bouwer had then taken a seat in the waiting room and noted in his journal: 'I was able to kill time by admiring the president's truly exceptional collection of paintings.'[16] The Australian artist and reporter Tony Rafty was also impressed by the paintings in Sukarno's home. Even the veranda of the Gedung Proklamasi (proclamation building) contained a monumental painting by the artist Henk Ngantung, entitled *Memanah* (Archery) [4]. Sukarno had bought the panel in 1944 at an exhibition of the Keimin Bunka Shidōsho and immediately given it a prominent spot on the wall of his veranda, where the archer formed the backdrop for the declaration of independence on 19 August 1945. Several weeks later, Rafty included the striking painting in his quick-fire sketch of the meeting of the Republican cabinet on 3 October 1945.[17]

Even after the core of the Republican government decamped to Yogyakarta in January 1946 and the Dutch tightened their grip on Jakarta, Indonesian artists, poets and writers were active in cosmopolitan Jakarta. A number of these artists, including the painters Mochtar Apin, Baharudin and Ngantung formed the collective Gelanggang Seniman

[4] *Memanah* (Archery), by Henk Ngantung, 1944

Merdeka (Arena of Independent Artists) that year. Apin and Baharudin specialized in making woodcuts and other graphic work. In 1946 they were commissioned to produce a series of linocuts, which the department of foreign relations of the Indonesian Bureau for Youth Affairs published in a portfolio. The publication served to celebrate the first anniversary of the Republic of Indonesia and was distributed abroad. It was a fine example of the cultural diplomacy with which the Republic aimed to establish a position in the world community. In the preface – in Indonesian, French and English – the famed Indonesian linguist Sutan Takdir Alisjahbana defends the youth of Indonesia and the Indonesian revolution, which, in his view, was being unfairly discussed in the outside world exclusively in terms of 'violence', 'bloodshed' and 'the burning down of towns and villages'. Much more fundamental than the physical fighting, he argued, was the spiritual revolution among the youth. This album of linocuts is an example of the desire for self-expression in Indonesian young people, Alisjahbana said.[18] Remarkably, among the portraits and folk scenes, only one of the works of art in the portfolio has the on-going reality of the revolution as its subject: a procession of people with flags and a banner bearing the words 'sekali merdeka, tetap merdeka' (once free, always free) [5]. The image seems to be based on a photo of the mass gathering on 19 September 1945 on Ikada Square in Jakarta, over a month after the declaration of independence.

TO YOGYAKARTA

Although some artists had remained in Jakarta, a number of significant artists left the city after the departure of the political leadership, as freedom of movement for revolutionaries became increasingly circumscribed by the Dutch. Several of them, including brothers Otto and Agus Djaya, enlisted in the Republican army, while others journeyed to Yogyakarta.[19] A further group of painters ventured eastwards from Bandung, towards Republican territory, and ultimately to Yogyakarta. Among them were Hendra Gunawan, Sudjana Kerton, Soeparto, Abedy, Barli, Toerkandi and Koestiwa. Prior to reaching Yogyakarta, they made a brief stop on the front lines to make drawings and paintings. In the city of Tasikmalaya, east of Bandung, they staged a temporary exhibition with the support of the Gaboengan Perdjoeangan Rakjat (Alliance of the People's Struggle) militia group. From Tasikmalaya the artists continued their journey to the Yogyakarta along with the troop of soldiers. The exhibition, entitled *Perdjoeangan Revolusi* (Struggle for the Revolution), was also shown in Yogyakarta in early May 1946.

In response to the exhibition, the newspaper *Kedaulatan Rakjat* (Sovereignty of the People) gave a striking description of the new orientation that now pervaded Indonesian art: 'The motto of the young Indonesian painters today is not *l'art pour l'art* (art for art's sake), but *l'art pour la révolution* (art for the revolution).'[20] It also reported on the presence of Sukarno, Mohammad Hatta and other important officials at the exhibition's opening. Sukarno did what he was best at and gave a speech elaborately praising the patriotic attitude of the artists and their active involvement with the revolution.[21]

[5] *Sekali Merdeka, Tetap Merdeka* (Once Free, Always Free), by Baharudin, 1946

Once in Yogyakarta, Affandi and Hendra Gunawan joined forces to form the association Seniman Masyarakat (Artists of the Community). In 1946 Affandi represented the spirit of the revolution on the front lines in a striking painting entitled *Laskar Rakyat Mengatur Siasat* (The People's Militia Decides Tactics) [P. 29 [4]]. Six guerrilla fighters are shown seated and standing around a map of Indonesia. Two lean against a wall on which a portion of a poster text is visible: 'tetap merdeka', possibly part of the slogan 'Sekali merdeka, tetap merdeka'. The image of the men united in purpose around the map of the country for which they are fighting is evocative. One of the men looks straight at the viewer. Affandi's guerrilla painting was given a prominent place in the front gallery of the presidential palace in Yogyakarta, immediately next to the entrance, where it reminded everyone who entered the palace how the struggle for a free Indonesia (the entire archipelago, visible on the map in the painting) was being fought in the field by anonymous fighters from the people.

Sudjojono followed a different path. He did not move to Yogyakarta but instead settled in the city of Madiun in East Java, where he joined the Pemuda Sosialis Indonesia (Pesindo, Socialist Youth of Indonesia), which was strongly supported by minister of defence Amir Sjarifuddin. In April 1946, Sudjojono founded the Seniman Indonesia Muda (SIM, Young Indonesian Artists) there with Trisno Sumardjo, Soedibio, Sunindyo, and D. Suradji.[22]

INDONESIAN MILITIA PORTRAIT

The artist comrades of SIM are depicted amid soldiers and civilians in Sudjojono's painted group portrait with the apt title *Kawan Kawan Repoloesi* (Comrades of the Revolution) [8]. His Indonesian militia portrait would become an icon of the Indonesian revolution.[23] Sudjojono painted this work in Solo. The Republican minister of youth affairs, Wikana, had called on artists to move to this sultanate city, situated closer to the front. At the same time, Amir Sjarifuddin, now the Republic's prime minister, had ordered Major Soegiri, the local military commander, to provide protection to the painters and *ketoprak* players (Javanese form of theatre) who were flocking to the city. Rumour has it that Sudjojono completed the painting in a single day, shortly after the first Dutch military offensive (21 July – 5 August 1947).[24]

In *Kawan Kawan Repoloesi* the revolution is given a face. Twenty Indonesian artists, soldiers and Sudjojono's son Tedjabayu (the youngest of the portrait subjects) are featured in the painting. The men seem inward-looking, but their gaze is determined. Sudjojono wrote in black paint above the heads of his comrades: 'The will of the time drives us toward *one* home, *one* place, *one* heaven, *one* revolution. This revolution is the Indonesian revolution.'[25]

REVOLUSI ABROAD

At the end of June 1947, several weeks before Sudjojono would work on his group portrait in Solo, the brothers Agus and Otto Djaya arrived in Amsterdam. While they were not the most talented artists of the

Indonesian revolution, they made their mark as cultural envoys of the Republic in the Netherlands. The Djaya brothers did not come without luggage. They brought more than one hundred of their paintings, gouaches and watercolours, as well as works by other Indonesian artists. Otto's paintings in particular included many works of an explicitly revolutionary character. These comrades of the revolution found their way to Amsterdam in this way.

The younger brother Otto was born in Rangkasbitung in West Java in 1916 [6]. As sons of a Javanese civil servant in the colonial administration, he and his elder brother Agus had access to a European education. Around 1940, as an autodidact, Otto managed to achieve a position as an artist. The brothers had known Sudjojono since the late 1930s through circles around the first Indonesian artists' association, Persatuan Ahli-Ahli Gambar Indonesia (Persagi, Union of Indonesian Painters), which Sudjojono had founded in 1938, and of which Agus Djaya was one of the most prominent members. In what was then Batavia (Jakarta), the brothers had been part of the (anticolonial) Indonesian cultural avant-garde, which was focused on the emancipation of the Indonesian arts. The careers of Agus and Otto flourished during the Japanese occupation of Indonesia and Agus secured a key position in the cultural centre established by the Japanese, the Keimin Bunka Shidōsho. In 1944, Otto joined the Pembela Tanah Air (PETA, Defenders of the Homeland), a Indonesian paramilitary organization founded by the Japanese, and received intensive military training in Bogor.

Not long after the Japanese surrender and the proclamation of Indonesian independence, both brothers served in the Indonesian army. They belonged to a regiment of the Republican Tentara Keamanan Rakjat (TKR, People's Security Army) in Sukabumi and would have carried out guerrilla operations in the vicinity of the city.[26] Here Agus, as chairman of the newly founded Balai Kesenian Oemoem (General Art Hall), organized a conference for revolutionary artists. With Otto in his wake, Agus became a cultural agent for the Republican cause [7].

When Otto and Agus Djaya boarded the ss *Nieuw Holland* in Tanjung Priok in June 1947 for the three-week voyage to the Netherlands, the brothers, by now over thirty years old, were registered as so-called Malino students. In 1947, besides the Djayas, another 158 Indonesian students resided in the Netherlands under the auspices of a grant programme named after the conference in Malino in Sulawesi in 1946, where this grant had been established. But Otto and Agus Djaya did not consider themselves students, as evidenced by the registration card of the Rijksakademie van Beeldende Kunsten (State Academy of Fine Arts), where Agus was expected to attend the painting course. The section 'particulars' notes 'seldom present'. That was not surprising, for the Javanese brothers had better things to do. From the moment they arrived, 'all the doors in Holland' had been opened to the two artists, as reported by a delegate for student affairs to the ministry.[27] One of these doors was that of the Stedelijk Museum in Amsterdam.

From 10 October to 10 November 1947 the exhibition *Agoes Djaya, Otto Djaya. Twee Indonesische schilders* (Agus Djaya, Otto Djaya: Two Indonesian Painters) was held there. The driving force behind the

[6] Otto Djaya at Rijswijk Palace in Jakarta at the signing of the Linggajati Agreement, photo by Cas Oorthuys, 25 March 1947

[7] Agus Djaya with his painting *Maya* at an exhibition in Jakarta, 1947

[8] *Kawan Kawan Repoloesi* (Comrades of the Revolution), by Sudjojono, 1947
Top, left to right: unknown, Marsudi Yudhokusomo (father of Kartono) / Rameli (?), Soeromo (green beret), Oesman Effendi (blue beret), unknown, Soedibio, Nashar, Soerono; middle: unknown, Sudarso (black beret), unknown, Dullah (not the painter), unknown, Rameli / Marsudi Yudhokusomo (father of Kartono) (?); bottom: Kartono Yudhokusomo, Basuki Resobowo, Tedjabayu (Sudjojono's son), Trisno Sumardjo, Major Soegiri

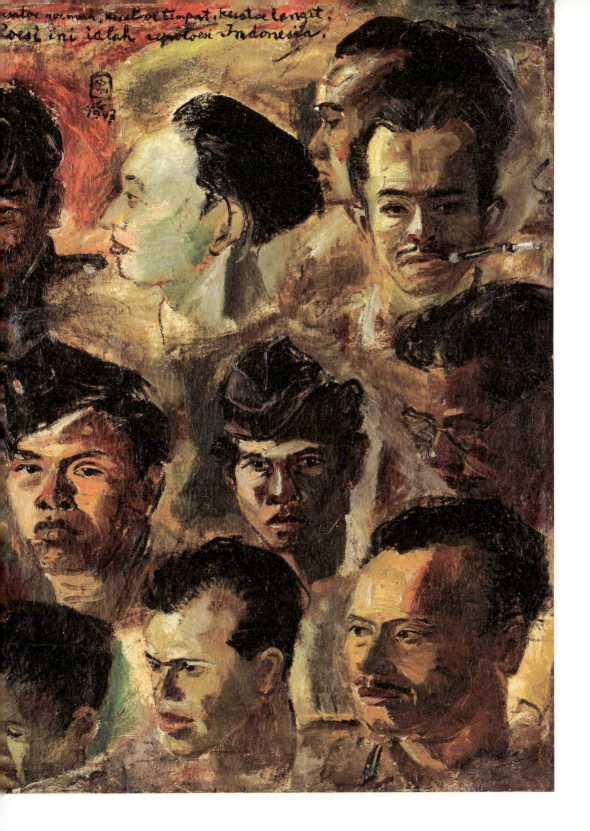

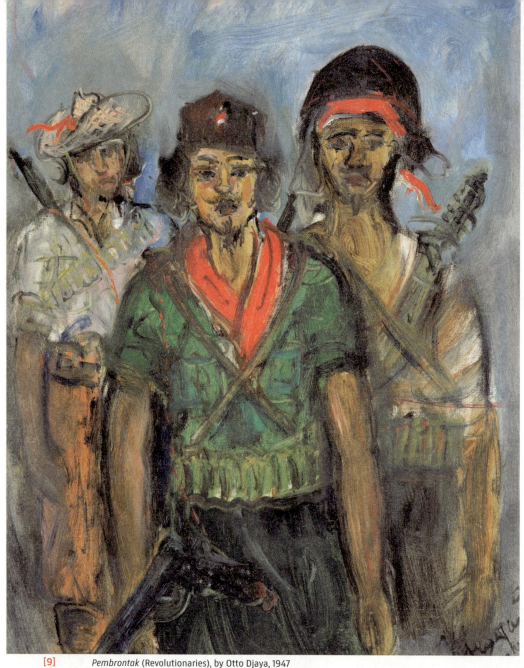

[9] *Pembrontak* (Revolutionaries), by Otto Djaya, 1947

presentation was the museum's director, Willem Sandberg, who felt that the exhibition 'substantiates an immeasurable contribution on the part of their country and their people, the Indonesians'.[28] The presentation was a political statement, a show of support for the Republic of Indonesia and a complete novelty in the Dutch museum world. It was the first time in history that contemporary work by Indonesian artists had been shown in a modern art museum.

On display were 137 works by the Djaya brothers, including 80 by Otto – the cargo of paintings they had carried with them had provided an ample supply. The exhibition poster, personally designed by Sandberg, was rendered in striking red and white, as was the accompanying catalogue. The listed titles and the translations in the booklet indicate that the subjects had a high 'revolutionary' quotient, especially in Otto's work. The titles ring out with *revolusi* and *merdeka*, *Lasjkar* (Fighters, 1946), *Pembrontakan* (Types from the Revolution, 1946), *Ahli Perjoangan* (Figures from the Revolution, 1946), *Potret Prajoerit* (Warrior, 1946), *Hari Merdeka* (Freedom Day at Buitenzorg, 1945) and *Pahlawan Goegoer* (Fallen Fighter, 1947).

One of the few works at the Amsterdam exhibition to have survived makes its revolutionary content powerfully clear to this day. It is probably the painting *Pembrontak*, anomalously translated as 'Revolutionaries' in the catalogue (no. 62) and dated 1947.[29] Otto must have painted this group portrait in 1946 or early 1947. The man in the middle may well be the painter himself, during his time as a soldier. The three men are portrayed in quick brushstrokes, facing forward, an impression of the combative, armed reputation of the national revolution. This naturally includes the red-and-white of the Indonesian flag with which the man in the middle is adorned [9].

The bellicose nature of a portion of the Indonesian art brought to the Netherlands by the Djayas did not negate the fact that the thinking within the Republican and Dutch governments was that cooperation in art and culture would in fact improve their difficult political relations. It had not been for nothing that a cultural clause had been added to the Linggajati Agreement signed at the end of 1946, outlining the first phase of the transition to independence.[30] In July 1947, shortly after the Djayas arrived in the Netherlands, a major offensive by the Dutch military in Indonesia sealed the temporary failure of the Linggajati Agreement, putting this cultural cooperation under tremendous pressure.

Once the conciliatory spirit of Linggajati seemed to have been extinguished from a political standpoint, Indonesian art nevertheless proved able, occasionally, to play a constructive role during the years of war and negotiations that followed. One good example of this is the work of the leading Javanese painter Basoeki Abdullah. He had completed his artistic training in the Netherlands before the war and had returned there in 1946. In a Dutch newspaper article from that year, he was described as a 'representative of the Indonesian government'.[31] On Sunday 2 January 1949, as the second Dutch military offensive raged across Indonesia, Queen Juliana posed for him in The Hague.[32] The picture was commissioned by the royal family, and Basoeki succeeded in painting an unusually glamorous portrait of the Dutch head of state with a Javanese

volcano furiously smoking in the background [11]. At the start of the
Dutch-Indonesian Round Table Conference in 1949 in The Hague, which
would ultimately result in the cession of sovereignty and the end of the
conflict between the Netherlands and Indonesia, Basoeki was given
another official portrait commission, this time a quadruple one. In early
September he made four pastel paintings of prominent Dutch and Indonesian participants at the conference, including the portrait of Mohammad
Hatta, the head of the Indonesian delegation [12].[33]

Basoeki's stay in the Netherlands, safely away from the frontline
of the revolution, was criticized by his Indonesian colleagues who were
participating in their country's struggle for independence. This is evident, for instance, in a satirical cartoon published in 1947 in the periodical *Seniman* (Artist) [10].[34] We see a portrait of the Dutch admiral
C.E.L. Helfrich on Basoeki's easel. The caption at the top of the cartoon
reads: 'Basoeki painted Helfrich in the Netherlands!' Basoeki, standing
before the easel, replies to Agus and Otto Djaya (also the subject of
mockery because of their trip to the Netherlands): 'So that my paintings
become popular and people want to buy them!' Whether Basoeki actually
painted a portrait of this notorious anti-Republican colonial hawk is
highly uncertain.[35]

BANDUNG

At an institutional level, there was still room for initiatives resulting from
combined Dutch and Indonesian efforts, including in Indonesia. This is
evidenced, for instance, by the founding in August 1947 of a new educa-
tional institution, the University Programme for the Training of Drawing
Teachers, in Bandung, a West Javanese city situated in the Dutch-sup-
ported region of Negara Pasundan, and therefore outside Republican
territory. This institution trained not only drawing teachers but autonomous artists as well. This had been urged by the Indo-Dutch drawing
teacher Simon Admiraal, who was appointed by the Department of
Education and Religion to develop the visual arts teaching programme.
He focused explicitly on two foundations: the local culture of the archipelago and the treasures of world art, especially Western modern art, for
the improvement of general knowledge.[36]

Admiraal was able to set his programme into motion as director
of the art school starting in autumn 1947.[37] Ries Mulder was appointed
to teach painting and art appreciation in 1948. During their internment
in a Japanese camp during the war, Admiraal and Mulder had made
plans for the future art education of Indonesians. The university programme in Bandung would evolve into the leading art academy in
Indonesia, and is today part of the Institut Teknologi Bandung (ITB,
Bandung Institute of Technology) as the Faculty of Arts and Design.

Simon Admiraal was unable to experience first-hand the blossom-
ing of the Bandung art school after the cession of sovereignty. In November 1949 he gave up work on the advice of doctors: he was suffering from
severe stress. The harsh period of time spent in internment camp during
the war and the loss of his eldest son, murdered in the street in October
1945, had taken their toll. Admiraal returned to the Netherlands, arriving

[10] Satirical cartoon of Basoeki Abdullah with Agus and Otto Djaya in *Seniman*, 1947

[11] Portrait of Queen Juliana, by Basoeki Abdullah, 1949

[12] Portrait of Mohammad Hatta, by Basoeki Abdullah, 1949

[13] *Studentenleven in de bergen* (Student Life in the Mountains), unknown artist, c. 1949

in early 1950. In his luggage was a portfolio of drawings. The portfolio bore a label that read: 'Presented to Mr S. Admiraal by the students of the Univers. Prog. for Drawing Teachers on his departure for the Netherlands, 3 December 1949'. The drawings varied in nature; they included figurative as well as more abstract work. One of the students had contributed a watercolour: a mountain landscape in which a couple of figures can be distinguished in the tall grass, one figure lying behind a machine gun reading a book, the other with a rifle on his knee, smoking a cigarette. In the bottom left corner, a caption notes: 'Student life in the mountains' [13].

The war was never far away. A number of students might have taken part in the revolutionary struggle as part of student militias. The military culture was familiar to them and inspired a generation of Indonesian artists (in training). In this context, however, we must not forget that the war had a devastating effect on the work and personal lives of various individual artists. During the second Dutch military offensive in late 1948, Yogyakarta was bombarded. Artists fled as fast they could, and some were taken prisoner. In the chaos that resulted from the Dutch occupation, seventy-one paintings disappeared from the SIM studio, which were later reported as missing.[38] Sudjojono was also severely affected by the war. In December 1948, his father was killed while trying to flee a Dutch bombardment in Bogem, a village near Yogyakarta. Around twenty of Sudjojono's paintings were destroyed by fire. Several of his sculptures were found to be vandalized when they were recovered. Sudjojono claimed that Dutch soldiers had used the sculptures for target practice.[39] In his painting *Biografi II di Malioboro* (Second Biography of Malioboro) Harijadi Sumadidjaja depicted the confusion among the citizens and fighters in Yogyakarta after the second military offensive by the Dutch [14].

The revolution also lived on after Indonesian independence in the work of the artists. After 1950, artists like Sudjojono and Dullah regularly returned to the domain of national independence in their work. In April 1957, a solo exhibition of work by Hendra Gunawan was held at the Hotel Duta Indonesia (the former Hotel des Indes), in the centre of Jakarta. Newspaper reports show that Sukarno was also in attendance. The president had always shown himself an important supporter of painting in his country. Over the course of the 1950s he built up a significant national art collection, which was partly rooted in the period of the struggle for independence. The Hendra Gunawan exhibition in Jakarta also included *Pengantin Revolusi* (Bride of the Revolution), a large canvas made especially for the exhibition [15]. Hendra made this painting more than seven years after the end of the revolution, which was more than simply a heroic rendition of fighters in battle. His predilection for scenes from the life of the Indonesian people is still identifiable: a bridal party walks along a muddy path; the bride sits on a bicycle in front, the groom walking next to her, dressed in his military uniform. They seem to be heading towards a somewhat uncertain future in the period following the revolution. The couple are observed by two rugged veterans of the struggle, who stand arm in arm, as comrades of the revolution, at a certain distance from the couple's civilian activities.

In another painting in the exhibition, entitled *Revolusi*, Hendra shows four guerrillas in the mountains [16]. As with the soldiers in

Pengantin Revolusi, there is visible camaraderie: this time the men are arranged fraternally at their machine-gun post above the river. We can see the devastation of war on the opposite bank. Two of the men are reading a letter together, the other two are jointly lighting a cigarette. A rifle rests in the lap of the man on the right. A small red-and-white flag flutters from the barrel.

[14] *Biografi II di Malioboro* (Second Biography of Malioboro), by Harijadi Sumadidjaja, 1949

[15]   *Pengantin Revolusi* (Bride of the Revolution), by Hendra Gunawan, 1957

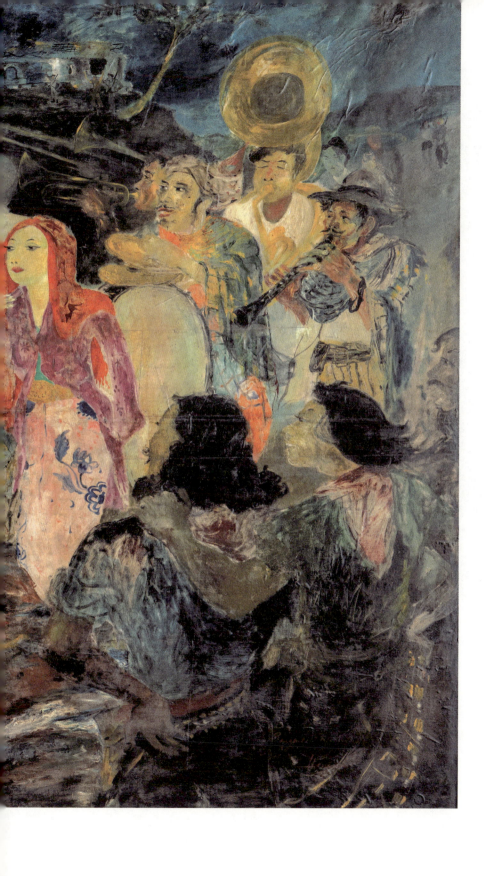

[16] *Revolusi* (Revolution), by Hendra Gunawan, 1951

FOUR TIMES 365 DAYS

SUKARNO'S RETURN TO JAKARTA CAPTURED

YUDHI SOERJOATMODJO

REVOLUSI!

For the forty-two-year-old Alex Mendur it was a scene reminiscent of another historic day he had been a part of, four years, four months and eleven days earlier at Jalan Pegangsaan Timur 56, Jakarta. There were the soldiers gripping their rifles, standing guard alongside the boy scouts in their khaki shorts. And, behind and to either side of him, the young men and women with expectant faces, crowding the front garden. There were the military officers up on the terrace, eyes alert, looking at something or someone beyond. Beside them were the dignitaries, some in Western-style jackets, standing close to Sukarno on the terrace steps, the latter resplendent in his characteristic black *kopiah* fez hat and white suit. Finally, there was the photojournalist himself, squinting through the viewfinder, patiently waiting for the right moment to click the shutter button of his Leica camera.

And yet, in many ways what Alex was observing on this day, 28 December 1949, could not have been more different from that morning of 17 August 1945, when he and his younger brother, Soemarto Frans Mendur, had been the only photographers to document Sukarno's proclamation of Indonesia's independence to an equally determined but much smaller and more subdued crowd. The Sukarno Alex was photographing on this occasion was not the pale exhausted man of yore, who had just emerged from his bedroom following several horrific days of being pressured and ultimately kidnapped by the *pemuda* (young freedom fighter), impatient for him to announce independence. Instead, the president and his entourage had flown in from Yogyakarta, Central Java, on a pair of silver Dakota aeroplanes, recently purchased for the newly established Garuda Indonesia Airways national carrier, their tails freshly painted with the twin colours of the Indonesian flag.

The planes had circled the clear skies above, raining streams of flyers bearing the word 'Merdeka' (freedom) onto the waiting crowds below, minutes before making their final descent to Kemayoran Airport at 11:42 a.m.[1] Alex Mendur quickly ran to the side of one of the aircraft, capturing the moment when an energized Sukarno appeared from within, waving and smiling to the rows of dignitaries, military officers, girl scouts and ordinary citizens welcoming him back to Jakarta with jubilant shouts of 'Merdeka! Merdeka!'[1]. The president stood at the door of the plane for a minute or two while a military officer preceded him down the steps, carefully carrying the red-and-white national flag used at the proclamation. Four years earlier, it had flown from a simple bamboo mast, freshly cut at dawn from Sukarno's own garden. This time it was transported on a silver tray like a national heirloom. Two Dutch attendants waited for him at the foot of the steps, which days before had been decorated with the letters 'G.I.A.' – the abbreviated name of the national carrier – in large sans-serif lettering on a red-and-white background.[2]

The president had not set foot in the capital city since the evening of 2 January 1946, when he and Vice President Mohammad Hatta and their families had been forced to decamp to the relative safety of Yogyakarta. As had been the case on the day of the proclamation, Sukarno was nervous, and this time the ever-loyal and level-headed Hatta would not be with him as he faced the crowd. The vice president, who eight days earlier had also been appointed prime minister, was in the Nether-

[1] President Sukarno arriving at Kemayoran Airport on his return to Jakarta, 28 December 1949, photo by Alex Mendur (IPPHOS)

[2] President Sukarno, accompanied by minister of defence Sultan Hamengkubowono IX, waving to the crowds on the ride from the airport to Koningsplein, Jakarta, 28 December 1949, photo by Melvin Jacob (IPPHOS)

lands where on 27 December 1949 at the Paleis op de Dam (the Royal Palace in Amsterdam) he and Queen Juliana had signed the official handover of the sovereignty of the former Dutch East Indies to the Republik Indonesia Serikat (RIS, Republic of the United States of Indonesia).[3] As Sukarno later recalled in his usual dramatic prose, his wide grin had camouflaged his nerves as he disembarked from the plane just as the spontaneous roar from the crowds drowned out 'the loud incessant thumping inside my chest'.[4]

But there was little time for reflection. Already on the tarmac, 'newsmen and cameramen went hither and thither', noted First Lady Fatmawati Sukarno of the numerous journalists interviewing and photographing Sukarno.[5] And after inspecting the honorary guards and a quick detour to the airport lounge for refreshments, handshakes and another short question-and-answer session with the gathered press, the president was soon escorted out, his movements tracked by the cameramen from Berita Film Indonesia (BFI, Indonesian News Films) filming on the ground and from the back of a purpose-built military truck.[6] Sukarno quickly climbed onto the spacious back seat of the car that had been loaned for the occasion by the Indonesian automobile importer, textile manufacturer and shipping magnate, Agus Musin Dasaad – a maroon, chrome-grilled, two-door 1949 Super Eight 160 Packard Convertible – that was to take him from the airport to the former residence of the Dutch East Indies governor-general at Koningsplein (which henceforth was to be renamed Merdeka Palace).[7]

'WEEPING, SCREAMING, CHEERING PEOPLE'

A huge mob had already formed along the seven-kilometre route, with various newspapers at that time putting the number at between 200,000 and 250,000; Sukarno himself later recalled being surrounded by 'millions of weeping, screaming, cheering people'. Whatever the true number, it was certainly more than the 800–1,000 people whom various observers had seen participating in the proclamation of independence on 17 August 1945.[8] The throng surged forwards, breaking the cordon that had been set up by the Indonesian police. Twenty people got crushed that day, *The New York Times* reported, as people swarmed Sukarno's car from all sides. Despite the considerable horsepower of its eight-cylinder, 5.3-litre engine the vehicle only managed to inch along, much like a dinghy, surrounded by wave after wave of joyous faces, raised fists and shouts of 'Merdeka!'

The fierce-looking Indonesian soldiers escorting the motorcade with their brand-new rifles and machine guns had been deployed from the Siliwangi Division in West Java. They included the combat-hardened Kala Hitam (Black Scorpion) battalion, which had not only fought the Dutch in their first and second military offensives of July 1947 and December 1948 but were also responsible for crushing the communist rebellion of September 1948 in East and Central Java.[9] That day, they were barely able to keep the mass of people clear of the road – as is shown in the photographs shot from a specially built platform by the young Melvin Jacob of Indonesia Press Photo Service (IPPHOS) [2].[10]

For months, Sukarno had distanced himself from the handover and its attendant ceremonies, arguing that Indonesia was already a sovereign nation the day he proclaimed its independence. Consequently, it had been left to the Sultan Hamengkubuwono IX – recently appointed as the RIS's minister of defence – to deal with that day's welcoming ceremony at the airport. The Sultan's other duties also included representing the Republic during the handover ceremony with the Dutch Crown's outgoing High Commissioner, A.H.J. Lovink, at Merdeka Palace, held in parallel to the one in the Netherlands the previous day. Meanwhile, the new interior minister, Ide Anak Agung Gde Agung, had been given responsibility for the welcome reception at Merdeka Palace.[11] And yet, faced with the adoring supporters shouting his name along the route of the cortège, Sukarno could not help but feel elated.[12] Time and time again he rose from the thickly upholstered seat he was sharing with his minister of defence and, with a broad smile on his face, waved to the crowd.

Alex Mendur was among the people on the street when Sukarno's car passed by just inches away from his Leica camera, allowing him to take a photograph up close. Two days later his picture would grace the front page of Surabaya's *De Vrije Pers* newspaper. It showed the president alongside the handsome Hamengkubuwono IX, waving to the crowd, while behind them we see what was perhaps the more interesting aspect of the image: two young men raising their fists, their lips forming the word 'Merdeka!', frozen for eternity.[13] The French Magnum photographer Henri Cartier-Bresson also got his 'decisive moment' as he accompanied Sukarno's car on foot. He had been in the country with his Indonesian-born Eurasian wife, the dancer Ratna Mohini, since 11 October 1949, reporting for *Life* magazine on the final days of the revolution in Jakarta, Yogyakarta, Semarang, Bandung, Bali and the island of Sumatra. He had timed his shot perfectly. The cleverly framed photograph leads our eye to follow the sleek, elongated shape of the dark-painted Packard's front bonnet all the way to its rear, contrasting with the standing figure of the white-suited Sukarno in the back seat, and finally ending with yet another visual surprise in the form of the running-jumping soldier trying his hardest to keep the crowd behind at bay [3].[14]

The motorcade took close to thirty minutes to pass through this celebration – twice the time the route would normally have taken – before arriving at the white portico of Merdeka Palace. Sukarno ascended the steps, which his wife, Fatmawati, later recalled were already filled with countless dignitaries and friends. She and their two young children – Guntur and Megawati, aged five and two respectively – were ushered into the safety of their rooms in the palace, which days before had been cleared of any items that might have reminded the new residents of its colonial past: emblems and decorations, as well as oil paintings depicting former Dutch Governors-General (now kept in the Rijksmuseum in the Netherlands) [4]. They were nearly crushed going up the steps: 'People jostled left and right; everybody wanted to shake our hands.'[15] Among this multitude was Alex Mendur, waiting at the top to photograph the still-beaming Sukarno – this time using his other camera, the Rolleiflex, with its 6 × 6 cm square format – just as the president was walking up. His

[3] President Sukarno is welcomed in Jakarta by an enthusiastic crowd, 28 December 1949, photo by Henri Cartier-Bresson (Magnum)

[4] The portrait of Governor-General Rooseboom being removed from the former Governor-General's Palace, Jakarta, 26 December 1949, photo by Henri Cartier-Bresson (Magnum)

[5] President Sukarno, accompanied by interior minister, Ide Anak Agung Gde Agung, ascending the steps of Merdeka Palace, Jakarta, 28 December 1949, photo by Alex Mendur (IPPHOS)

[6] View of the crowd and photographers at the Merdeka Palace steps, Jakarta, 28 December 1949, photo by Frans 'Nyong' Umbas (IPPHOS)

picture shows Sukarno preceded by a uniformed military adjutant and accompanied by his interior minister, Ide Anak Agung Gde Agung [5].[16]

Across the road, the BFI cameramen recorded the moment when the already-flimsy cordon broke and the sky once again rang with echoing cries of 'Merdeka! Merdeka!'. Thousands of people began to run, jump and trample on the well-manicured garden of the palace. Those who were too slow or too far away to get into the compound occupied the boulevard and the immense square in front of the palace, the now-renamed Medan Merdeka, as Sukarno commenced his speech. The president started off by demanding silence and invoking the grace of Allah (God). Seconds later he aroused the crowds' already strong emotions when he said:

> I have been separated from the people of Jakarta for four times three-hundred-and-sixty-five days that felt like more than forty years ... To my *Marhaen* [proletarian] brothers and sisters; my brethren, the *becak* [pedicab] drivers; my kin, the vegetable-sellers; and even to you my brothers and sisters, the humblest of labourers. I come bearing this greeting to you all! It is with God's blessing that our Red-and-White [flag] now flies from this lawn ... because seventy million Indonesians fought for it with all their might!

The IPPHOS photographer, Frans 'Nyong' Umbas, had taken the astute preparation of perching himself on the balustrade to the right of the palace steps, equipped with the Busch Pressman he had purchased just days earlier for 7,500 Dutch guilders from his drinking companion and close friend, Johnny Waworuntu, photographer for the Regeringsvoorlichtingsdienst (RVD, Government Information Service).[17] With the 6 × 9 cm large-format camera, 'Nyong' only needed to shift his aim very slightly – pointing it towards the square on his left, or to the palace's colonnade at the centre and to his right – to make half a dozen photographs which more than seventy years later would clearly reveal the truth: witnesses had not been exaggerating when they spoke of 'oceans of people' that day. Medan Merdeka was filled to bursting with people [7]. And as he focused his camera below him, there was yet another crowd that had spilled out from the palace's vast portico, steps, and even the cool dark nooks under the shadows of its six tall columns: ministers and military officers; soldiers and boy scouts; diplomats and foreign observers; as well as housewives, workers and students.

All were in the grip of the long-awaited celebration. All stood shoulder to shoulder with every inch of space taken up, save for the one slight gap at the centre – a narrow passage that ran in a straight line from the top of the terrace (where Sukarno now stood) to the bottom of the steps. On the one day when even the most ordinary citizen of Jakarta might consider her or himself the most privileged as they stood within a hair's breadth from the president, this spot – at the heart of the action, less than a metre away from the electrifying, crowd-swaying, Sukarno – was still the best seat in the house. And it was reserved for the few professionals whom the president always seemed to love the most, from youth until his death nearly two decades later: photographers and film cameramen.[18] Raden Mas Soeharto of BFI remembered it well. 'Oh, those were special days', he recounted with a gleam in his eyes, many years later. 'The editors and writers, those he tolerated; but only if they stood behind or to the side of him. Us cameramen and photojournalists he treated as kings, always at the front and up close to him.'[19]

The eighteen or so photojournalists and cameramen that 'Nyong' Umbas captured in his photographs would all experience the full force of Sukarno's bewitching charisma and mastery of the dramatic as he stood there, confident that their lenses would always have a clear line of sight to his every gesture and expression. Johnny Waworuntu chose to position himself close to the now-stationary Packard, where minutes before he had cheekily mounted its hood as Sukarno was about to step out. Standing on the vehicle's wide running board gave the RVD photographer the vantage point he needed to record the moment with his big Speed Graphic camera [6]. 'It got me some incredible photos that day!' he chuckled during his interview in 1996, still amazed at the incredible moment he had witnessed. Not far away from him the lean, immaculately dressed Henri Cartier-Bresson stood on a specially raised platform. In one of 'Nyong' Umbas's pictures he is shown carefully assessing the scene, his hands setting the aperture and shutter buttons of his small Leica camera, looking cool and collected in his pale linen suit even though he had earlier run alongside Sukarno's procession to the palace.[20]

Among these privileged groups were Abdoel Wahab Saleh and Mohammad Sayuti of the Antara news photography bureau, both of whom had hitched a ride on the second of the two presidential aeroplanes that day as well as the Dutch photographer, Willem Boshouwers,[21] who had been covering the transfer of sovereignty in Jakarta on 27 December 1949.[22] And of course there was Alex Mendur, positioned dead centre at the bottom of the steps, perpendicular to where Sukarno was giving his speech, the most senior and perhaps most experienced Indonesian photojournalist that day. Alex was switching back and forth between the two cameras he had brought – now looking down through the square focusing mirror of his Rolleiflex; now picking up his Leica to squint through its small viewfinder, his forefinger hovering lightly over the shutter button, waiting for that one-hundredth-second of a moment that would perfectly encapsulate the historic event. It was similar to the morning of 17 August 1945, when he and his brother, Soemarto Frans Mendur, then the *Asia Raya* daily photographer, had photographed and experienced the hopeful optimism of the beginning of Indonesia's independence. On that occasion, in just a matter of hours, they also had to face the arduous and sometimes tragic realities of defending it when Alex's Japanese bosses at the Domei news agency confiscated and destroyed his negatives of the proclamation.

But that incident had merely strengthened their resolve. And what the Mendur brothers then did (as well their peers who later went on to establish the photography bureau at Antara and the cine-news agency, BFI) refutes the long-held theory that in the days, weeks and months after the proclamation it had been the passionate *pemuda* who first took matters into their own hands. They had been impatient with the slow pace of Sukarno, Hatta and other senior politicians who seemed to take their time deliberating the formation of a functioning government while

[7] View of the crowd on Merdeka Square listening to Sukarno's speech, Jakarta, 28 December 1949, photo by Frans 'Nyong' Umbas (IPPHOS)

Allied fighters were circling the sky, dropping Dutch and Allied paratroopers as well as leaflets about the imminent liberation of the Dutch East Indies.[23] By September 1945, the *pemuda* had organized themselves to take over the radio station, railway depot and various other public facilities from the Japanese.

Yet, we might have no visual proof of their initiatives – of the young women and men riding with their rifles atop cars and trucks captured from the Japanese; of the anti-Dutch and anti-colonial slogans in English painted on government buildings, monuments and statues; or of the trams and trains scrawled with the words 'Property of the Republic of Indonesia' – if the Indonesian photographers and cameramen had not first gone into action weeks before the *pemuda* hatched their plan. They pilfered anything they could get their hands on: cameras, lenses, light bulbs, film, batteries for cinematic equipment, and even printing paper. They raided their former offices to set up the Republic's first photo and cinematic news agencies. On 29 September 1945, Frans Mendur had even led the seizure of the *Asia Raya* and Djawa Shimbun Sha bureaus and printing shop at the Unie building on Molenvliet Oost 8. Two days later, he and several editors and journalists who had worked at *Asia Raya* – B.M. Diah, Yep Kamsar, Dal Bassa Pulungan and Rosihan Anwar among them – published the *Merdeka* newspaper.[24]

AUTONOMOUS

Frans and Alex joined *Merdeka* from the newspaper's first edition on 1 October 1945 until the festive reception on 2 October 1946, when they announced the establishment of the Indonesia Press Photo Service company in partnership with the brothers Justus and Frans 'Nyong' Umbas, their friends from before the war. However, unlike Antara and BFI, which were on the payroll of the Indonesian Minister of Information, IPPHOS had decided to remain autonomous. In contrast to Antara and BFI, which had relocated to Central Java, they maintained two main offices of equal status, making them the most unique among the three *Kiblik* (a play on the word 'Republic', popular among pro- as well as anti-Republican journalists of the time) agencies. Their bureau in the Republican stronghold of Yogyakarta was headed by Soemarto Frans Mendur – a down-to-earth type, conversant in the Javanese language – who by that time had become a favourite of President Sukarno. The other, in Jakarta, was led by Alex and the Umbas brothers who in contrast to Frans Mendur spoke fluent Dutch and whose diplomatic skills, demeanour and love of fashionable Western attire made them particularly well suited to successfully navigate the intricacies of operating in what was then an occupied territory [8, 9].[25]

Certainly, the choice to stay autonomous had not been without its challenges particularly since IPPHOS had been set up in the midst of one of the worst economic crises the country had experienced since its independence. In addition to their embargo, the Dutch had flooded the market with confiscated Japanese reserves – the currency then still used by all pro-Republicans – to create hyperinflation and weaken the Indonesians.

[8] Frans 'Nyong' Umbas, Alex Mendur and Justus Umbas with Alex Mamusung (front left to right) in front of the IPPHOS office at Molenvliet Oost 30, Jakarta 1951

[9] Justus Umbas, Frans 'Nyong' Umbas and Alex Mendur (left to right) at the IPPHOS office at Molenvliet Oost 30, Jakarta, 1948

By October 1946 a litre (approximately 0.8 kg) of rice, which at the start of the revolution had been sold for 25 cents, could not be had for less than 60 guilders.[26] The Mendur and Umbas brothers did not have the benefit of government salaries or operational funds enjoyed by their peers at Antara and BFI. Neither could they rely solely on regular sales or subscriptions of their photographs as most newspapers managed to print no more than four pages of news per day. Many of the *Kiblik* press had been using the remaining wartime paper stock they had seized from the Japanese and, when that finally ran out, had resorted to using cheap *merang* parchment made locally from the pulp of dried rice stalks, too thin and easily torn to be used for printing photographs.

IPPHOS survived in spite of this because of an entrepreneurial attitude, which grew from its founders' long experience and unique yet complementary skill sets. In Jakarta, Alex pulled favours from friends such as the Antara editor, Mochtar Loebis, to help them sell to his network of sympathetic newspapers in India and the Philippines pictures of the revolution and of Sukarno, Hatta and the Sultan Hamengkubuwono (from whom Frans Mendur had already secured creation, duplication and distribution rights for the photographs).[27] The agency also published custom-made albums featuring portraits of Republican leaders, Indonesian troops and other images of the Revolusi, which they openly advertised in newspapers and happily sold to Indonesians as well as to foreign visitors, such as the Dutch politician and *Het Parool* journalist, Frans Goedhart.[28] As evidenced in a couple of examples now kept in the collection of the National Archives in The Hague,[29] IPPHOS even produced photo albums beautifully embellished with hand-drawn lettering and decoration in the Art-Deco style [10]. Because of the lack of proper production and distribution at that time, these albums – with their photographs of leaders and soldiers and important events that projected a sense of authority and legitimacy – might even have served as almanacs, substitutes for official publications of the Indonesian Republic. The Netherlands Forces Intelligence Service (NEFIS) had thought it important to seize many of them during the war.

Alex also convinced some well-known local businessmen, such as Dasaad and the textile magnate Rahman Tamin, to lend them money, with which the shrewd Justus Umbas – a former bookkeeper at the Koninklijke Paketvaart-Maatschappij (KPM), a Dutch Shipping Company based in the Dutch East Indies – took to markets on the outskirts of the city at dawn to purchase vegetables for resale in the capital. 'Nyong' Umbas, would then use some of that profit to bargain for hard-to-get things (such as photographic film or car tyres) on Jakarta's black market. The younger Umbas also had a reputation as a 'fixer'. At the beginning of the revolution he had successfully negotiated the release of Menadonese and Ambonese families wrongly suspected as Dutch agents and taken hostage by local inhabitants in Sukabumi and Bandung for the Kebaktian Rakjat Indonesia Sulawesi (KRIS). Those goods Alex would dispatch to his brother in Yogyakarta – smuggled by Indonesian government officials on the special trains they used when travelling between Yogyakarta and Jakarta for negotiations and meetings – which Frans Mendur then used or sold at a premium in the blockaded city.[30]

But what had truly set IPPHOS apart from Antara and BFI was its willingness and ability to engage with the enemy. This was not limited to providing services for Dutch and British soldiers, who needed to have their photographs made at their studio for identification cards or keepsakes, or sending out one of their photographers to document celebrations of the various Netherlands national day parades or visits from Sinterklaas (Saint Nicholas) to the children's hospital in Jakarta. Alex Mendur had even joined press jaunts organized by the Dutch, for example to document the destruction on the city of Semarang wrought by the bombs of the Indonesian Air Force – which Frans Mendur had photographed in the morning as they took off from Yogyakarta – during the first Dutch military offensive in July 1947. Or the time during the second military offensive in December 1948 when he photographed the mournful Siliwangi Division troops who had to vacate their guerrilla strongholds in West Java as they boarded the Yogyakarta-bound train (whom his younger brother would photograph later that evening, showing the beaming soldiers welcomed at the railway station in the Republican capital by pony-tailed young women and Republican officials).[31]

Such images had led to IPPHOS being described as 'two-faced' and 'treacherous'; charges that all Indonesian journalists who had spent the war years in Jakarta suffered, particularly from their own Republican peers in Yogyakarta. For the three friends who managed IPPHOS in Jakarta it had been especially painful. Their status as triple minorities – Christians, Minahasans (from a region in North Sulawesi often stereotyped as being culturally close to the Dutch) and Dutch-speaking former employees of the colonizers – had led to some hair-raising situations. In 1946, a mob nearly executed Alex Mendur as he was reporting on the battle between Indonesian and the Dutch and British soldiers in Masing, West Java. The locals had been suspicious of Alex simply for his appearance: a fair-skinned, neatly dressed man carrying a camera, who spoke fluent Dutch. Critics tended to forget that the Dutch had also raided the IPPHOS archive in Jakarta during the second military offensive and even put Alex and Justus and both their young sons in jail after they arrested them during the first offensive. The historian Robert Cribb, who had studied this dichotomy, later wrote that this sort of indictment had ignored the personal loyalty professed by people like Alex, Justus and 'Nyong', whose real intentions had always been to defeat the enemy. 'Acting passively caused the Dutch to continually second-guess themselves while working for them meant infiltrating the enemy.'[32]

In the long run, the strategy paid off thanks to the nearly 250,000 photographs that IPPHOS managed to create between 1945 and 1949, which have since formed the canon of the iconography of the Indonesian revolution. The collection is important because of its size; because it became the only surviving visual archive to survive from the war of independence (Antara and BFI had lost theirs, seized by the Dutch during their second military offensive in 1948); and finally, because the photographers had been able to capture the rich nuances of life during wartime from both sides of the divide.[33] The IPPHOS photographers not only documented many of the events and incidents that are now considered important milestones in the history of the Indonesian revolution – the proclamation of

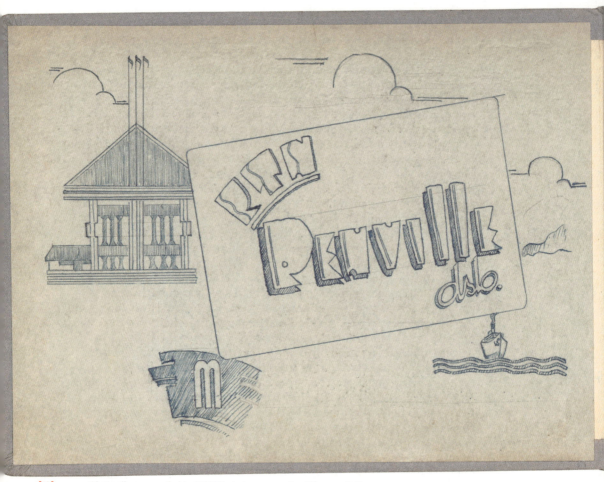

[10] Photo album compiled by IPPHOS photo agency, about the negotiations aboard the USS *Renville*, 1947/1948

Gambar Atas:

Kedua Consul tiba dilapangan Neguwo. Menteri Negara S.P. Hamengku Buwono berdjabatan tangan dengan Consul djendral Rorentjis ditangga tampak cons. Dj. Australia.

Gambar Atas:

Kedua consul meninggalkan lapangan bersama Wk. Perdana Menteri Setiadjit dan menteri negara Hamengku Buwono.

Gambar bah:

Kedua Consul diterima oleh P.J.M. Presiden didjalan. Dari kiri kekanan: P.M. Mr. Amir Sjarifoedin, Consul djendral Perentjis, P.J.M. Presiden dan Consul Australia Eton.

independence in 1945, the burning of the city of Bandung by retreating Indonesian army and militias in 1946, the recapture of Yogyakarta in 1949 – but also the often surprisingly normal daily lives of the Indonesians, Dutch, Eurasians and Chinese, who continued to go to work, study, watch movies, attend dances, play sports and even socialize with one another. IPPHOS had shown how throughout the war both the Indonesians and the Dutch had been capable of inflicting the same violence and atrocities as well as experiencing the same suffering, kindness, joy and lust for life.

FULL CIRCLE

In the grand narrative of Indonesia's historiography, it follows that President Sukarno's return to Jakarta on 28 December 1949 has always been and continues to be treated as the closing of the chapter of the four and a half years of the *revolusi*, its description and images always chronologically placed in the last few pages of history books and photo albums. It did mark the end of many things: the dispersal of the Antara photographers, some of whom, like Sayuti, would join the country's ministry of information photo bureau, led by the former RVD photographer, Johnny Waworuntu. Or the merging of BFI into the Perusahaan Film Negara (PFN, the state film company) where Wahab would later serve as still-cameraman.[34] Although in his speech Sukarno had graciously acknowledged Dutch goodwill in the transfer of power, he and the Indonesian people have largely, and perhaps intentionally, chosen to forget about this day. The nation's stance had always been clear: the celebration of 28 December 1949, and the parallel handover of sovereignty on the previous day, had been mere formalities. No piece of paper could substitute for the fact that Indonesia had always been free and established since Sukarno and Hatta proclaimed its independence on 17 August 1945.

For Alex Mendur, however, it was less about the end of a chapter than about coming full circle from that day, when he had stood in the front garden of Jalan Pegangsaan Timur 56, his right index finger clicking the shutter button of his Leica as Sukarno – solemn, restrained, exhausted, his voice raspy – announced the terse, matter-of-fact words of the proclamation that finally set the nation free, only to have his photograph taken away, obliterated, for eternity. Today, once again he stood in front of Sukarno, his eyes squinting through the small viewfinder, his finger clicking the button of his Leica camera at the moment when the Indonesian president – his left fist resting on his hip and the index finger of his right hand raised to the sky; bold, confident and exuberant – spoke his final words to the crowd [11], this time in his famously barking thunderous voice:

'Sekali merdeka, tetap merdeka!' (Once free, always free!)

[11] President Sukarno giving his speech on the steps of Merdeka Palace, Jakarta, 28 December 1949, photo by Alex Mendur (IPPHOS)

NOTES

FACES OF THE REVOLUTION
(PP. 8–17)

1. Anouk Mansfeld, 'Een vriendenboekje als oorlogsbuit. Koloniaal erfgoed in de Bijzondere Collecties in Leiden', *Indische letteren* 36 (2021), no. 3, pp. 151–162, esp. 155.
2. Ibid., p. 162.
3. Ibid., p. 156.
4. Executions of prisoners were in contravention of the prevailing laws of war. The killing of prisoners by Dutch military personnel took place with impunity and on a large scale. See Rémy Limpach, *De brandende kampongs van generaal Spoor*, Amsterdam 2016, pp. 439–449.
5. Mansfeld 2021 (note 1), p. 158
6. An Advisory Commission on National Policy on Colonial Collections was established in the Netherlands in 2019. On 7 October 2020, commission chair Lilian Gonçalves-Ho Kang You presented the report *Koloniale Collecties en Erkenning van Onrecht* (Colonial Collections and Recognition of Injustice) to minister Ingrid van Engelshoven (OCW).
7. Mansfeld 2021 (note 1), p. 158.
8. The reference 'the blinding light of the revolution' is borrowed from William H. Frederick, 'Weerspiegelingen in stromend water. Indonesische herinneringen aan de oorlog en Japanners', in Remco Raben (ed.), *Beelden van de Japanse bezetting. Persoonlijke getuigenissen en publieke beeldvorming in Indonesië, Japan en Nederland*, Zwolle 1999, pp. 16–35.
9. More or less recent exceptions include the exhibitions *Beyond the Dutch* at the Centraal Museum, Utrecht (2009–2010), and *Gebroeders Djaya. Revolusi in het Stedelijk* at the Stedelijk Museum, Amsterdam (2018).
10. You could say that the choice for this photo as the image for the exhibition and book demonstrates that the Rijksmuseum has a certain penchant for 'radical chic', the term coined by Tom Wolfe in a 1970 essay about the infatuation of the upper classes with revolutionary, often leftist, popular movements.
11. See Remco Raben, 'The Spirit of the Revolusi', pp. 18–49, in this book.
12. See David van Reybrouck, *Revolusi. Indonesië en het ontstaan van de moderne wereld*, Amsterdam 2020, p. 22. The exhibition *Nederlanders, Japanners, Indonesiërs. De Japanse bezetting van Nederlands-Indië herinnerd* and the accompanying publication (see Raben 1999, note 8), which the Rijksmuseum made in 1999 in collaboration with the Netherlands Institute for War, Holocaust and Genocide Studies (NIOD), can be seen as an exception to the rule. The exhibition explicitly focused on examining Japanese and Indonesian perspectives, as well as Dutch, on the years of the Japanese occupation of Indonesia, 1942–1945.
13. One example of the continuation of this unilateral viewpoint was unintentionally provided in the newspaper *de Volkskrant* of 28 November 2020, in an interview with David van Reybrouck, author of the book *Revolusi* (Van Reybrouck 2020, note 12). The title of the article is 'In Indonesië was Nederland kortzichtig en hardvochtig' (In Indonesia the Netherlands was short-sighted and cold-hearted). The accompanying illustration seemed to underscore that the picture editors of *de Volkskrant* suffered from the same myopia. In this photo by a Dutch photographer from the Military Contacts Service, Dutch soldiers, some laughing at the photographer, hold six Indonesians (members of the TNI, according to the caption) sitting on the ground with their hands on their heads at gunpoint. The Indonesians in the photo, as a result of this picture they did not want, are placed in a position that is entirely humiliating. The placement of the photo, with a proper explanation of its origin, is short-sighted and cold-hearted.
14. The title is taken from a verse in the poem 'Semangat' (Spirit, 1943) by the poet Chairil Anwar (1922–1949).

THE SPIRIT OF THE REVOLUSI
(PP. 18–49)

1. 'Surat kepertjajaan Gelanggang', *Siasat*, 22 October 1950; Jennifer Lindsay, 'Heirs to World Culture. An Introduction', in Jennifer Lindsay and Maya H.T. Liem (eds.), *Heirs to World Culture. Being Indonesian 1950–1965*, Leiden 2012, pp. 1–27, esp. p. 10.
2. The first use of this term was probably by Rosihan Anwar in his article 'Angkatan 45 buat martabat manusia', *Siasat*, 26 December 1948. Martina Heinschke, 'Between Gelanggang and Lekra. Pramoedya's Developing Literary Concepts', *Indonesia* 61 (April 1996), pp. 145–169, esp. p. 147.
3. Chairil Anwar, *The Voice of the Night. Complete Poetry and Prose of Chairil Anwar* (trans. Burton Raffel), Athens (OH) 1993, pp. 74–76.
4. Chairil Anwar, 'Hoppla!!' (trans. Burton Raffel), *Pembangoenan* 1 (10 December 1945), p. 13; see also Hendrik M.J. Maier, *We Are Playing Relatives. A Survey of Malay Writing*, Leiden 2004, pp. 286–287.
5. More than an handful of spectators, as has been claimed, e.g. by David van Reybrouck in *Revolusi. Indonesië en het ontstaan van de moderne wereld*, Amsterdam 2020, p. 289.
6. Imrad Idris et al. (eds.), *Herinneringen aan 17 Augustus 1945. Oud-leerlingen van de Koning Willem III School (Batavia) aan het woord*, Jakarta 2000, p. 2.
7. Des Alwi and Barbara S. Harvey (eds.), *Friends and Exiles. A Memoir of the Nutmeg Isles and the Indonesian Nationalist Movement*, Ithaca (NY) 2008, pp. 156–157; H. Untung Rahardjo (ed.), *Ketika Rakjat Bantul membela Republik*, Bantul 2008, p. 4.
8. Minarsih Wiranatakusuma, diary, personal collection.
9. Anton Lucas, *One Soul One Struggle. Region and Revolution in Indonesia*, Sydney 1991, p. 67; Else Ensering, 'Banten in Times of Revolution', *Archipel* 50 (1995) pp. 131–164.
10. Remco Raben, 'Decolonization and the Roots of Democracy', in Alfred W. McCoy, Josep M. Pradera and Stephen Jacobson (eds.), *Endless Empire. Spain's Retreat, Europe's Eclipse, America's Decline*, Maddison

2012, pp. 276–291, esp. p. 286.

11 Elien Utrecht, *Twee zijden van een waterscheiding. Herinneringen aan Indonesië voor en na de onafhankelijkheid*, Amsterdam 1991, p. 75.

12 Ethan Mark, *Japan's Occupation of Java in the Second World War. A Transnational History*, London 2018.

13 Soewarsih Djojopuspito, *Buiten het gareel*, Utrecht 1940. See also Harry A. Poeze, 'Political Intelligence in the Netherlands Indies', in Robert Cribb (ed.), *The Late Colonial State in Indonesia. Political and Economic Foundations of the Netherlands Indies 1880–1942*, Leiden 1994, pp. 229–245; Marieke Bloembergen, *De geschiedenis van de politie in Nederlands-Indië. Uit zorg en angst*, Amsterdam 2009.

14 E.B. Locher-Scholten, 'De Stuw, tijdstekening en teken des tijds', *Tijdschrift voor geschiedenis* 84 (1971) pp. 36–65.

15 Susan Blackburn, *Women and the State in Modern Indonesia*, Cambridge 2004, p. 149.

16 Anton Lucas and Robert Cribb, 'Women's Roles in the Indonesian Revolution. Some Historical Reflections', in Taufik Abdullah (ed.), *The Heartbeat of Indonesian Revolution*, Jakarta 1997, pp. 70–93, esp. pp. 75–76.

17 Srikandi was the name of a corps of female fighters. Ans M. Gommers-Dekker, *Indonesische volksliederen. Een bijdrage aan de nationale identiteit*, Utrecht 2011, p. 81.

18 Sri Margono, 'Corat-coret revolusi. Seniman dalam Revolusi Indonesia di Yogyakarta', in *Gelora di Tanah Raja. Yogyakarta pada masa revolusi 1945–1949*, Yogyakarta 2017, pp. 45–72.

19 Agus Dermawan T., *Surga kemelut pelukis Hendra. Dari pengantin revolusi sampai terali besi*, Jakarta 2018, pp. 28–29.

20 A.D. Pirous, 'Sejarah Poster Sebagai Alat Propaganda Perjuangan Di Indonesia', *Jurnal Ilmu Desain, FSRD-ITB* 1 (2006), no. 3, pp. 139–158, esp. p. 141.

21 Letter from the chairman of the commission-general, W. Schermerhorn, to the minister of overseas territories, J. Jonkman, 17 July 1947, in S.L. van der Wal, P.J. Drooglever and M.J.B. Schouten (eds.), *Officiële bescheiden betreffende de Nederlands-Indonesische betrekkingen 1945–1950 – deel 9. 21 mei–20 juli 1947*, The Hague 1981, p. 707.

22 Letter from Van Mook to the minister of overseas territories, J. Jonkman, 8 August 1947, in P.J. Drooglever and M.J.B. Schouten (eds.), *Officiële bescheiden betreffende de Nederlands- Indonesische betrekkingen 1945–1950, deel 10. 21 juli–31 augustus 1947*, The Hague 1982, p. 294.

23 Pieter 't Hoen [=Frans Goedhart], *Terug uit Djokja*, Amsterdam, n.d. [1947], passim and p. 5; Madelon de Keizer, *Frans Goedhart. Journalist en politicus (1904–1990). Een biografie*, Amsterdam 2012, p. 181.

24 Suhartono et al., *Parlemen desa. Dinamika DPR kalurahan dan DPRK-Gotong, Royong*, Yogyakarta 2000, pp. 60–61 and 67.

25 The Hague, National Archives, Archief Mariniersbrigade Nederlands-Indië: interview with Pak Sudardji, dusun Wates Lor, 24 August 2019, 2.13.126, inv. no. 637.

26 The exact number of victims in Rawagede is a controversial matter. Indonesian sources report 431 killed; Dutch accounts give a much lower number. The figures for South Sulawesi are also uncertain. Willem IJzereef, *De Zuid-Celebes affaire. Kapitein Westerling en de standrechtelijke executies*, Dieren 1984, pp. 140–141; Manon van den Brekel, *Massa-executies op Sulawesi. Hoe Nederland wegkwam met moord in Indonesië*, Zutphen 2017, p. 18.

27 Rémy Limpach, *De brandende kampongs van generaal Spoor*, Amsterdam 2016.

28 The long-established estimate is 100,000, a figure based on official records of the Dutch military and civilian authorities. According to Christiaan Harinck, Nico van Horn and Bart Luttikhuis, 'Wie telt de Indonesische doden?', *De Groene Amsterdammer*, 26 July 2017, this is at the lower end of the plausible range. See www.groene.nl/artikel/wie-telt-de-indonesische-doden (consulted on 17 August 2021).

29 G.C. Zijlmans, *Eindstrijd en ondergang van de Indische bestuursdienst. Het corps binnenlands bestuur op Java 1945–1950*, Amsterdam/Dieren 1985, p. 213.

30 Remco Raben and Peter Romijn, *Talen van geweld. Stilte, informatie en misleiding in de Indonesische onafhankelijkheidsstrijd, 1945–1949*, Amsterdam 2022 (forthcoming).

31 Jeroen Kemperman, 'De slachtoffers van de Bersiap', niod bibliotheek.blogspot.com/2014/05/de-slachtoffers-van-de-bersiap_16.html (consulted on 17 August 2021). Higher figures are extremely speculative and undocumented. See H.T. Bussemaker, *Bersiap! Opstand in het paradijs. De Bersiap-periode op Java en in Sumatra 1945–1946*, Zutphen 2005, p. 342; Robert Cribb, 'The Brief Genocide of Eurasians in Indonesia, 1945/46', in A. Dirk Moses (ed.), *Empire, Colony, Genocide. Conquest, Occupation, and Subaltern Resistance in World History*, New York 2008, pp. 424–436, esp. p. 432; William H. Frederick, 'The Killing of Dutch and Eurasians in Indonesia's National Revolution (1945–49). A "Brief Genocide" Reconsidered', *Journal of Genocide Research* 14 (2012), no. 3/4, pp. 359–380, esp. p. 369.

32 See for instance Abdul Wahid, 'The Untold Story of the Surabaya Battle of 1945', *The Jakarta Post*, 12 November 2013.

33 Y.B. Mangunwijaya, *Burung-burung manyar*, Jakarta 1981; Iksaka Banu, *Semua untuk Hindia*, Jakarta 1914.

34 Geoffrey Robinson, *The Dark Side of Paradise. Political Violence in Bali*, Ithaca/London 1995, pp. 122–127.

35 See e.g. Oei Hiem Hwie, *Memoar Oei Hiem Hwie. Dari pulau Buru sampai Medayu Agung*, n.p. (Wastu Lanas Grafika) 2015, pp. 49–53.

36 The name Ikada is not Japanese in origin but stands for Ikatan Atletik Djakarta (Jakarta Athletic Bond), which managed an athletics track in the square.

37 On Ratna Mohini's background, see Kunang Helmi, 'Ratna Cartier-Bresson. A Fragmented Portrait', *Archipel* 54 (1997), pp. 253–268.

38 Video, 'Pidato Presiden Soekarno 28 Desember 1949', www.youtube.com/watch?v=PbRttU1dccA (consulted on 6 July 2021, transcript by Amir Sidharta).

39 Sita van Bemmelen and Remco Raben (eds.), *Antara daerah dan negara. Indonesia tahun 1950-an*, Jakarta 2011.

40 Benedict Anderson, *Imagined Communities. Reflections on the Origin and Spread of Nationalism*, London/New York 2006, p. xiv.
41 Huw Bennett and Peter Romijn, '"Liever geen onderzoek". Hoe schandalen over koloniaal geweld in de Britse en Nederlandse politiek onschadelijk gemaakt konden worden (1945–1960)', *BMGN – Low Countries Historical Review* 135 (2020), no. 2, pp. 52–71.
42 A.H. Nasution, *Sekitar perang kemerdekaan Indonesia*, 11 vols., Bandung 1977–1979.
43 One favourable exception is Harry A. Poeze's impressive study, *Verguisd en vergeten. Tan Malaka, de linkse beweging en de Indonesische Revolutie, 1945–1949*, 3 vols., Leiden 2007.
44 Michael Joseph Karabinos, 'Displaced Archives, Displaced History. Recovering the Seized Archives of Indonesia', *Bijdragen tot de Taal-, Land- en Volkenkunde* 169 (2013), pp. 279–294.

PROKLAMASI
(PP. 50–75)

1 Soemarto F. Mendur, 'Kesaksian Frans Mendur Ketika Detik-Detik Proklamasi, 17 Agustus 1945 Di Jalan Pegangsaan Timur No. 56', *IPPHOS Report*, Jakarta 1962, unpag.
2 Cindy Adams, *Bung Karno Penyambung Lidah Rakjat Indonesia*, Yogyakarta 2007, pp. 267–268.
3 Nidjo Sandjojo, *Abdul Latief Hendraningrat*, Jakarta 2011, pp. 162–163.
4 Shigeru Sato, 'The PETA', in Peter Post et al., *The Encyclopedia of Indonesia in the Pacific War*, Leiden 2010, p. 134.
5 David Jenkins, 'Soeharto and the Japanese Occupation', *Indonesia* 88 (2009–2010), p. 61; John Lee, '"A Spirit of Destruction". The Origins of the Indonesian Military's Institutional Culture', Ithaca (NY) (master's thesis Correll University) p. 30.
6 Sato 2010 (note 4), pp. 133, 140–141. See also Edy Burhan Arifin, 'Pemberontakan Tentara Peta di Blitar: Sebuah Kesaksian Sejarah', in *PETA Tentara Sukarela Pembela Tanah Air Di Jawa Dan Sumatera 1942–1945*, Jakarta 1996, pp. 163–174, and Suwondo et al., 'Peristiwa Pemberontakan Peta di Cileunca-Pangalengan, Bandung Selatan, Jawa Barat', in ibid., pp. 175–191.
7 Sandjojo 2011 (note 3), p. 161. The Japanese 16th Army provided its PETA battalions with about 40% of the weapons they possessed. In Java these comprised 17,218 rifles, 687 heavy machine guns and 93 mortars, mostly originating from those they confiscated from surrendered KNIL troops. See Sato 2010 (note 4), pp. 132, 139, and Philip Jowett and Stephen Walsh, *Japan's Asian Allies 1941–45*, London 2020, p. 23. For a list of Japanese weapons terminology see also G.L. Rottman, *Japanese Army in World War II. The South Pacific and New Guinea, 1942–43*, London 2013, pp. 35–36. Unfortunately, Hendraningrat did not specify the type of rifles they had managed to steal from their garrison though most probably it would have been the KNIL's *Mannlicher M1895 Geweer carbines*, not the *Arisaka* rifles of the Japanese Imperial Army, as these were the ones they provided for their *Heiho* and PETA battalions.
8 Mendur 1962 (note 1).
9 Wiwi Kuswiah, *Alexius Impurung Mendur (Alex Mendur)*, Jakarta 1986, p. 22.
10 Ibid., pp. 16–17; Debra H. Yatim, *Kembara Tiada Berakhir, Herawati Diah Berkisah*, Jakarta 2021 (original ed. 1993), p. 56; Ethan Mark, *Japan's Occupation of Java in the Second World War. A Transnational History*, London 2018, pp. 147, 154.
11 Mohammad Sayuti and Abdoel Kadir Said, former photographers at Domei (1943–1945) and Antara (1945–1949), interview by the author, 28 September 1996.
12 Hatta described it as a special gift because the announcement was made by Field Marshal Hisaichi Terauchi, Commander of the Southern Expeditionary Army Group in Dalat on 12 August, which happened to be his own 43rd birthday, Mohammad Hatta, *Memoir*, Jakarta 1982 (original ed. 1979), p. 437.
13 Sukarno, 'Indonesia Pasti Merdeka, Sebeloem Djagoeng Berboenga', *Tjahaja* daily (Bandung), 15 August 1945, p. 1.
14 Dal B. Pulungan, 'Soeasana Sekitar Proklamasi Kemerdekaan Indonesia Di Pegangsaan Timoer', in *Merdeka* (Independence Special), Jakarta 1946, p. 70.
15 Arifin 1996 (note 6), pp. 72–73.
16 Minarsih Soedarpo-Wiranatakoesoema in Imrad Idris (ed.), *Aku Ingat ... Rasa dan Tindak Siswa Sekolah Kolonial di Awal Merdeka Bangsa*, Jakarta 1996, p. 44; Amir Pamoentjak in ibid., p. 120.
17 Soemarto Frans Mendur's house was at Jalan Petodjo Oedik VII no. 2, Jakarta; Titin Mendur, daughter of Soemarto Frans Mendur, interview by the author, 11 November 2014; S.F. Mendur, 'Questionnaire Sekitar Proklamasi Kemerdekaan', Jakarta, 10 October 1970, Frans Mendur family archive, Jakarta.
18 A.P. Audretsch, 'Kesaksian Shigetada Nishijima: Pemberontakan Melawan Jepang?', in *Seputar Proklamasi Kemerdekaan: Kesaksian, Penyiaran, Dan Keterlibatan Jepang*, Jakarta 2015, p. 221; Adolf Heuken, *Atlas Sejarah Jakarta*, Jakarta 2014, pp. 42–43.
19 Etty Rachman in Idris 1996 (note 16), p. 1.
20 Sudiro, 'Saat-Saat Proklamasi Sangat Mendebarkan', in Hendri F. Isnaeni (ed.), *Seputar Proklamasi Kemerdekaan: Kesaksian, Penyiaran, Dan Keterlibatan Jepang*, Jakarta 2015, p. 74.
21 Soebagijo I. Notodijoyo, *S.K. Trimurti Wanita Pengabdi Bangsa*, Jakarta 1985, pp. 30–33, 60–61.
22 B.E. Matindas and Bert Supit, *Ventje Sumual Pemimpin Yang Menatap Hanya Ke Depan*, Jakarta 1998, pp. 27, 29–32.
23 S.K. Trimurti, 'Iuranku Bagi Ibu Pertiwi', in *Sumbangsihku Bagi Ibu Pertiwi, Kumpulan Pengalaman Dan Pemikiran, Buku V*, Jakarta 1985, pp. 74–75.
24 The would-be revolutionaries were also appeased by the news that Sukarno and Hatta would proclaim independence that very morning.
25 Sayuti Melik, 'Kenangan Pribadi Sekitar Proklamasi: Menyongsong Kemerdekaan Dari Balik Terali Penjara', in *Seputar Proklamasi Kemerdekaan: Kesaksian, Penyiaran, Dan Keterlibatan Jepang*, Jakarta

25 2015, p. 100; Hendri F. Isnaeni, *In 17-8-45 Fakta, Drama, Misteri*, Jakarta 2015, p. 199.
26 Sandjojo 2011 (note 3), p. 164; R.H.A.A D Tandikusumah in Idris 1996 (note 16), p. 232.
27 R.M.A. Soetrisno Mangoendihardjo in Idris 1996 (note 16), pp. 139–141.
28 O.E. Engelen, *Lahirnya Satu Bangsa dan Negara*, Depok 1997, p. 86.
29 Audretsch 2015 (note 18), p. 221; Lambert Giebels, *Soekarno Biografi 1901–1950*, Jakarta 2001, p. 356.
30 Toeti Kakiailatu, *B.M. Diah Wartawan Serba Bisa*, Jakarta 1997, pp. 119–121.
31 Ibid.
32 Hatta 1982 (note 12), p. 452.
33 The PETA soldiers were led by *shodan-cho* Singgih from the same Jaga Monyet Battalion as acting *daidan-cho* Hendraningrat. The Japanese purposely kept their PETA battalions separate to prevent them from conspiring with one another. PETA also consisted of many factions – some of which were even loyal to the Japanese – hence Hendraningrat's ignorance about Singgih's involvement in the 'kidnapping' of Sukarno and Hatta. See Sandjojo 2011 (note 3), p. 155. See also Sidik Kertapati, *Sekitar Proklamasi 17 Agustus 1945*, Jakarta 2000, pp. 80–81.
34 Fatmawati Sukarno, *Catatan Kecil Bersama Bung Karno*, Jakarta 1978, p. 24.
35 Hatta 1982 (note 12), p. 450.
36 Adams 2007 (note 2), p. 332.
37 Sudiro, *Pengalaman Saya Sekitar 17 Agustus 1945*, Jakarta 1994, pp. 31–44.
38 Isnaeni 2015 (note 25), pp. 188–190. The sound men were hired by Wilopo, a staff member at the Jakarta municipality under deputy mayor Suwiryo (who gave one of the speeches during the proclamation of independence), and Njonoprawoto, a lecturer at the Perguruan Rakjat (People's School) an adult education institute under the sponsorship of the Partai Nasional Indonesia (Indonesian National Party).
39 Soerasto Soerjokoesoemo in Idris 1996 (note 16), p. 25.
40 Aboe B. Loebis, *Kilas balik revolusi: kenangan, pelaku dan saksi*, Depok 1992, p. 96.

41 Sudiro recalled that some people had initially thought Suroto to be an agent from the *Kempeitai*.
42 A.B. Lapian, *Semangat 45 Dalam Rekaman Gambar IPPHOS*, Jakarta 1985, pp. 14–17.
43 Mendur 1962 (note 1).
44 Etty Rachman in Idris 1996 (note 16), p. 1.
45 Pulungan 1946 (note 14), p. 70.
46 Onghokham, *Runtuhnya Hindia Belanda*, Jakarta 1989, p. 64.
47 The Political Intelligence Bureau, part of the colonial police and main security agency, was set up in 1916 until its disbandment in 1945.
48 By the mid-1960s Mendur got caught up in Sukarno's anti-West movement and demonstrations. After the so-called failed communist coup of 1965 he was branded a leftist, which ultimately destroyed his reputation until his death in 1971. See Soebagijo I. Notodidjoyo, *Jagat Wartawan Indonesia*, Jakarta 1981, p. 124.
49 J. Mendur, *Riwayat Hidup Singkat*, Frans Mendur family archive, Jakarta 1986.
50 Notodijoyo 1981 (note 48), p. 124.
51 Titin Mendur 2014 (note 17).
52 Kuswiah 1986 (note 9), p. 7.
53 Titin Mendur 2014 (note 17).
54 Notodijoyo 1981 (note 48), p. 121.
55 Pramoedya A. Toer, *Nyanyi Sunyi Seorang Bisu II*, Jakarta 1997, p. 115.
56 Jowett and Walsh 2020 (note 7), p. 46.
57 Mangoendihardjo recalled he only realized the gravity of the situation when the flag ceremony did not include the Japanese Hinomaru. The second of these pictures would be dragged into controversy 30 years later when Suharto's New Order regime reproduced the image with half of Sukarno's body cropped out in the book, *30 Years of Indonesia's Independence*. This was a period when Sukarno and all things related to him were being suppressed by the regime because of his alleged connection to the so-called '30 September' communist coup of 1965.
58 Jusuf-Wirjosapoetro in Idris 1996 (note 16), p. 54; Hatta 1982 (note 12), p. 456.
59 Giebels 2001 (note 29), p. 359.
60 The officers – surrounded by angry-looking Barisan Pelopor – had quickly left after Sukarno had told

them they had already completed the proclamation: Mendur 1962 (note 1); Sudiro 2015 (note 20), p. 71.
61 Pulungan 1946 (note 14), p. 71.
62 Kuswiah 1986 (note 9), p. 123.
63 Titin Mendur 2014 (note 17).
64 The Galeri Foto Jurnalistik Antara (GFJA) team surveyed the IPPHOS collection from 1 September 1997 to 1 February 1998.
65 The same two photographs were reproduced in the *Lukisan Revolusi* of 1949 and other photo albums over the next decades, including the commemorative *50 Years of Indonesia's Independence* of 1995.
66 The two images are of Suwiryo giving his speech and of Fatmawati Sukarno standing near S.K. Trimurti at the start of the flag ceremony. See Lapian 1985 (note 42), pp. 20–21, 24–25.
67 That survey was the first ever conducted by an external organization. The three photographs were of Sukarno reading the proclamation, of Hendraningrat raising the flag, and another of Fatmawati Sukarno standing near S.K. Trimurti at the start of the flag ceremony.
68 Kristupa Saragih, 'Pejuang Bersenjatakan Kamera', *Kompas.com*, 17 August 2010. https://nasional.kompas.com/read/2010/08/17/17314678/pejuang.bersenjatakan.kamera?page=all (consulted on 9 August 2021).
69 Sandjojo 2011, pp. 167–168.
70 Oscar Motuloh, *70th Histori Masa Depan*, Jakarta (Galeri Foto Jurnalistik Antara) 2015, pp. 24, 28–39.
71 Sadly, they did not keep the purchase records.
72 IPPHOS officially sold its collection to the National Archive of the Republic of Indonesia (ANRI), licensed the digitized version of a select number of photographs to the Antara News Agency Photo Bureau, and somehow also managed to sell an undisclosed number of negatives to the art dealer and collector Binton Nadapdap in Depok, West Java. See Yudhi Soerjoatmodjo, *IPPHOS Remastered*, Jakarta (Galeri Foto Jurnalistik Antara) 2013, p. 10.

FREEDOM THE GLORY OF ANY NATION (PP. 76–97)

1. Interview with Affandi by the Australian historian Robert Cribb, Yogyakarta, 8 November 1982, The Hague, National Archives, 'Losse aanwinsten vanaf 1980', 2.22.06, inv. no. 188, interviews R. Cribb 1978–1984. My thanks to Remco Raben for pointing out this interview.
2. Robert Cribb, *Gangsters and Revolutionaries. The Jakarta People's Militia and the Indonesian Revolution 1945–1949*, Singapore 2009, pp. 60–61.
3. Before the war, the Menteng 31 building was Hotel Schomper I, owned by L.C. Schomper. During the Japanese occupation, the hotel was used as a headquarters for youth groups. For more details, see A.M. Hanafi, *Menteng 31. Markas Pemuda Revolusioner Angkatan 45. Membangun Jembatan Dua Angkatan*, Jakarta 1996.
4. Ibid., pp. 59–60.
5. Dajal is a figure from Islamic eschatology, a false messiah.
6. Sidik Kertapati, *Sekitar Proklamasi 17 Agustus 1945*, Jakarta 2000, pp. 99–100.
7. Ahmad Subardjo Djoyoadisuryo, *Kesadaran Nasional. Sebuah Otobiografi*, Jakarta 1978, p. 359.
8. Benedict R.O'G. Anderson, *Java in a Time of Revolution. Occupation and Resistance 1944–1946*, Jakarta 2006, pp. 270–277.
9. Djoyoadisuryo 1978 (note 7), p. 361.
10. Harry A. Poeze, *Tan Malaka, Gerakan Kiri dan Revolusi Indonesia, deel 1. Agustus 1945–Maret 1946*, Jakarta 2008, p. 3.
11. Ibid., p. 53.
12. Ibid., p. 192.
13. Ibid., p. 198.
14. Tan Malaka, *Moeslihat*, Jakarta 2005 [1st ed. 1945].
15. Ibid.
16. Poeze 2008 (note 10), pp. 219–220.
17. Kees Snoek, 'Sjahrir (1909–1966), Strijder in een overgangstijd. Een biografische schets', in Sjahrir, *Sjahrir. Wissel op de toekomst. Brieven van de Indonesische nationalist aan zijn Hollandse geliefde*, Kees Snoek (ed.), Amsterdam 2021, pp. 169–247, esp. pp. 230–231.
18. George McTurnan Kahin, *Nationalism and Revolution in Indonesia*, Ithaca (NY) 2003, p. 147.
19. Sjahrir, *Perdjoeangan Kita*, 1945, see https://serbasejarah.files.wordpress.com/2014/12/sutan-sjahrir-perjoeangan-kita-libre.pdf (consulted on 25 March 2021).
20. Sjahrir, *Onze strijd*, Amsterdam 1946.
21. Snoek 2021 (note 17), p. 181.
22. *Merdeka*, 10 November 1945. See also Ben Anderson, *Revoloesi Pemoeda. Pendudukan Jepang dan Perlawanan di Jawa 1944–1946*, Jakarta 1988, pp. 219–230.
23. Rosihan Anwar, *Kisah-Kisah Jakarta Setelah Proklamasi*, Jakarta 1977, p. 70.
24. Sjahrir 1946 (note 20), p. 20.
25. Ibid., p. 14
26. Snoek 2021 (note 17), p. 235.

THE SIGNAL TO RISE UP (PP. 98–119)

1. Details about Letty Kwee and her family are taken from the baby book now in the possession of her family, which she kept from 12 August 1945, supplemented with oral information from Kwee Tjoe Houw, Letty Kwee's son.
2. Roger Cribb, *Gangsters and Revolutionaries. The Jakarta People's Militia and the Indonesian Revolution 1945–1949*, Singapore 2009, p. 66.
3. Ibid., pp. 64–65.
4. The first film in which the sequence occurs is a report entitled *Werkzaamheden Japanse krijgsgevangenen*. There is no sound. See https://zoeken.beeldengeluid.nl/program/urn:vme:default:program:2101608040030628931 (with thanks to Gerda Jansen Hendriks).
5. Mary Somers Heidhues, 'Anti-Chinese Violence in Java during the Indonesian Revolution, 1945–1949', in Bart Luttikhuis and A. Dirk Moses (eds.), *Colonial Counterinsurgency and Mass Violence. The Dutch Empire in Indonesia*, London/New York 2014, pp. 155–175, esp. p. 155.
6. Ibid., p. 170.
7. Rémy Limpach, *De brandende kampongs van generaal Spoor*, Amsterdam 2016, pp. 215–225.
8. Ibid., p. 156.
9. Margaret Leidelmeijer (comp. and ed.), *Het verhaal van Indië*, Arnhem s.a., p. 55.
10. Letter from Peu de Loos to her parents, Batavia, 3 December 1945, private archive.
11. Cribb 2009 (note 2), p. 63.
12. Ibid.
13. Louis Zweers, *Buit. De roof van Nederlands-Indisch erfgoed 1942–1950*, Amsterdam 2020, pp. 151 ff.
14. The names Uhlenbusch and Anna Sofia are spelt in different ways in the historical documents known to us. Here we have chosen to follow the spelling given in the 'Oorlogsgravenstichting' (War Graves Foundation) website: oorlogsgravenstichting.nl/persoon/200809/anna-sofia-uhlenbusch (consulted on 3 October 2021).
15. G. Roger Knight, 'Death in Slawi. The "Sugar Factory Murders". Ethnicity, Conflicted Loyalties and the Context of Violence in the Early Revolution in Indonesia, October 1945', *Itinerario* 41 (2017), no. 3, pp. 606–626, esp. pp. 609–617.
16. Ibid., p. 618.
17. See Remco Raben, 'The Spirit of the Revolusi' in this book, p. 41.
18. For more about the term *Bersiap*, see Harry A. Poeze, 'Walking the Tightrope. Internal Indonesian Conflict, 1945–1949', in Luttikhuis and Moses 2014 (note 5), pp. 176–197, esp. p. 180.
19. Anton Lucas, *One Soul One Struggle. Region and Revolution in Indonesia*, Sydney 1991, pp. 140–141.
20. Kevin W. Fogg, 'Decolonization and Religion. Islamic Arguments for Indonesian Independence', *Leidschrift* 31 (October 2016), no. 3, pp. 109–124, esp. p. 115.
21. Idrus, 'Surabaja', in *Oriëntatie. Literair-cultureel tijdschrift in Indonesië (1947–1953). Een bloemlezing samengesteld en ingeleid door Peter van Zonneveld*, Schoorl 1988, pp. 212–249, esp. p. 228.
22. Ibid., p. 212.
23. Benedict R.O'G. Anderson, *Java in a Time of Revolution. Occupation and Resistance 1944–1946*, Jakarta 2006, pp. 155–157, 185–186.
24. Quoted (in English) in William H. Frederick, *Visions and Heat. The Making of the Indonesian Revolution*, Ohio 1989, p. 255.

25 J.J.P. de Jong, *De terugtocht. Nederland en de dekolonisatie van Indonesië*, Amsterdam 2015, pp. 39–40.
26 Idrus 1988 (note 21), pp. 215–216.

PROPAGANDA FOR THE REPUBLIC (PP. 120–139)

1 Baskoro Suryo Banindro, 'Daya Gagas Poster dalam Pergerakan dan Kebebasan Revolusi Indonesia 1945–1965', *ARS Jurnal Seni Rupa dan Desain* 21 (2018), no. 1, p. 70, see https://tinyurl.com/yc5xapwx (consulted on 3 October 2021).
2 The Hague, National Archives, NEFIS and CMI, 2.10.62, inv. no. 7265.
3 A.D. Pirous, 'Sejarah Poster Sebagai Alat Propaganda Perjuangan Di Indonesia', *Jurnal Ilmu Desain, FSRD-ITB* 1 (2006), no. 3, p. 141.
4 The Hague, National Archives, NEFIS and CMI, 2.10.62, inv. no. 4070.

CAUGHT IN THE NET (PP. 140–165)

1 Sjahrir, *Onze strijd*, Amsterdam 1946, p. 20.
2 Okeu Yulianasar, *Deciphering the NEFIS Archives. Investigating Dutch Information Gathering in Indonesia 1945–1949*, Leiden (unpublished master's thesis, Leiden University) 2012, p. 25.
3 The Hague, National Archives, NEFIS and CMI, 2.10.62, 'Beschrijving' (P.L. Groen 2001), 'Geschiedenis van de archiefvormer', see https://www.nationaalarchief.nl/onderzoeken/archief/2.10.62/ (consulted on 8 July 2021)
4 The Hague, National Archives, NEFIS and CMI, 2.10.62, inv. no. 3034.
5 Rosihan Anwar, *Napak Tilas ke Belanda. 60 Tahun Perjalanan Wartawan KMB 1949*, Jakarta 2010.
6 R.J.J. Stevens, 'Manipulatie van informatie? De rol van de Nederlandse militaire inlichtingendienst in Indonesië ten tijde van het Nederlands-Indonesisch conflict 1945–1949', *Politieke opstellen* 11/12 (1992), pp. 149–168, esp. p. 155, see http://hdl.handle.net/2066/93668 (consulted on 8 July 2021).
7 Anwar 2010 (note 5).
8 Rosihan Anwar, *Sejarah Kecil Indonesia. Kisah-Kisah Zaman Revolusi Kemerdekaan*, vol. 7, Jakarta 2015, pp. 135, 138.
9 Information about and quotations from Simon Admiraal are taken from letters and documentation supplied to the author by his granddaughter Marjon Berkenvelder.
10 Rémy Limpach, *De brandende kampongs van generaal Spoor*, Amsterdam 2016, p. 517.
11 Ibid., p. 513.
12 Ibid., p. 515.
13 A. Teeuw, *Pramoedya Ananta Toer. De verbeelding van Indonesië*, Breda 1993, p. 345.
14 Ibid., p. 21.
15 The rest of the book was later published under the title of *Ditepi Kali Bekasi* (On the Banks of the Bekasi), see ibid., p. 86.
16 Ibid., p. 87.
17 Ibid., p. 248.
18 Pramoedya Ananta Toer, *In de fuik*, Breda 1994, p. 584.
19 Ibid., p. 7.
20 The Hague, National Archives, NEFIS and CMI, 2.10.62, inv. no. 3585.
21 Stevens 1992 (note 6), p. 150.
22 Harry A. Poeze, 'De geheimen van het NEFIS-archief', 2019 (unpublished memorandum), p. 1.
23 Groen 2001 (note 3).

DIPLOMASI AND AGRESI (PP. 166–199)

1 Tanja Dezentjé was married several times and therefore went by a number of different surnames, including MacGillavry, Sanstranegara and Rahman.
2 The Hague, National Archives, personal file for T.E.C.C. Dezentjé, 2.10.62, inv. no. 2555.
3 www.alamy.com/mahatma-gandhi-at-prayer-meeting-bhangi-colony-delhi-india-asia-july-10-1947-image330810085 (consulted on 17 September 2021).
4 Transcript of a letter from Tanja Dezentjé to her mother, New Delhi, 14 July 1947. The Hague, National Archives, personal file for T.E.C.C. Dezentjé, 2.10.62, inv. no. 2555.
5 The Hague, National Archives, collection 570, F.J. Goedhart, 2.21.285, inv. no. 52 A.
6 C. Smit (ed.), *Het dagboek van Schermerhorn*, vol. 2, Utrecht 1970, appendix 3, p. 873.
7 Ibid., vol. 1, p. 116.
8 J.J.P. de Jong, *De terugtocht. Nederland en de dekolonisatie van Indonesië*, Amsterdam 2015, p. 93.
9 Ibid., p. 109.
10 Ibid., p. 108. English translation from https://indonesia-nederland.org/archive/foundation-friends-of-linggadjati/speech-upik-sjahrir-on-exhibition-the-linggadjati-conference-in-the-hague/ (consulted on 18 November 2021).
11 Anne-Lot Hoek, *De strijd om Bali. Imperialisme, verzet en onafhankelijkheid 1846–1950*, Amsterdam 2021, p. 209.
12 Ibid., p. 195.
13 Ibid., p. 135.
14 Ibid., p. 357.
15 Anthony Reid, *The Blood of the People. Revolution and the End of the Traditional Rule in Northern Sumatra*, Oxford 1980.
16 Mary Margaret Steedly, *Rifle Reports. A Story of Indonesian Independence*, Berkeley (CA) 2013, p. 44.
17 Ibid., p. 245.
18 Ibid., p. 246.
19 Ibid., p. 244.
20 Ibid., p. 334.
21 Ibid., p. 214.
22 silima-merga.blogspot.com/2018/08/operasi-bukit-bertah.html (consulted on 1 October 2021).
23 Interviews with Benamuli Ginting, Eben Hezer Sinuraya's wife, in August 2018, and with Evlina Sinuraya, his daughter, on 12 September 2021.
24 Letter from Hans van Santen to his parents, 28 July 1947, private archive.
25 Ibid., 23 April 1946.
26 Ibid., 11 September 1946.
27 Ibid., 28 July 1947.
28 Ibid.
29 Ibid.
30 Rémy Limpach, *De brandende kampongs van generaal Spoor*, Amsterdam 2016, pp. 663–669.
31 Harry A. Poeze, 'Walking the Tightrope. Internal Indonesian Conflict, 1945–1949', in Bart Luttikhuis and A. Dirk Moses (eds.), *Colonial Counterinsurgency and Mass Violence. The Dutch Empire in Indonesia*, London/New York 2014,

pp. 176–197, esp. p. 194.
32 Petra Groen et al., *Krijgsgeweld en kolonie. Opkomst en ondergang van Nederland als koloniale mogendheid, 1816–2010*, Amsterdam 2021, p. 348, esp. note 235 on p. 558.
33 Christiaan Harinck, Nico van Horn and Bart Luttikhuis, 'Wie telt de Indonesische doden?', *De Groene Amsterdammer*, 26 July 2017. For more insight into the Indonesian fatality figures and the debate surrounding them, see Groen et al. 2021 (note 32), p. 348, esp. note 236 on p. 558.
34 Letter from Adriana Nasoetion-van der Have to the Maas family, 23 January 1949, The Hague, National Archives, 2.10.14, inv. no. 2748.
35 Frank Vermeulen, 'Afgemaakt als een dolle hond', *NRC Handelsblad*, 17 January 2020 (online version).
36 Nasoetion-van der Have 1949 (note 34).
37 Kees Kuiken, '*Have, Adriana van der*', in *Digitaal Vrouwenlexicon van Nederland*, resources.huygens.knaw.nl/vrouwenlexicon/lemmata/data/HaveAdriana, 25 June 2018 (consulted on 17 September 2021).
38 Nasoetion-van der Have 1949 (note 34).
39 Frank Vermeulen, 'Hoe een weduwe de Nederlandse staat deed buigen', *NRC Handelsblad*, 27 January 2017 (online version). Geelhoed, Nasoetion's murderer, received a Bronze Lion for his military service in 1949.
40 This biographical sketch of Petrus Akihary was put together with the help of his daughter, Ms M. Anthony-Akihary, and grandson Huib Akihary, curator at Museum Maluku in The Hague.

COMRADES OF THE REVOLUTION (PP. 200–229)

1 *The Voice of Free Indonesia*, January 1946, p. 2.
2 In the final months of their occupation, the Japanese permitted the flying of the Indonesian flag, albeit exclusively alongside the Japanese flag.
3 Interviews with Monica Daryati (daughter of Trubus Soedarsono) by Amir Sidharta, 11–16 December 2019. The appellation of a Javanese grandparent often refers to his/her first child. Soma Podho is the name of Mbah Podho's first child.
4 Claire Holt, *Art in Indonesia. Continuities and Change*, Ithaca (NY) 1967, p. 201.
5 Amir Sidharta, 'Acquisitions: no. 10', *The Rijksmuseum Bulletin* 68 (2020), no. 3, p. 296.
6 *Het Inzicht*, 26 March 1947, p. 9.
7 Remco Raben speaks of 'guided emancipation', see Remco Raben, 'Geleide emancipatie', in Meta Knol, Remco Raben and Kitty Zijlmans, *Beyond the Dutch. Indonesië, Nederland en de beeldende kunsten van 1900 tot nu*, Amsterdam/Utrecht 2009, pp. 92–93, esp. p. 92.
8 'minshin ha'aku' and 'senbu kōsaku', in Aiko Kurasawa, *Mobilisasi dan Kontrol. Studi Perubahan Sosial di Pedesaan Jawa 1942–1945*, Jakarta 1993, p. 229.
9 See *Asia Raya*, 22 September 1944.
10 Rosihan Anwar, 'Sekelumit Kenang-kenangan Kegiatan Sastrawan di Zaman Jepang (1943–1945)', *Budaya Djaya* 65 (1973), pp. 595–596.
11 Ibid., p. 596.
12 In his memoirs, Sudjojono mentioned Chairil Anwar's involvement. See S. Sudjojono, *Cerita Tentang Saya dan Orang-orang Sekitar Saya*, Jakarta 2017, p. 84. See also Anwar 1973 (note 10), p. 596.
13 Rosihan Anwar, 'Seniman dan Wartawan dalam Perjuangan 1942–1950', *Makalah Seminar Peranan Generasi Muda dalam Perjuangan Bangsa 1942–1950*, Jakarta 1990, p. 8.
14 M. Balfas, 'Mendjelang Seniman Sudjojono', *Masjarakat* 1 (1947).
15 Dullah, 'Mas Affandi', in Ajip Rosidi et al., *Affandi 70 Tahun*, Jakarta 1978, p. 8.
16 Jan Bouwer, *Het vermoorde land*, Franeker 1988, p. 394.
17 Amir Sidharta and Waty Moerany, *Indonesia Semangat Dunia. Pameran Kolleksi Seni Rupa Istana Kepresidenan Republik Indonesia*, Jakarta 2018, pp. 20–23.
18 Takdir Alisjahbana, 'Preface', in *Linoleographs. Baharoedin / Mochtar Apin*, Bandung 1946.
19 Anwar 1990 (note 13), p. 8.
20 'Seni Oentoek Revoloesi, Boekan Seni Oentoek Seni', *Kedaulatan Rakjat*, 24 April 1946.
21 'Pertoendjoekkan Seni Loekis Perdjoeangan', *Kedaulatan Rakjat*, 2 April 1946.
22 Suromo, 'Timbul dan Tumbuhnya Seni Lukis Indonesia', *Mimbar Indonesia*, 27 July 1949.
23 Remco Raben called the painting 'a modern militia portrait'. See Remco Raben, 'Op zoek naar de vrijheid', in Knol, Raben and Zijlmans 2009 (note 7), pp. 83–91, esp. p. 87.
24 Tedjabayu (son of Sudjojono), interview by Amir Sidharta through social media, 20 May 2019.
25 Claire Holt, 'In Memoriam. Trisno Sumardjo (December 6, 1916 – April 21, 1969)', *Indonesia* 8 (1969), pp. 212–216.
26 Solichin Salam, *Agus Djaya dan Sejarah Seni Lukis Indonesia*, Jakarta 1994, p. 20.
27 Delegate for student affairs to the Amsterdam municipal museums bureau chief, 29 August 1947. See Britte Sloothaak, *Tempo Doeloe? Kunstenaars, guerrilla-strijders en spijbelaars*, Stedelijk Museum (2018), www.stedelijk.nl/nl/digdeeper/tempo-doeloe-agus-en-otto-djaya (consulted on 4 October 2021).
28 Willem Sandberg in *Agoes Djaya en Otto Djaya*, exh. cat. Amsterdam (Stedelijk Museum) 1947, p. 4, trans. Steve Green, see www.stedelijk.nl/en/digdeeper/agoes-djaya-en-otto-djaya-stedelijk (consulted on 3 December 2022).
29 Ibid., p. 9. *Pembrontak* actually means rebel.
30 Lizzy van Leeuwen, *Indra. Een wayangleven. Biografie van Leo Broekveldt 1906–1992*, Amsterdam 2020, p. 188.
31 *Het Dagblad*, 18 November 1946.
32 *Algemeen Handelsblad*, 3 January 1949.
33 *De Gooi- en Eemlander. Nieuws- en Advertentieblad*, 5 September 1949.
34 On the periodical *Seniman*, see Helena Spanjaard, *Artists and their Inspiration. A Guide through Indonesian Art History (1930–2015)*, Volendam 2016, pp. 39–40.
35 *Seniman* 1 (1947), no. 3. *Seminam* was published by the art association SIM from 1947 to 1949.
36 Helena Spanjaard, 'Ries Mulder en

de ontwikkeling van de moderne kunst in Bandung', in Knol, Raben and Zijlmans 2009 (note 7), pp. 106–115, esp. pp. 108–109.
37 Essay by Eddie Kartasubarna in the brochure *Solo Exhibition of Eddie Kartasubarna*, 1980. See also Department of Fine Art, *Art Education Catalogue*, Bandung (Bandung Institute of Technology) 1988.
38 Sudarmadji, *Dullah. Raja Realisme Indonesia*, Bali 1988, pp. 18–19.
39 Mia Bustam, *Sudjojono dan Aku*, Jakarta 2013, pp. 115–123.

FOUR TIMES 365 DAYS
(PP. 230–251)

1 'Indonesia Throng Acclaims Sukarno', *The New York Times*, 29 December 1949, p. 12, see https://timesmachine.nytimes.com/timesmachine/1949/12/29/84581913.html?pdf_redirect=true&ip=0&pageNumber=12 (consulted on 27 October 2021); 'Juichende menigte begroet president Sukarno', *Java Bode*, 29 December 1949, p. 1, see https://resolver.kb.nl/resolve?urn=ddd:010864921:mpeg21:p001 (consulted on 27 October 2021); Cindy Adams, *Bung Karno Penyambung Lidah Rakjat Indonesia* (trans. Mayor Abdul B. Salim), Jakarta 1966, p. 390.
2 Yudhi Soerjoatmodjo, *IPPHOS Remastered*, Jakarta (Galeri Foto Jurnalistik Antara) 2013, p. 183.
3 Republik Indonesia Serikat was a federation established by the *Bijeenkomst voor Federaal Overleg*, the Federal Consultative Assembly, between the Indonesians and the Dutch. Its territories included those controlled by the Republic, seven federal administrations and nine special regions, but excluded Netherlands New Guinea, which was still under Dutch control.
4 Adams 1966 (note 1), p. 390.
5 Fatmawati Sukarno, *Fatmawati: Catatan Kecil Bersama Bung Karno, Bagian 1*, 3rd ed. Jakarta 1985, pp. 170–171.
6 Interview with Raden Mas Soeharto, cameraman at Berita Film Indonesia (1945–1950), 18 August 2000. BFI was established by Raden Mas Soetarto, Soeharto's half-brother and former documentary film-maker at Multi film (1939–1942) and Nippon Eiga Sha (1942–1945), on 6 October 1945. It was one of the three important pro-Republican news agencies alongside Antara and the Indonesia Press Photo Service (IPPHOS).
7 Interview with Johnny Waworuntu, former photographer for the Regeringsvoorlichtingsdienst (1946–1949) and later chief of the photo division at the Kementerian Penerangan RI (1949–1952), 14 August 1996; *The New York Times* 1949 (note 1), p. 12.
8 Adams 1966 (note 1), p. 390; Nidjo Sandjojo, *Abdul Latief Hendraningrat*, Jakarta 2011, p. 164.
9 Rosihan Anwar, Ramadhan K.H., Ray Rizal, Din Madjid (comp.), *Kemal Idris: Bertarung Dalam Revolusi*, Jakarta 1996, pp. 125–126.
10 Interview with Melvin Jacob, son of Rev. Jacob, whose house in Jalan Sayidan, Yogyakarta, was used as IPPHOS Yogyakarta's office. Melvin later joined as an assistant photographer in Yogyakarta and became a full-time member of IPPHOS (1948–1967), 17 May 1996; Soerjoatmodjo 2013 (note 2), pp. 184–185. IPPHOS was one of the three pro-Republican news agencies, established on 1 October 1946.
11 J.G. de Beus, *Morgen, bij het aanbreken van de dag, Nederland driemaal aan de vooravond van oorlog*, Rotterdam 1977, pp. 239–240.
12 Adams 1966 (note 1), p. 390.
13 'Woensdag precies om 11:42 uur, kwam President Soekarno...', *De Vrije Pers*, 30 December 1949, p. 1, see https://resolver.kb.nl/resolve?urn=ddd:011210314:mpeg21:p001 (consulted on 27 October 2021).
14 John Bloom, 'Henri Cartier-Bresson, Primacy of the Other Over Fact', in Jane L. Reed (ed.), *Toward Independence. A Century of Indonesia Photographed*, San Francisco 1991, p. 113.
15 Sukarno 1985 (note 5), p. 171.
16 Soerjoatmodjo 2013 (note 2), p. 188.
17 Waworuntu 1996 (note 7).
18 Yudhi Soerjoatmodjo, 'Bung Karno dan Fotografi', *Majalah Tempo* (2001), no. 4, pp. 72–81.
19 Interview with Raden Mas Soeharto, cameraman at Berita Film Indonesia (1945–1950), 2 October 1996.
20 Soerjoatmodjo 2013 (note 2), pp. 186–187.
21 See also https://www.rijksmuseum.nl/nl/collectie/NG-2004-40-100 and https://www.rijksmuseum.nl/nl/collectie/NG-2004-40-99.
22 Interview with Mohammad Sayuti and Abdoel Kadir Said, former photographers at Domei (1943–1945) and Antara (1945–1949), 28 September 1996; 'Bij de geboorte van de R.I.S', *Java Bode*, 30 December 1949, p. 3, see https://resolver.kb.nl/resolve?urn=ddd:010864922:mpeg21:p005 (consulted on 27 October 2021).
23 Soetomo, *Bung Tomo, Dari 10 Nopember 1945 ke Orde Baru, Kumpulan Karangan*, Frans M. Parera (ed.). Jakarta 1982, p. 14.
24 Sayuti and Said (note 22); Toeti Kakiailatu, *B.M. Diah Wartawan Serba Bisa*, Jakarta 1997, p. 122; Soebagijo I. Notodidjojo, *Jagat Wartawan Indonesia*, Jakarta 1981, p. 472.
25 Interview with Rosihan Anwar, former editor at *Asia Raya* (1943–1945) and *Merdeka* newspaper (1945–1946), 14 August 1996; interview with Soebagijo I. Notodidjojo, former reporter at Antara news agency (1946–1949 and 1957–1981), 7 August 1996; interview with Des Alwi, Indonesian historian, diplomat and documentary film-maker, sometimes described as 'the adopted son of former Vice President Mohammad Hatta and Prime Minister Sutan Sjahrir', 13 September 1996.
26 Rosihan Anwar, *Kisah-Kisah Jakarta Menjelang Clash ke-1*, Jakarta 1979, pp. 95, 98.
27 Interview with Mochtar Lubis, former editor at Antara news agency (1945–1949), 6 August 1996; Wiwi Kuswiah, *Alexius Impurung Mendur (Alex Mendur)*, Jakarta 1986, pp. 34–35.
28 'Kennisgeving van IPPHOS', *Het Inzicht*, 29 January 1947, unpag.
29 The Hague, National Archives, inv. nos. 7272 and 7275.
30 Lubis 1996 (note 27); interview with Rudy Umbas, son of Justus Umbas and former director of IPPHOS (1961–1968), 7 May 1996; interview with Ines Mendur, former IPPHOS

photographer (1949–1950) and second wife of Alex Mendur, 28 July 2000; Waworuntu 1996 (note 7); Jozef A. Warouw et al., *KRIS 45 Berjuang Membela Negara. Sebuah Refleksi Perjuangan Revolusi KRIS (Kebaktian Rakjat Indonesia Sulawesi)*, Jakarta 1999, pp. 66, 140. KRIS was a social and military organization set up by politicians, professionals and students from the island of Sulawesi to support the Republic, while safeguarding their ethnic groups who were often suspected of colonial sympathies.

31 Soerjoatmodjo 2013 (note 2), pp. 130–131, 140, 153.

32 Interview with Raden Mas Soetarto, former documentary film-maker at Multi film (1939–1942) and Nippon Eiga Sha (1942–1945), 30 September 1996; interview with Mohammad Sayuti and Mudijanto, former photographers at Domei (1943–1945) and Antara (1945–1949), 8 August 1996; Mochtar Lubis, Mohammad Said, Suardi Tasrif, *Visi Wartawan 45*, Andy Zoeltom (ed.), Jakarta 1992, p. 34; Kuswiah 1986 (note 27), p. 30; interview with Lexy Mendur, son of Alex Mendur and former director of IPPHOS (1959–1967), 10 May 1996; Umbas 1996 (note 30); Robert B. Cribb, *Gejolak Revolusi di Jakarta 1945–1949. Pergulatan antara otonomi dan hegemoni* (trans. Hasan Basari), Jakarta 1990, pp. 40, 60, 63.

33 The Galeri Foto Jurnalistik Antara research team, *1945, Inventory of Negatives in the IPPHOS (Indonesian Press Photo Service) Archive*, Jakarta 1998, unpag.; Sayuti and Mudijanto 1996 (note 32); Soeharto 1996 (note 19); Raden Mas Soetarto, 'Cerita Ringkas Tugas BFI Yang Berhubungan Dengan Rapat Raksasa IKADA 19 September 1945', unpublished manuscript, unpag.

34 Sayuti and Said 1996 (note 22); Soebagijo I. Notodidjojo, *Lima Windu 'Antara' (Sejarah & Perjuangannya)*, Soendoro (ed.), Jakarta 1978, p. 71; Notodidjojo 1996 (note 25); interview with Abdoel Moentalib, younger brother of Abdoel Wahab Saleh, 9 August 1998; Soetarto 1996 (note 32).

• LIST OF ILLUSTRATIONS

**FACES OF THE REVOLUTION
(PP. 8–17)**

[1] Cover of Sutarso Nasrudin's book of friends, c. 1948. Photo album, 10 × 8 cm (closed). Leiden, Leiden University Libraries, inv. no. KITLV A1070

[2] Sutarso Nasrudin, portrait from his book of friends, c. 1948. Photo album, 10 × 8 cm (closed). Leiden, Leiden University Libraries, inv. no. KITLV A1070

[3] S. Munif, portrait from Sutarso Nasrudin's book of friends, c. 1948. Photo album, 10 × 8 cm (closed). Leiden, Leiden University Libraries, inv. no. KITLV A1070

[4] Three women and two boys, portrait from Sutarso Nasrudin's book of friends, c. 1948. Photo album, 10 × 8 cm (closed). Leiden, Leiden University Libraries, inv. no. KITLV A1070

[5] Group of soldiers, portrait from Sutarso Nasrudin's book of friends, 26 August 1948. Photo album, 10 × 8 cm (closed). Leiden, Leiden University Libraries, inv. no. KITLV A1070

[6] Three men, portrait from Sutarso Nasrudin's book of friends, c. 1948. Photo album, 10 × 8 cm (closed). Leiden, Leiden University Libraries, inv. no. KITLV A1070

[7] Three young Indonesians on the street in Yogyakarta, December 1947. Hugo Wilmar. Gelatin silver print, 17.2 × 23.4 cm. The Hague, National Archives of the Netherlands / Collectie Spaarnestad

**THE SPIRIT OF THE REVOLUSI
(P. 18–49)**

[1] Gelanggang Seniman Merdeka (Arena of Independent Artists), Jakarta, 1948. Charles Breijer. Original negative from the archive of Charles Breijer, 6 × 6 cm. Rotterdam, Nederlands Fotomuseum, inv. no. CHB-5152-3. © Charles Breijer / Nederlands Fotomuseum

[2] Mass gathering on Ikada Square in Jakarta, 19 September 1945. Unknown photographer. Gelatin silver print. The Hague, National Archives of the Netherlands, Collection 570, F.J. Goedhart, 2.21.285, inv. no. 52A

[3] Indonesian propaganda poster: 'Darahkoe merah-ta'soedi didjadjah!' (My blood is red, unwilling to be conquered!), c. 1945–1949. Koempoel Sujatno. Print, 62 × 43 cm. The Hague, National Archives of the Netherlands, Collection 215, Ch.O. van der Plas, 2.21.266, inv. no. 175A

[4] *Laskar Rakyat Mengatur Siasat I* (The People's Militia Decides Tactics I), 1946. Affandi. Oil on canvas, 130 × 155 cm. Jakarta, Presidential Palace Collection, inv. no. 00276.02.01.02.003.482 © Kartika Affandi

[5] *Persiapan Gerilya* (Preparations for the Guerrilla), 1949. Dullah. Oil on canvas, 178 × 197 cm. Jakarta, Presidential Palace Collection, inv. no. 08296.02.01.02.003.185. © Ir Sawarno

[6] *Seko Perintis Gerilya (Prambanan)* (Guerrilla Vanguard, Prambanan), 1949. Sudjojono. Oil on canvas, 173 × 194 cm. Jakarta, Presidential Palace Collection, inv. no. 31056.02.01.02.003.061

[7] *Mengungsi* (The Refuge or Seeking for Refuge), 1947. Henk Ngantung. Oil on canvas, 95 × 119 cm. Jakarta, Presidential Palace Collection, inv. no. 02066.02.01.02.003.335. © Sena Meaya Ngantung, Geniati Heneve Ngantung, Kamang Solana Ngantung, Karno Putra Ngantung †

[8] The lead Republican and Dutch negotiators in Linggajati, 11–13 November 1946. Unknown photographer. Gelatin silver print. The Hague, National Archives of the Netherlands, Collection 570, F.J. Goedhart, 2.21.285, inv. no. 52A

[9] Mohammad Hatta and Huib van Mook during the negotiations in Linggajati, 11–13 November 1946. Henk Ngantung. Pen and ink, 41 × 28 cm. Jakarta, Museum Seni Rupa Dan Keramik, inv. no. 010/SK/MSRK/08. © Sena Meaya Ngantung, Geniati Heneve Ngantung, Kamang Solana Ngantung, Karno Putra Ngantung †

[10] *Pembersihan Desa* (Purge of the Village), 1949. Soerono. Oil on canvas, 133.5 × 195.5 cm. Tangerang, Museum Universitas Pelita Harapan. © Dewi Puspasari SP. Photo: Kurniawan Wigena

[11] Hizbullah march, Islamic armed forces, presumably Yogyakarta, 1946/1947. Unknown photographer. Gelatin silver print. The Hague, National Archives of the Netherlands, Collection 570, F.J. Goedhart, 2.21.285, inv. no. 52A

[12] Enthusiastic crowd in Yogyakarta in the period around Sukarno's inauguration as president of the Republik Indonesia Serikat, 1949. Henri Cartier-Bresson (Magnum). Gelatin silver print, 16.8 × 24.8 cm. The Hague, National Archives of the Netherlands / Collectie Spaarnestad, SPA035 VINT INT, inv. no. 0048. © Henri Cartier-Bresson © Fondation Henri Cartier-Bresson / Magnum Photos

[13] An Indonesian kneels surrounded by Dutch marines. A propaganda poster is seized, c. 1946–1949. Unknown photographer. Photograph, 5.5 × 6.2 cm. Rotterdam, Marines Museum, inv. no. 14996

**PROKLAMASI
(PP. 50–75)**

[1] Soemarto Frans Mendur, with Indonesian police officers, probably Yogyakarta, 1946. Unknown photographer (IPPHOS, Indonesia Press Photo Service). Photograph. Collection Yudhi Soerjoatmodjo. © Antara/IPPHOS

[2] The draft of the *Proklamasi*, 17 August 1945. Sukarno. Manuscript, 25.7 × 21.3 cm. Jakarta, ANRI, Koleksi Khusus

[3] Sukarno and Dr Moewardi on the veranda of Sukarno's house at the start of the proclamation, Jakarta, 17 August 1945. Soemarto Frans Mendur (IPPHOS, Indonesia Press Photo Service). Gelatin silver print, 11.5 × 16.5 cm. The Hague, The Netherlands Institute for Military History, inv. no. 2164-003-004. © Antara/IPPHOS

[4] Mohammad Hatta, Sukarno and Dr Moewardi on the veranda of Sukarno's house at the start of the proclamation, Jakarta, 17 August 1945. Soemarto Frans Mendur (IPPHOS, Indonesia Press Photo Service). Gelatin silver print, 11.5 × 16.5 cm. The Hague,

The Netherlands Institute for Military History, inv. no. 2164-003-005. © Antara/IPPHOS

[5] Photo 3: Sukarno, guarded by Abdul Latief Hendraningrat, on the veranda of his house at the start of the proclamation, Jakarta, 17 August 1945.
Soemarto Frans Mendur (IPPHOS, Indonesia Press Photo Service). Gelatin silver print, 11.5 × 16.5 cm. The Hague, The Netherlands Institute for Military History, inv. no. 2164-003-006.
© Antara/IPPHOS

[6, 7] Suwiryo giving his speech at the start of the proclamation, Jakarta, 17 August 1945. Soemarto Frans Mendur (IPPHOS, Indonesia Press Photo Service)

[6] Gelatin silver print, 11.5 × 16.5 cm. The Hague, The Netherlands. Institute for Military History, inv. no. 2164-003-007.
© Antara/IPPHOS

[7] Photograph.
Jakarta, Collection Yayasan Bung Karno. © Antara/IPPHOS

[8, 9] Sukarno reading the text of the proclamation from the veranda of his house, Jakarta, 17 August 1945. Soemarto Frans Mendur (IPPHOS, Indonesia Press Photo Service).

[8] Photograph.
Jakarta, Collection Yayasan Bung Karno. © Antara/IPPHOS

[9] Gelatin silver print, 11.5 × 16.5 cm. The Hague, The Netherlands Institute for Military History, inv. no. 2164-003-008.© Antara/IPPHOS

[10, 11] Sukarno conducting prayers on the veranda of his house after the proclamation, Jakarta, 17 August 1945. Soemarto Frans Mendur (IPPHOS, Indonesia Press Photo Service).
Gelatin silver print, 11.5 × 16.5 cm. The Hague, The Netherlands Institute for Military History, inv. nos. 2164-003-009, 010.
© Antara/IPPHOS

[12] Mohammad Hatta giving a short speech on the veranda of Sukarno's house following Sukarno's proclamation, Jakarta, 17 August 1945. Soemarto Frans Mendur (IPPHOS, Indonesia Press Photo Service). Gelatin silver print, 11.5 × 16.5 cm. The Hague, The Netherlands Institute for Military History, inv. no. 2164-003-011

[13] S.K. Trimurti and Fatmawati Sukarno with other participants waiting for the flag ceremony in the front garden of Sukarno's house, Jakarta, 17 August 1945. Soemarto Frans Mendur (IPPHOS, Indonesia Press Photo Service). Photograph.
Jakarta, Collection Yayasan Bung Karno. © Antara/IPPHOS

[14, 15] Abdul Latief Hendraningat and Soehoed of the Barisan Pelopor preparing to raise the Indonesian flag in the front garden of Sukarno's house, Jakarta, 17 August 1945. Soemarto Frans Mendur (IPPHOS, Indonesia Press Photo Service).

[14] Gelatin silver print, 11.5 × 16.5 cm. The Hague, The Netherlands Institute for Military History, inv. no. 2164-003-013. © Antara/IPPHOS

[15] Photograph.
Jakarta, Collection Yayasan Bung Karno. © Antara/IPPHOS

[16] The flag-raising ceremony following the proclamation, viewed from the veranda, Jakarta, 17 August 1945. Soemarto Frans Mendur (IPPHOS, Indonesia Press Photo Service). Photograph.
Jakarta, Collection Yayasan Bung Karno. © Antara/IPPHOS

[17] Abdul Latief Hendraningrat raising the Indonesian flag, Jakarta, 17 August 1945. Soemarto Frans Mendur (IPPHOS, Indonesia Press Photo Service). Photograph.
Jakarta, Collection Yayasan Bung Karno. © Antara/IPPHOS

[18] Following the flag-raising ceremony, Sukarno and other dignitaries on the veranda raise their arms and shout 'Merdeka!' (Freedom), Jakarta, 17 August 1945. Soemarto Frans Mendur (IPPHOS, Indonesia Press Photo Service). Gelatin silver print, 11.5 × 16.5 cm. The Hague, The Netherlands Institute for Military History, inv. no. 2164-003-012. © Antara/IPPHOS

[19, 20] Members of the Preparatory Committee for Indonesian Independence (PPKI): Teuku Muhammad Hasan, Dr Radjiman Wediodiningrat and Dr Sam Ratulangi, with troops of the Barisan Pelopor who arrived late for the proclamation at Sukarno's house, Jakarta, 17 August 1945.

Soemarto Frans Mendur (IPPHOS, Indonesia Press Photo Service). Gelatin silver print, 11.5 × 16.5 cm. The Hague, The Netherlands Institute for Military History, inv. nos. 2164-003-002, 003.
© Antara/IPPHOS

FREEDOM THE GLORY OF ANY NATION (PP. 76–97)

[1] Slogan on the wall of the Hotel des Galeries in Jakarta, from *British Troops Arrive in Batavia*. September 1945. Duncan MacTavish. Film still. London, Imperial War Museum, inv. no. JFU 385

[2] Banner on the wall of the Hotel des Galeries in Jakarta, from *British Troops Arrive in Batavia*, September 1945. Duncan MacTavish. Film stills. London, Imperial War Museum, inv. no. JFU 385

[3] Poster on the wall of the Hotel des Galeries in Jakarta, from *British Troops Arrive in Batavia*, September 1945. Duncan MacTavish. Film still. London, Imperial War Museum, inv. no. JFU 385

[4] Sudjojono, 1951. Unknown photographer. Photograph. Unknown collection

[5] Affandi, 1949. Unknown photographer. Photograph. Yogyakarta, Affandi Museum.
© Affandi Foundation
© Kartika Affandi

[6] Indonesian nationalists ride through the streets with the 'Boeng, Ajo Boeng' poster. Photo in *Life*, 12 November 1945. Unknown photographer.

[7] The monument in Jakarta to J.B. van Heutsz, governor-general of the Dutch East Indies, painted in revolutionary slogans, October 1945. Unknown photographer, NIGIS (Netherlands Indies Government Information Service). Photograph, 11.1 × 16.4 cm. Leiden, Nationaal Museum voor Wereldculturen, inv. no. 7082-nf-683-14-1

[8] Slogan on a city tram in Java: 'Van Mook and Plas cause a Rebellion in Indonesia', 1945. H. Ripassa. Photograph. Amsterdam, NIOD, WW2 image database

[9] Photos of Tan Malaka from various periods, taken from his personal file in the archives of the NEFIS

REVOLUSI!

military intelligence service. Gelatin silver prints and negatives. The Hague, National Archives of the Netherlands, Netherlands Forces Intelligence Service [NEFIS] and Centrale Militaire Inlichtingendienst [CMI] in the Dutch East Indies, 2.10.62, inv. no. 2747
[10] *Moeslihat* (Tactics), 1945. Tan Malaka. Book, 15 × 12 cm. Collection Harry Poeze
[11] *Onze strijd* (Our Struggle), 1946. Sjahrir. Book. Amsterdam, Harm Stevens collection
[12] Sjahrir, in Cas Oorthuys, *Een staat in wording*, 1947. Photo book, h. 25 cm. Amsterdam, Rijksmuseum Research Library, 575 D 41

THE SIGNAL TO RISE UP (PP. 98–119)

[1] Letty Kwee, Jakarta, August 1945. Unknown photographer. Photograph, 5.3 × 5.3 cm. Kwee family collection
[2] Letty Kwee with daughter Tjoe and domestic servants, Jakarta, August 1945. Unknown photographer. Photograph, 5.7 × 8.3 cm. Kwee family collection
[3] Mateni, the Javanese domestic, hand in hand with Tjoe on the Joos Banckersweg, Amsterdam, 1948. Unknown photographer. Photograph, 5.3 × 5.3 cm. Kwee family collection
[4] The Kwee family, Amsterdam, 1949. Unknown photographer. Photograph, 4.9 × 8 cm. Kwee family collection
[5] Jeanne (Peu) van Leur-de Loos after her return from Indonesia, c. 1946. Unknown photographer. Photograph, 5.3 × 3.6 cm. Leiden, P.A. Terwen collection
[6] House dress of silk maps, Jakarta, 1945. Jeanne (Peu) van Leur-de Loos. 155 (l) × 40 (shoulder) cm. Amsterdam, Rijksmuseum, inv. no. NG-2000-5. Gift of P.A. Terwen, Leiden and J.W. Terwen, Nieuwegein
[7] List of victims of the violence in Tegal, including the Uhlenbusch family, December 1945 or later. Typescript, 33.5 × 20.9 cm. The Hague, National Archives of the Netherlands, Netherlands Forces Intelligence Service [NEFIS] en Centrale Militaire Inlichtingendienst [CMI] in Nederlands-Indië, 2.10.62, inv. no. 4932
[8] The Uhlenbusch sisters, before 1942. John Thiessen. Gelatin silver print, 12.5 × 17.5 cm. Amsterdam, Rijksmuseum, inv. no. NG-2018-331-87. Private Gift
[9] Sutomo (Bung Tomo), 1947. Alex Mendur (?). Photograph. Yudhi Soerjoatmodjo collection
[10] Idrus, 1948. Unknown photographer. Photograph. Idrus family collection
[11] Studio portrait of nx111341 sergeant Tony Rafty, official war artist, military history, c. 1944. Unknown photographer. Photograph. Campbell, Australian War Memorial, inv. no. P00968.001
[12] *Battle of Surabaya*, 14 November 1945. Tony Rafty. Pen and ink, 27.9 × 39.8 cm. Canberra, National Library of Australia, inv. no. 1191138
[13] *Evacuation of the Muntilan camp on Java*, 1945. Tony Rafty. Pen and ink, 19 × 27 cm. Canberra, National Library of Australia, inv. no. 2713385
[14] *'Dutch soldier fully armed and on the elert [alert] throughout the streets'*, 1945. Tony Rafty. Pen and ink, 15.8 × 23.5 cm. Canberra, National Library of Australia, inv. no. 2928058
[15] *An Indonesian policeman in Jakarta*, 1945. Tony Rafty. Pen and ink, 32.2 × 24.6 cm. Canberra, National Library of Australia, inv. no. 1191104

PROPAGANDA FOR THE REPUBLIC (PP. 120–139)

[1] Cas Oorthuys in Indonesia, January 1947. Original negative from the archive of Cas Oorthuys, 6 × 6 cm. Rotterdam, Nederlands Fotomuseum, inv. no. CAS-10047-4. © Cas Oorthuys / Nederlands Fotomuseum
[2] Portraits of Indonesians, in Cas Oorthuys, *Een staat in wording*, 1947. Photo book, h. 25 cm. Amsterdam, Rijksmuseum Research Library, 575 D 41. © Cas Oorthuys / Nederlands Fotomuseum
[3] Sukarno and the Indonesian parliament, in Cas Oorthuys, *Een staat in wording*, 1947. Photo book, h. 25 cm. Amsterdam, Rijksmuseum Research Library, 575 D 41. © Cas Oorthuys / Nederlands Fotomuseum
[4] A poster workshop, in Cas Oorthuys, *Een staat in wording*, 1947. Photo book, h. 25 cm. Amsterdam, Rijksmuseum Research Library, 575 D 41. © Cas Oorthuys / Nederlands Fotomuseum
[5] Indonesian soldiers, in Cas Oorthuys, *Een staat in wording*, 1947. Photo book, h. 25 cm. Amsterdam, Rijksmuseum Research Library, 575 D 41. © Cas Oorthuys / Nederlands Fotomuseum
[6] Template for poster, with picture of a mosque and the text 'Kemerdekaan, keadilan dan sediahtera' (Freedom, justice and welfare) on letterhead of S.M. Kartosoewirjo, secretary of the Partij Sarekat Islam Hindi Timoer, c. 1948. Spray paint on paper, 30 × 23 cm. The Hague, National Archives of the Netherlands, Netherlands Forces Intelligence Service [NEFIS] en Centrale Militaire Inlichtingendienst [CMI] in Nederlands-Indië, 2.10.62, inv. no. 6441
[7] Production of a poster in a workshop, 1947. Cas Oorthuys. Original negative from the archive of Cas Oorthuys, 6 × 6 cm. Rotterdam, Nederlands Fotomuseum, inv. no. CAS-10357-1. © Cas Oorthuys / Nederlands Fotomuseum
[8] 'Flying Dutchman' poster in a workshop in Yogyakarta, 1947. Cas Oorthuys. Original negative from the archive of Cas Oorthuys, 6 × 6 cm. Rotterdam, Nederlands Fotomuseum, inv. no. CAS-10358-4. © Cas Oorthuys / Nederlands Fotomuseum
[9, 10, 11] Posters in the album *Kami Berdjuang Dengan Poster/We Struggle with Posters*, 1947. Pusat Tenaga Pelukis Indonesia (PTPI). Watercolour on paper. Jakarta, collection Amir Sidharta
[12] Cover of the album *Kami Berdjuang Dengan Poster/We Struggle with Posters*, 1947. Pusat Tenaga Pelukis Indonesia (PTPI). Album, crocodile leather or imitation leather, 31 × 40 cm (closed). Jakarta, collection Amir Sidharta
[13] Exhibition of posters by Pusat Tenaga Pelukis Indonesia (PTPI) in the Kedu region, Central Java,

1946/1947. Unknown photographer. Gelatin silver print.
The Hague, National Archives of the Netherlands, Netherlands Forces Intelligence Service [NEFIS] en Centrale Militaire Inlichtingendienst [CMI] in Nederlands-Indië, 2.10.62, inv. no. 7265

[14] Propaganda poster with the text 'Pertahankanlah kampoeng halamanmoe' (Defend your village), 1946. Pusat Tenaga Pelukis Indonesia (PTPI).
Watercolour, 60 × 42 cm.
The Hague, National Archives of the Netherlands, Netherlands Forces Intelligence Service [NEFIS] en Centrale Militaire Inlichtingendienst [CMI] in Nederlands-Indië, 2.10.62, inv. no. 4070

[15] Propaganda poster with the text 'Adalah 3 sendi oentoek menjoesoeh kemakmoeran desa kembali' (Three principles for the reorganization of welfare in the villages), 1946. Pusat Tenaga Pelukis Indonesia (PTPI).
Watercolour, 60 × 42 cm.
The Hague, National Archives of the Netherlands, Netherlands Forces Intelligence Service [NEFIS] en Centrale Militaire Inlichtingendienst [CMI] in Nederlands-Indië, 2.10.62, inv. no. 4070

[16] Propaganda poster with the text 'Padi oentoek India bahan pakaian oentoek Indonesia' (Rice for India, clothing for Indonesia), 1946. Pusat Tenaga Pelukis Indonesia (PTPI).
Watercolour, 60 × 42 cm.
The Hague, National Archives of the Netherlands, Netherlands Forces Intelligence Service [NEFIS] en Centrale Militaire Inlichtingendienst [CMI] in Nederlands-Indië, 2.10.62, inv. no. 4070

[17] Propaganda poster with the text 'Aman di desa karena pendjaga' (Thanks to the guards it is safe in the villages), 1946. Pusat Tenaga Pelukis Indonesia (PTPI).
Watercolour, 60 × 42 cm.
The Hague, National Archives of the Netherlands, Netherlands Forces Intelligence Service [NEFIS] en Centrale Militaire Inlichtingendienst [CMI] in Nederlands-Indië, 2.10.62, inv. no. 4070

[18] Propaganda poster with the text 'Naskah djembatan tjita 2 kita' (The draft [of the Linggajati agreement] is the bridge to our goal), 1946. Seniman Indonesia Muda (SIM). Print, 30 × 21 cm.
Amsterdam, International Institute of Social History, inv. no. BG H20/289

[19] Propaganda poster with the text 'Hai...! Penghianat bangsa! Aku telah menggabung kan diri, guna meng hakimi jang sebaja dosamu' (Hey traitors! I've joined [the armed forces] to bring justice to people with sins like yours), 1946. Army unit (name unknown). Paint on paper, 41 × 30 cm.
The Hague, National Archives of the Netherlands, Netherlands Forces Intelligence Service [NEFIS] en Centrale Militaire Inlichtingendienst [CMI] in Nederlands-Indië, 2.10.62, inv. no. 848

[20] Propaganda poster with the text 'Djangan desik Indonesia!' (Don't mess with Indonesia!), 1945–1949. Penerangan Tentara information service.
Watercolour on paper, 56 × 42 cm.
The Hague, National Archives of the Netherlands, Netherlands Forces Intelligence Service [NEFIS] en Centrale Militaire Inlichtingendienst [CMI] in Nederlands-Indië, 2.10.62, inv. no. 4690

CAUGHT IN THE NET (PP. 140–165)

[1] Rosihan Anwar, 29 July 1939, portrait photo from his photo album, seized by NEFIS in April 1946 (Jakarta). Unknown photographer. Gelatin silver print.
The Hague, National Archives of the Netherlands, Netherlands Forces Intelligence Service [NEFIS] en Centrale Militaire Inlichtingendienst [CMI] in Nederlands-Indië, 2.10.62, inv. no. 3034

[2] Rosihan Anwar and his classmates, 1939, photo from his photo album. Unknown photographer
Gelatin silver print.
The Hague, National Archives of the Netherlands, Netherlands Forces Intelligence Service [NEFIS] en Centrale Militaire Inlichtingendienst [CMI] in Nederlands-Indië, 2.10.62, inv. no. 3034

[3] Rosihan Anwar and his classmates on a school trip, 10 September 1939, page from his photo album. Unknown photographer.
Gelatin silver prints in album, 24 × 28 cm (closed).
The Hague, National Archives of the Netherlands, Netherlands Forces Intelligence Service [NEFIS] en Centrale Militaire Inlichtingendienst [CMI] in Nederlands-Indië, 2.10.62, inv. no. 3034

[4] Pamphlet seized by NEFIS on 20 January 1948 (location unknown). Pencil on paper, 30 × 57 cm.
The Hague, National Archives of the Netherlands, Netherlands Forces Intelligence Service [NEFIS] en Centrale Militaire Inlichtingendienst [CMI] in Nederlands-Indië, 2.10.62, inv. no. 5821

[5A] Anti-Dutch pamphlet, seized by NEFIS on 4 October 1947 (Semarang). Typescript, watercolour on paper (sheets stuck together), 24 × 31 cm.
The Hague, National Archives of the Netherlands, Netherlands Forces Intelligence Service [NEFIS] en Centrale Militaire Inlichtingendienst [CMI] in Nederlands-Indië, 2.10.62, inv. no. 5418

[5B] Anti-Dutch pamphlet, seized by NEFIS on 15 December 1947 (Pasuruan). Typescript (sheets stuck together), 39 × 21 cm.
The Hague, National Archives of the Netherlands, Netherlands Forces Intelligence Service [NEFIS] en Centrale Militaire Inlichtingendienst [CMI] in Nederlands-Indië, 2.10.62, inv. no. 5507

[5C] Anti-Dutch pamphlet, seized by NEFIS on 8 March 1948 (Tjikampek). Typescript, watercolour on paper (sheets stuck together), 37 × 20 cm.
The Hague, National Archives of the Netherlands, Netherlands Forces Intelligence Service [NEFIS] en Centrale Militaire Inlichtingendienst [CMI] in Nederlands-Indië, 2.10.62, inv. no. 5821

[6] Poster (reverse side), seized by NEFIS on 10 March 1948 (Sukaratu). Paint/ink on paper, 25 × 17 cm.
The Hague, National Archives of the Netherlands, Netherlands Forces Intelligence Service [NEFIS] en Centrale Militaire Inlichtingendienst [CMI] in Nederlands-Indië, 2.10.62, inv. no. 5825

[7] Red armband with the letters P.K.M., seized by NEFIS on 15 August

1946 (Bandung). Cotton, paper, 10 × 28 cm. The Hague, National Archives of the Netherlands, Netherlands Forces Intelligence Service [NEFIS] en Centrale Militaire Inlichtingendienst [CMI] in Nederlands-Indië, 2.10.62, inv. no. 3585

[8] Album about the Indonesian declaration of independence, 1945–1946, seized by NEFIS, date unknown. Indonesia Press Photo Service (IPPHOS). Photo album, 24.7 × 54.5 cm (open). The Hague, National Archives of the Netherlands, Netherlands Forces Intelligence Service [NEFIS] en Centrale Militaire Inlichtingendienst [CMI] in Nederlands-Indië, 2.10.62, inv. no. 7270

[9] Rosihan Anwar delivers a speech at the Malino conference, July 1946. Unknown photographer. Photograph. Leiden, Leiden University Libraries, inv. no. KITLV 157731

[10] Series of photos taken at the unveiling of a stone monument to celebrate one year of independence, Jakarta, 17 August, 1946. Unknown photographer. Photo album, 20 × 56 cm (open). The Hague, National Archives of the Netherlands, Netherlands Forces Intelligence Service [NEFIS] en Centrale Militaire Inlichtingendienst [CMI] in Nederlands-Indië, 2.10.62, inv. no. 7276

[11] Simon Admiraal in his office at the university library in Jakarta, 1947. Unknown photographer. Photograph, 8.5 × 13 cm. Collection Marjon Berkenvelder

[12] Pramoedya Ananta Toer, 1951. Unknown photographer. Photograph. Jakarta, Pusat Dokumentasi Sastra H.B. Jassin

[13] Military identification card of Sergeant Major A. Emoeh, seized by NEFIS on 15 August 1946 (Bandung). Typescript, photograph, 11 × 14 cm. The Hague, National Archives of the Netherlands, Netherlands Forces Intelligence Service [NEFIS] en Centrale Militaire Inlichtingendienst [CMI] in Nederlands-Indië, 2.10.62, inv. no. 3585

[14] Notebook of Sergeant Major Emoeh, seized by NEFIS on 15 August 1946 (Bandung). c. 14 × 22 cm (open). The Hague, National Archives of the Netherlands, Netherlands Forces Intelligence Service [NEFIS] en Centrale Militaire Inlichtingendienst [CMI] in Nederlands-Indië, 2.10.62, inv. no. 3585

[15] Exhibition of seized Indonesian propaganda posters in the Security Museum in Surabaya, June 1947. Hugo Wilmar. Gelatin silver print. The Hague, National Archives of the Netherlands / Collectie Spaarnestad

[16] Portraits of Lenin and Stalin at an exhibition on Indonesian communism at the Security Museum in Surabaya, June 1947. Hugo Wilmar. Gelatin silver print. The Hague, National Archives of the Netherlands / Collectie Spaarnestad

DIPLOMASI AND AGRESI (PP. 166–199)

[1] *Portrait of Tanja Dezentjé*, 1947. Sudarso. Oil on canvas, 100 × 68 cm. Jakarta, Christin Kam, inv. no. SDRS 001. Photo: Kurniawan Wigena

[2] Tanja Dezentjé with an earlier portrait of her, 1946. Unknown photographer Gelatin silver print. The Hague, National Archives of the Netherlands, collection 250 P. Sanders, 2.21.147, inv. no. 8

[3] Henk Ngantung with KRIS fighters, 1946/1947. Unknown photographer. Gelatin silver print The Hague, National Archives of the Netherlands, collection 570, F.J. Goedhart, 2.21.285, inv. no. 52A

[4] Sukarno, Schermerhorn and Lord Killearn seated at a table for lunch during the negotiations in Linggajati, 1946. Henk Ngantung. Pen and black ink, 39 × 28 cm. Jakarta, Museum Seni Rupa Dan Keramik, inv. no. 042/SK/MSRK/08. © Sena Meaya Ngantung, Geniati Heneve Ngantung, Kamang Solana Ngantung, Karno Putra Ngantung +

[5] *Portrait of Sjahrir*, 1946. Henk Ngantung. Pen and black ink, 41 × 28 cm. Jakarta, Museum Seni Rupa Dan Keramik, inv. no. 062/SK/MSRK/08. © Sena Meaya Ngantung, Geniati Heneve Ngantung, Kamang Solana Ngantung, Karno Putra Ngantung +

[6] *Portrait of Willem Schermerhorn*, 1946. Henk Ngantung. Pen and black ink, 41 × 28 cm. Jakarta, Museum Seni Rupa Dan Keramik, inv. no. 035/SK/MSRK/08. © Sena Meaya Ngantung, Geniati Heneve Ngantung, Kamang Solana Ngantung, Karno Putra Ngantung +

[7] *Portrait of Johannes Leimena*, 1946. Henk Ngantung. Pen and black ink, 47 × 28 cm. Jakarta, Museum Seni Rupa Dan Keramik, inv. no. 015/SK/MSRK/08. © Sena Meaya Ngantung, Geniati Heneve Ngantung, Kamang Solana Ngantung, Karno Putra Ngantung +

[8] *Portrait of Hadji Agus Salim*, 1946. Henk Ngantung. Pen and black ink, 29 × 29 cm. Jakarta, Museum Seni Rupa Dan Keramik, inv. no. 019/SK/MSRK/08. © Sena Meaya Ngantung, Geniati Heneve Ngantung, Kamang Solana Ngantung, Karno Putra Ngantung +

[9] *Portrait of Mohammad Roem*, 1946. Henk Ngantung. Pen and black ink, 41 × 27.5 cm. Jakarta, Museum Seni Rupa Dan Keramik, inv. no. 024/SK/MSRK/08. © Sena Meaya Ngantung, Geniati Heneve Ngantung, Kamang Solana Ngantung, Karno Putra Ngantung +

[10] Tjokorda Rai Pudak, 1927. Unknown photographer. Photograph. Ubud, Gianyar, Bali, collection Tjokorda Gde Dalem Pudak

[11] Tjokorda Rai Pudak's shredded army shirt. Textile, 70 × 60 cm. Ubud, Gianyar, Bali, collection Tjokorda Gde Dalem Pudak

[12] Eben Hezer Sirunaya with his fellow fighters, 1949 or later. Unknown photographer. Photograph. Medan, Collection Ebenhezer Sinuraya family

[13] Hans van Santen, 1945. Unknown photographer. Photograph, 13 × 8.1 cm. Collection Van Santen family

[14] Hans van Santen, near Surabaya, 1946. Unknown photographer. Photograph, 5.7 × 8 cm. Collection Van Santen family

[15] Funeral of Private Reint Wolf in Medan, 2 December 1946. Unknown photographer. Photograph, 5.3 × 8.3 cm. Collection Van Santen family

[16] Mohammad Toha and his mother, date unknown. Photograph, from: Dullah, *Karya Dalam Peperangan Dan Revolusi*, Bali 1982. Unknown photographer.

[17] *A Squadron of Dutch Bombers over Yogyakarta at Sunrise*, 1948. Mohammad Toha. Watercolour on hardboard, 7 × 10.3 cm. Amsterdam, Rijksmuseum, inv. no. NG-1998-7-1. © Heirs Mohammed Toha Adimidjojo

[18] *Dutch Soldiers Forcing Indonesian Civilians together*, 1948–1949. Mohammad Toha. Watercolour on hardboard, 7.4 × 10.7 cm. Amsterdam, Rijksmuseum, inv. no. NG-1998-7-12. © Heirs Mohammed Toha Adimidjojo

[19] *Dutch Soldiers Searching Mohammad Toha's Home*, 1949. Mohammad Toha. Watercolour on hardboard, 7 × 9.9 cm. Amsterdam, Rijksmuseum, inv. no. NG-1998-7-40. © Heirs Mohammed Toha Adimidjojo

[20] *Dutch Troops Surrounding the City Forcing the Indonesians to Hand over their Weapons*, 1948–1949. Mohammad Toha. Watercolour on hardboard, 7.3 × 10.3 cm. Amsterdam, Rijksmuseum, inv. no. NG-1998-7-15. © Heirs Mohammed Toha Adimidjojo

[21] *Republican Troops Returning to Yogyakarta*, June 1949. Mohammad Toha. Watercolour on hardboard, 17.3 × 27.1 cm. Amsterdam, Rijksmuseum, inv. no. NG-1998-7-43. © Heirs Mohammed Toha Adimidjojo

[22] Masdoelhak Nasoetion, Kaliurang, 1948. Unknown photographer. Gelatin silver print. The Hague, National Archives of the Netherlands, Netherlands Forces Intelligence Service [NEFIS] en Centrale Militaire Inlichtingendienst [CMI] in Nederlands-Indië, 2.10.62, inv. no. 7265

[23] Adriana Nasoetion-van der Have and her four children at the grave of her husband Masdoelhak Nasoetion, Yogyakarta, 1949. Unknown photographer. Photograph. Collection S.H. Nasution

[24] Petrus Akihary, 1949/1950. Unknown photographer. Photograph. Culemborg, Collection of Ms E. Supusepa-Akihary

[25] Body tag of Petrus Akihary with service book number 20574, issued at his entry into service, 1926. Metal.

Maarssen, Collection Ms M. Anthony-Akihary

[26] Military identity card (KNIL) of Sergeant Major Instructor Petrus Akihary, July 1950 – March 1950. Typescript, c. 10 × 15 cm. Maarssen, Collection Ms M. Anthony-Akihary

COMRADES OF THE REVOLUTION (PP. 200–229)

[1] *Portrait of Sukarno on Proclamation Day*, 1945. Basoeki Abdullah. Oil on canvas, 111 × 75 cm. Jakarta, Presidential Palace Collection, inv. no. 29796.02.01.02.003.233. © Cecilia Sidhawati

[2] *Iboekoe* (My Mother), 1946. Trubus Soedarsono. Oil on panel, 50.5 × 36 cm. Amsterdam, Rijksmuseum, inv. no. SK-A-5068. © Heirs Trubus Soedarsono

[3] Indonesian street vendors sell pins with the red-and-white flag, 1945/1946. Unknown photographer. Gelatin silver print. The Hague, National Archives of the Netherlands, Collection 570, F.J. Goedhart, 2.21.285, inv. no. 52A

[4] *Memanah* (Archery), 1944. Henk Ngantung. Oil on hardboard, 152 × 152 cm. Jakarta, Presidential Palace Collection. © Sena Meaya Ngantung, Geniati Heneve Ngantung, Kamang Solana Ngantung, Karno Putra Ngantung †

[5] *Sekali Merdeka, Tetap Merdeka* (Once Free, Always Free), from Mochtar Apin and Baharudin, *Linoleographs*, 1946. Baharudin. Paper, linocut, 43.5 × 38.2 cm. Amsterdam, Stedelijk Museum, inv. no. A 40126(1-25)

[6] Otto Djaya at Rijswijk Palace at the signing of the Linggajati Agreement, 25 March 1947. Cas Oorthuys. Original negative from the archive of Cas Oorthuys, 6 × 6 cm. Rotterdam, Nederlands Fotomuseum, inv. no. CAS-10078-6. © Cas Oorthuys / Nederlands Fotomuseum

[7] Agus Djaya with his painting *Maya* at an exhibition in Jakarta, 1947. Unknown photographer. Gelatin silver print, 17.2 × 12.5 cm. Nationaal Museum van Wereldculturen, inv. no. TM-33000028

[8] *Kawan Kawan Repoloesi* (Comrades of the Revolution), 1947. Sudjojono. Oil on canvas, 95 × 149 cm. Jakarta, Presidential Palace Collection, inv. no. 01476.02.01.02.003.057

[9] *Pembrontak* (Revolutionaries), 1947. Otto Djaya. Oil on canvas, 48.1 × 39.2 cm. Amsterdam, Rijksmuseum, inv. no. NG-2018-569. Purchased with the support of Pon Holdings B.V. © Asoka Djaya

[10] Satirical cartoon of Basoeki Abdullah with Agus and Otto Djaya in *Seniman* 1 (1947), no. 3.

[11] *Portrait of Queen Juliana*, 1949. Basoeki Abdullah. Oil on canvas, 162 × 127 cm. The Hague, Koninklijke Verzamelingen, inv. no. SC1367. © Cecilia Sidhawati

[12] *Portrait of Mohammad Hatta*, 1949. Basoeki Abdullah. Pastel, 100 × 60 cm. Jakarta, collection Hatta family. © Cecilia Sidhawati

[13] *Studentenleven in de bergen* (Student life in the mountains), c. 1949. Unknown artist. Watercolour. Bandung, Institut Teknologi Bandung; gift of Marjon Berkenvelder

[14] *Biografi II di Malioboro* (Second Biography of Malioboro), 1949. Harijadi Sumadidjaja. Oil on canvas, 180 × 200 cm. Jakarta, Presidential Palace Collection, inv. no. 01486.02.01.02.003.316. © Harijadi's family

[15] *Pengantin Revolusi* (Bride of the Revolution), 1957. Hendra Gunawan. Oil on canvas, 225 × 296 cm. Jakarta, Museum Seni Rupa Dan Keramik, inv. no. 1/LK/MSR

[16] *Revolusi* (Revolution), 1951. Hendra Gunawan. Oil on canvas, 130 × 293 cm. Jakarta, Museum Seni Rupa Dan Keramik, inv. no. 53/LK/MSR

REVOLUSI!

**FOUR TIMES 365 DAYS
(PP. 230–249)**

[1] President Sukarno arriving at Kemayoran Airport on his return to Jakarta, 29 December 1949.
Alex Mendur (IPPHOS, Indonesia Press Photo Service).
Photograph. Jakarta, Antara.
© Antara/IPPHOS

[2] President Sukarno, accompanied by minister of defence Sultan Hamengkubowono IX, waving to the crowds on the ride from the airport to Koningsplein, Jakarta, 28 December 1949.
Alex Mendur (IPPHOS, Indonesia Press Photo Service).
Photograph. Jakarta, Antara.
© Antara/IPPHOS

[3] President Sukarno is welcomed in Jakarta by an enthusiastic crowd, December 1949.
Henri Cartier-Bresson (Magnum).
Photograph. Paris, Magnum Photos
© Henri Cartier-Bresson
© Fondation Henri Cartier-Bresson / Magnum Photos

[4] The portrait of Governor-General Rooseboom being removed from the former Governor-General's palace, Jakarta, 26 December 1949.
Henri Cartier-Bresson (Magnum).
Photograph. Paris, Magnum Photos.
© Henri Cartier-Bresson
© Fondation Henri Cartier-Bresson / Magnum Photos

[5] President Sukarno, accompanied by interior minister, Anak Agung Gde Agung, ascending the steps of Merdeka Palace, Jakarta, 28 December 1949.
Alex Mendur (IPPHOS, Indonesia Press Photo Service). Photograph. Jakarta, Antara © Antara/IPPHOS

[6] View of the crowd and photographers at the Merdeka Palace steps, Jakarta, 28 December 1949.
Frans 'Nyong' Umbas (IPPHOS, Indonesia Press Photo Service).
Photograph. Jakarta, Antara.
© Antara/IPPHOS

[7] View of the crowd on Merdeka Square listening to Sukarno's speech, Jakarta, 28 December 1949.
Frans 'Nyong' Umbas (IPPHOS, Indonesia Press Photo Service).
Photograph. Jakarta, Antara.
© Antara/IPPHOS

[8] Frans 'Nyong' Umbas, Alex Mendur and Justus Umbas with Alex Mamusung in front of the IPPHOS office at Molenvliet Oost 30, Jakarta, 1951.
Unknown photographer (IPPHOS, Indonesia Press Photo Service).
Photograph. Collection Yudhi Soerjoatmodjo. © Antara/IPPHOS

[9] Justus Umbas, Frans 'Nyong' Umbas and Alex Mendur at the IPPHOS office at Molenvliet Oost 30, Jakarta, 1948. Unknown photographer (IPPHOS, Indonesia Press Photo Service). Collection Yudhi Soerjoatmodjo.
© Antara/IPPHOS

[10] Album about the negotiations aboard the USS *Renville*, 1947/1948.
Indonesia Press Photo Service (IPPHOS).
Photo album, 24.7 × 54.5 cm (open). The Hague, National Archives of the Netherlands, Netherlands Forces Intelligence Service [NEFIS] en Centrale Militaire Inlichtingendienst [CMI] in Nederlands-Indië, 2.10.62, inv. no. 7275. © Antara/IPPHOS

[11] President Sukarno giving his speech on the steps of Merdeka Palace, Jakarta, 28 December 1949.
Alex Mendur (IPPHOS, Indonesia Press Photo Service). Photograph. Jakarta, Antara. © Antara/IPPHOS

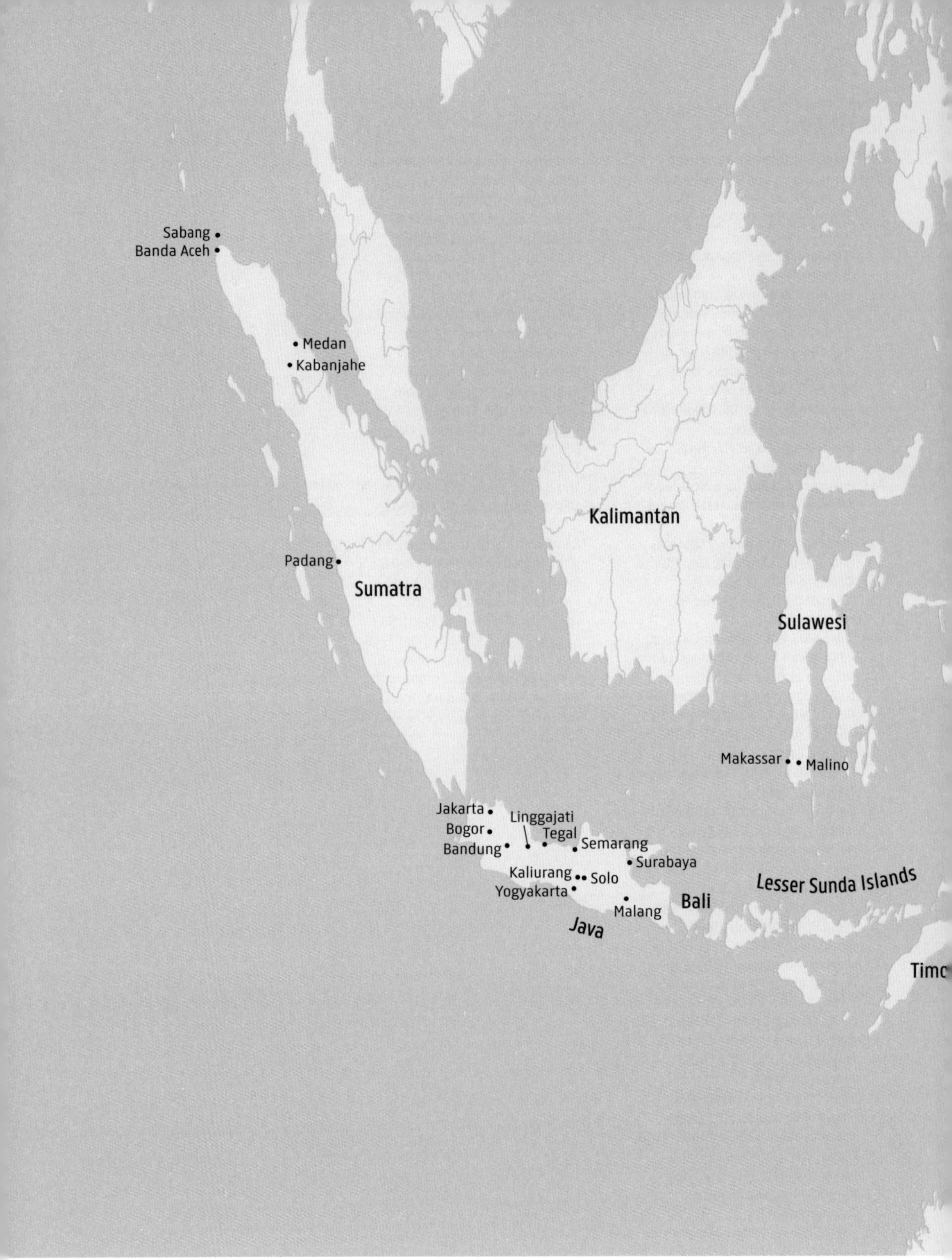
Sabang
Banda Aceh
Medan
Kabanjahe
Padang
Sumatra
Kalimantan
Sulawesi
Makassar
Malino
Jakarta
Bogor
Bandung
Linggajati
Tegal
Semarang
Surabaya
Kaliurang
Solo
Yogyakarta
Malang
Java
Bali
Lesser Sunda Islands

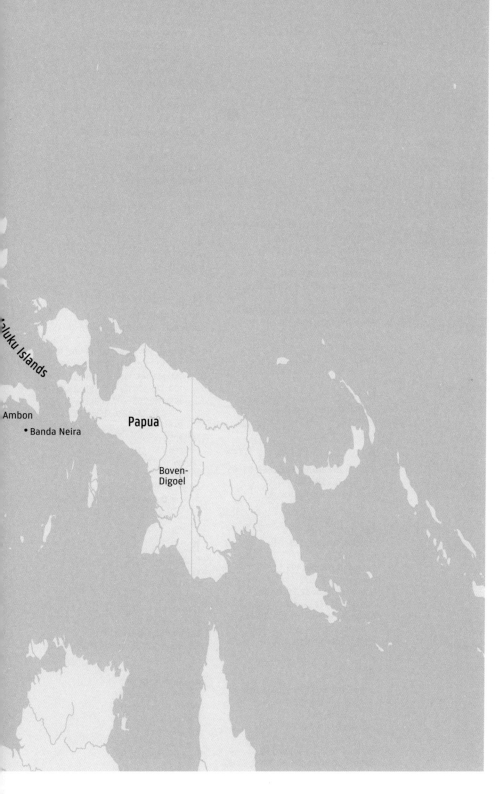

Map of Indonesia in the Gall Peters projection.
The places indicated play a role in this book.

INDEX
of people and places

A

Abdurachman, Arifin 51
Abedy 209
Aboru 195, 199
Admiraal, Jan 153
Admiraal, Simon 153, 156–157, 159, 218, 223
Affandi, Muhammed 28–29, 77, 80–81, 85, 170, 186, 201, 205–207, 211
Akihary, Petrus 195–199
Alisjahbana, Sutan Takdir 209
Amir 9
Amsterdam 89, 93, 101, 103–104, 121, 136, 192, 195, 211–212, 217, 223
Anak Agung Gde Agung, Ide 43, 177, 234, 236, 238
Anderson, Benedict 47
Anwar, Chairil 20–21, 24, 27, 80, 207
Anwar, Rosihan 93, 141–144, 150–152, 156, 160, 165, 206, 242
Apin, Mochtar 20, 205, 207, 209

B

Bagan Siapiapi 44
Baharudin 20, 207, 209–210
Baheramsjah, Noor 127
Balapulang 105
Balaraja 56
Balfas, Muhammad 207
Balongwono 37
Banda Aceh 199
Bandung 32, 93, 147, 162–163, 170, 206, 209, 218, 234, 244, 248
Bangkok 89, 167, 169
Banten 22, 55–56, 90
Banu, Iksaka 42
Barli 209
Basoeki Abdullah 202, 205, 217–221
Batavia see Jakarta
Bekasi 32, 159
Berastagi 179
Berlin 123, 170
Boedikadjo 12
Bogem 223
Bogor 21, 91, 105, 170, 212
Boshouwers, Willem 239
Bot, Ben 47
Bouwer, Jan 207
Breijer, Charles 19
Buitenzorg see Bogor
Bukit Bertah 181
Bukittinggi 89, 192
Bung Tomo see Sutomo

C

Canton 89
Cartier-Bresson, Henri 45–46, 234–236, 239
Cideng 55
Cikampek 159
Cirebon 37, 171
Cribb, Robert 245
Culemborg 196

D

Dalat 54, 57
Daljono 28
(Pulau) Damar 160
Dasaad, Agus Musin 45, 233, 244
De la Court, Albert 121, 126
Delacroix, Eugène 77
Delhi 169
Dezentjé, Tanja 167–170
Diah, Burhanuddin Mohammad 57, 242
Djajengasmoro 127
Djaya, Agus 205, 209, 211–213, 217–219
Djaya, Otto 205, 209, 211–213, 216–219
Djojopuspito, Soewarsih 26
Djokosajano 9
Dullah 30, 32, 186, 207

E

Effendi, Oesman 205, 214
Emoeh, A. 161–163, 165

F

Fatmawati Sukarno 59, 62–63, 65–66, 68–71, 233–234
Fort de Kock see Bukittinggi

G

Gandhi, Mahatma 169
Garut 162
Geelhoed, Marinus 193
Gianyar 43, 177–178
Goedhart, Frans 32, 73, 75, 244
Guangzhou see Canton
Gunawan, Hendra 32, 209, 211, 223, 226, 228
Guntur Sukarnoputra 234

H

Hague, The 22, 37, 75, 151, 153, 162, 165, 167, 170, 183–184, 195, 217–218, 244
Hamengkubuwono IX, Sultan 32, 44, 234, 244
Hasan, Teuku Muhammad 69, 74
Hatta, Mohammad 21, 36–37, 51, 54–57, 59–66, 68–71, 86, 90–91, 93, 118, 152, 170, 186, 192–193, 209, 218, 221, 231, 239, 244, 248
Have, Adriana van der 193–195
Hawthorn, D.C. 118
Helfrich, C.E.L. 128
Hendraningrat, Abdul 52, 55–56, 59, 62–64, 66–68, 70–71, 73
Heutsz, J.B. van 80, 84–85, 236
Hirohito, Emperor 54
Hisaichi, Terauchi 54
Hitler, Adolf 94
Hoesein, Rushdy 73
Hoesman, Mas 37
Hussein, Iljas see Tan Malaka

I

Ichsani 12
Idrus 111–113, 115

J

Jacob, Melvin 233
Jakarta 13, 16, 19–23, 32–33, 37, 44–45, 51, 56–57, 59–60, 62, 69, 73, 77–80, 84–86, 89–91, 93, 96, 99–102, 104–105, 107, 109, 115, 117–118, 121, 127, 141–142, 144, 151–154, 156–157, 159–160, 170–171, 177–178, 181, 183, 185, 193, 196, 206–207, 209, 212–213, 223, 231–232, 234–236, 238–239, 242–245, 248
Jaksa 153
Janssen v E[...] 9
Jatinegara 59
Jerusalem 89
Jonge, Bonifacius Cornelis de 60
Juliana, Queen of the Netherlands 217, 220, 233

K

Kabanjahe 179, 181
Kaliurang 192–194
Kamsar, Yep 242
Kamsidi 28
(Tanah) Karo 179, 181
Karta Legawa 162
Kartodirdjo, Oerip 43
Kartosoewirjo, Sekarmadji Maridjan 44, 128
Kediri 91
Kertapati, Sidik 86
Kerton, Sudjana 209
Killearn, Lord 172–173
Klender 56
Klungkung 60
Koestiwa 209
Kompoel Sujatno 25
Kubang Nan Dua 141

REVOLUSI!

Kuningan 171, 173
Kusno, Timoteus Anggawan 16
Kwee, Laetitia/Letty 99, 101-102, 104
Kwee Thian Yoe/Jan 99, 104
Kwee, family 99-101, 103

L

Laluasan, Anna 151
Laluasan, A.E. 151
Langkat 183
Lapi 109
Lapian, A.B. 73
Lasmo, Mbok 37
Lawang 193
Leiden 13, 89, 93, 169, 192
Leimena, Johannes 174
Lenin, Vladimir 161, 164
Leur, Job van 105
Leur-de Loos, Jeanne/Peu van see Loos, Jeanne/Peu de
Lim Him Nio see Kwee, Laetitia/Letty
Lincoln, Abraham 85
Linggajati 36-37, 121, 123, 136-137, 144, 151-152, 171-173, 178, 184-185, 213, 217
Loebis, Mochtar 244
Logemann, Johann 26
Loos, Jeanne/Peu de 104-107
Lovink, A.H.J. ('Tony') 44, 234

M

Maas, Tono 193
MacTavish, Duncan 77
Madiun 9, 133, 201, 211
Madrid 126
Maeda, Tadashi 54-57
Magelan 196
Makassar 133, 144
Malacca 183
Malang 99, 112, 123, 193
Malik, Adam 32
Malino 150-152, 212
Mallaby, A.W.S. 111, 118
Mamusung, Alex 243
Mangoendihardjo 56, 63
Mangunwijaya, Y.B. 42
Manila 89
Mansfeld, Anouk 13
Manuhutu, Jan 109
Marx, Karl 90
Marzuki, Ismail 28
Masing 245
Mateni 103-104
Mauk 56
Medan 89, 144, 178-179, 181-184
Megawati Sukarnoputri 234
Melaka see Malacca
Melik, Sayuti 56-57
Mendur, Alex 54, 55, 59-61, 73, 231-232, 234, 236, 239, 242-245, 248-249
Mendur, Soemarto Frans 21, 51-55, 59-75, 231, 239, 242, 244-245
Moewardi 61, 63-64, 67-68
Mohini, Ratna 234
Mojokerto 37
Mook, Huib van 9, 26, 32, 36-37, 43, 85, 87, 151, 162
Moriën, Joop 136
Moscow 44, 89, 93
Mountbatten, Pamela 169
Mulder, Ries 218
Munif 11
Musso 9, 44
Mussolini, Benito 94

N

Nahumury, Jacoba 196
Nashar 214
Nasoetion, Masdoelhak 192-195
Nasoetion-van der Have, Adriana see Have, Adriana van der
Nasrudin, Sutarso 9-13
Nasution, Abdul Haris 47
Nehru, Jawaharlal 167
New Delhi 167
New York 43, 185
Ngantung, Henk 20, 34, 36-37, 170-175, 177, 207-208
Ngurah Rai, I Gusti 178

O

Oemar 12
Oorthuys, Cas 32, 95, 121-126, 129, 133, 213

P

Padang 111, 141
Palar, Nico 43
Parepare 144
Paris 192
Pasuruan 146
Pekalongan 22
Penjaringan 69
Plas, Charles van der 85, 162
Pramoedya Ananta Toer 61, 158-160
Prawito 127
Pudak, Tjokorde Gede Dalem 177
Pudak, Tjokorda Rai 176-178
Pulungan, Dal Bassa 55, 59, 69, 242

R

Rachman, Etty Abdul 21, 55-56, 59
Radjiman Wediodiningrat 69, 74
Rafty, Tony 114-119, 207
Rai, Tjokorda Gede 177-178
Rameli 214
Rangkasbitung 90, 212
Rasjid, Gadis 171
Ratulangi, Sam 69, 74
Rawagede 38
Rengasdengklok 56-57
Rengat 185
Resobowo, Basuki 205, 214
Riwu Ga 59, 69
Rizal, José 152
Roem, Mohammad 175, 181, 186
Roijen, Jan Herman van 181
Ronodipuro, Muhammad Jusuf 22

S

Sabang 196, 199
Salam, Abdul 207
Saleh, Chaerul 90
Saleh, Raden 205
Salim, Hadji Agus 175
Sandberg, Willem 217
Sanders, Piet 167
Sani, Asrul 20-21
Santen, Hans van 182-184
Sardjito 186
Saseo, Ono 205
Sayuti Mohammad 239, 248
Schermerhorn, Willem 37, 171-174
Selopanggung 91
Semarang 24, 118, 146, 195, 234, 245
Senduuk 109
Sindusiswoyo 127
Singapore 62, 89, 167, 169
Sinuraya, Eben Hezer 179-181
Sjahrir, Sutan 56, 60, 86, 89, 91-96, 101, 144, 151, 153, 169, 173-174, 177, 185-186
Sjarifuddin, Amir 44, 118, 133, 136, 169, 211
Soedibio 32, 133, 211, 214
Soedjijo 12
Soegiri 211, 214
Soeharto, Raden Mas 238
Soehoed 59, 63, 70-71
Soeparto 209
Soeromo 214
Soerono 39, 214
Soetomo 60
Solo 133, 211
Stalin, Joseph 161, 164
Subandrio 127
Subardjo Djoyoadisuryo, Achmad 55-57, 89-90
Sudarso 167-168
Sudiro 59
Sudjojono 31-32, 80-81, 133, 201, 205, 207, 211-212, 214, 223
Sugianto 12
Sugondo, Setyadjit 9
Sukabumi 212, 244
Sukaratu 147
Sukarni 90

Sukarno, President 9, 16–17, 19, 21–22, 27–28, 37, 44–46, 51–52, 54–74, 77, 80, 86, 89–91, 99, 115, 118, 121, 124, 152, 167, 171–173, 178–179, 186, 201–202, 207, 209, 223, 231–236, 238–240, 242, 244, 248–249
Sukotjo 91
Sumadidjaja, Harijadi 223, 225
Sumardjo, Trisno 211, 214
Sunindyo 211
Supono Siswosoeharto, F.X. 186
Surabaya 60, 91, 93, 111–112, 114–115, 118, 161, 164, 182–183, 234
Suradji, D. 211
Surjosugondo 127
Suromo 207
Suroto 59
Sutiksna 205
Sutomo 112–113, 177
Suwarno, Sri 186
Suwiryo 62, 65

T

Takashi, Ohno 205
Tamin, Rahman 244
Tan Malaka, Ibrahim Gelar Datuk 86, 88–94
Tangerang 56, 186
Tas, Salomon 93
Tasikmalaya 209
Tedjabayu 211, 214
Tegal 108–109
Tekebek, Suradi 91
Ternate 144
Tiga Binanga 181
Tjikampek 146
Tjipanas 91
Toerkandi 209
Toha, Mohammad 186–190, 192
Tomohon 170
Trimurti, S.K. 55–56, 63, 68, 70, 169
Trubus Soedarsono 201, 203, 205, 207

U

Ubud 177
Uhlenbusch, Anna Sofia 105, 109
Uhlenbusch, Christina 105
Uhlenbusch, Wilhelm Friedrich 105
Uhlenbusch, familie 105, 108–110
Ullfah, Maria 28, 169
Umbas, Frans 'Nyong' 237–240, 242–244
Umbas, Justus 242–245

V

Visscher, Elien 24

W

Wahab Saleh, Abdoel 239, 248
Wates 201
Wates Lor 37–38
Wates, Mbah Podho 201
Waworuntu, Johnny 238–239, 248
(Pulau) Weh 196
Wenghart, Rudolf 170
Westerling, Raymond 38, 133
Widjojoatmodjo, Abdulkadir 43
Wikana 9, 211
Wilhelmina, Queen of the Netherlands 27
Wilmar, Hugo 15, 161, 164
Wiranatakusuma, Minarsih 22, 43
Wolf, Reint 182, 184

Y

Yogyakarta 15–16, 19, 21, 28, 32–33, 40, 44, 46, 53, 126, 129, 133, 141, 144, 148, 153, 167, 171, 185–186, 188, 190, 192–193, 195, 201, 207, 209, 211, 223, 231, 234, 242, 244–245, 248
Yudhokusomo, Kartono 214
Yudhokusomo, Rameli/Marsudi 214

Z

Zaini 205

271

This book was published on the occasion of the exhibition
REVOLUSI! INDONESIA INDEPENDENT
at the Rijksmuseum in Amsterdam, 11 February–6 June 2022

The appointment of the Indonesian curators Amir Sidharta and Bonnie Triyana has been made possible by the Johan Huizinga Fund / RijksmuseumFund. The additional programme accompanying the exhibition with room for dialogue has been made possible in part by vfonds and DutchCulture.

AUTHORS
MARION ANKER
junior curator of history, Rijksmuseum
ANNE-LOT HOEK
historian and investigative journalist
REMCO RABEN
professor of colonial and postcolonial literary and cultural history at the University of Amsterdam and lecturer in Asian history at Utrecht University
AMIR SIDHARTA
curator and researcher, director Museum Lippo/Museum Universitas Pelita Harapan, Tangerang, Jakarta
YUDHI SOERJOATMODJO
producer and curator
AMINUDIN T.H. SIREGAR
PhD Candidate Art History, Leiden University
HARM STEVENS
curator of history, Rijksmuseum
BONNIE TRIYANA
historian and editor in chief Historia.Id

TRANSLATION
Pierre Bouvier (Foreword, Faces of the Revolution, The Signal to Rise Up, Propaganda for the Republic, Comrades of the Revolution)
David McKay (The Spirit of the Revolusi, Freedom the Glory of any Nation, Caught in the Net, Diplomasi and Agresi)

EDITING
Geri Klazema, Barbera van Kooij, Rijksmuseum

ENGLISH TEXT EDITING
Kate Bell

IMAGE RESEARCH
Ellen Slob, Rijksmuseum

INDEX
Miekie Donner

PHOTOGRAPHY
Image Department of the Rijksmuseum and other institutions and individuals as indicated in the list of illustrations (pp. 259–265). For the maps on pp. 266–267, the following should be added: Carto Studio BV, Utrecht.

COVER
Three young Indonesians on the street in Yogyakarta, December 1947 (detail, see p. 15)

DESIGN
Irma Boom Office
(Irma Boom, Anna Moschioni)

LITHOGRAPHY
BFC, Bert van der Horst

PRINTING AND BINDING
Drukkerij Wilco

PUBLISHER
Atlas Contact, Amsterdam/Antwerp

WITH THANKS TO
Huib Akihary, M. Anthony-Akihary, Marjon Berkenvelder, Martine Gosselink, Elwin Hendrikse, Gerda Jansen Hendriks, Kwee Tjoe Houw, Anouk Mansfeld, Margaret Leidelmeijer, S.H. Nasution, Merapi Obermayer, Harry Poeze, Tjokorda Gde Dalem Pudak, Ellen van Sambeek, Gerard van Santen, Iris van Santen, Mirjam Shatanawi, Evlina Sinuraya, Ni Ketut Sudiani, Pier Terwen, Frank Vermeulen, Bas van Wersch, A. van der Zande †

SPELLING
Since the proclamation of independence in 1945 Indonesian spelling has changed three times. In 1947 the Soewandi (or Republican) Spelling System replaced the Ophuijsen spelling, whereby 'oe' was changed to 'u' amongst others. In 1972, the Enhanced Spelling System was introduced, changing the spelling of 'tj' to 'c', 'dj' to 'j', 'j' to 'y', and 'ch' to 'kh'. In 2015, the Indonesian Spelling System was introduced, with some minor changes.
For geographical names, we followed the modern Indonesian spelling, so Surabaya instead of Soerabaja. With people's names, we used the spelling preferred by the individuals themselves or their families as much as possible. For publications, we kept the spelling of the title as originally published, for organisations we use the last known spelling while in existence. As a result, old and new spellings are sometimes mixed in this book.

© 2022 text: Rijksmuseum, Amsterdam
© 2022 images: Rijksmuseum, Amsterdam, and other institutions and individuals as indicated in the list of captions and the photography credits

Every effort has been made to find the various right holders of the photographs, works of art and objects reproduced in this book. In case of error of omission, please contact the Rijksmuseum: publicaties@rijksmuseum.nl

ISBN 978 90 450 4575 7
NUR 688

All rights reserved. No part of this publication may be transmitted in any form or by any means, electronic or mechanical, including photocopy, recording, or any storage and retrieval system, without prior permission from the publisher.

FOUNDER
PHILIPS

MAIN SPONSORS
VRIENDENLOTERIJ   ING   kpn